D1233213

Hitchcock's Partner in Suspense

# HITCHCOCK'S PARTNER IN SUSPENSE

The Life of Screenwriter
CHARLES BENNETT

CHARLES BENNETT

EDITED BY
JOHN CHARLES BENNETT

 UNIVERSITY PRESS OF KENTUCKY

Copyright © 2014 by The University Press of Kentucky

Scholarly publisher for the Commonwealth,
serving Bellarmine University, Berea College, Centre College of Kentucky,
Eastern Kentucky University, The Filson Historical Society, Georgetown College,
Kentucky Historical Society, Kentucky State University, Morehead State
University, Murray State University, Northern Kentucky University, Transylvania
University, University of Kentucky, University of Louisville, and Western
Kentucky University.
All rights reserved.

*Editorial and Sales Offices:* The University Press of Kentucky
663 South Limestone Street, Lexington, Kentucky 40508-4008
www.kentuckypress.com

Cataloging-in-Publication data is available from the Library of Congress.

978-0-8131-4449-8 (hardcover : alk. paper)
978-0-8131-4479-5 (epub)
978-0-8131-4480-1 (pdf)

This book is printed on acid-free paper meeting the requirements of the American
National Standard for Permanence in Paper for Printed Library Materials.

Manufactured in the United States of America.

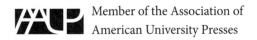 Member of the Association of
American University Presses

# Contents

*Illustrations follow page 128*

# To Charles at Eighty

When, crowned with laurel as a youth
Our Charles bestrode the London stage,
He was, despite his tender age,
Most eager, beautiful, and couth.
Rather a dear—
As many maidens gone to rest,
Would so attest, if they were here.

The stage's fairest sought for space
In his productions—and no wondra!
Joan, Edna, Paulette, Annie Ondra,
The Pride of England—Boniface![1]

He *reaped a wilder wind,* a vine
Of sweeter wine along the way.
His step was always light and gay,
From infancy to *thirty-nine.*

Those were the golden years, by Gad!
They are not easy to forget,
For there's a light of glory yet
Around that plump and humming lad—

Whom now we welcome to *our* play
That opens on each eightieth year
For those we love and hold most dear—
And on *this* marquee, bold and clear,
Is "*Live Forever and a Day!*"
*A Hopeful Tenet,* by Charles Bennett.

With Love,
Robert Nathan,
Author of *Portrait of Jenny, Dunkirk,* and much more

# Preface

AMIENS: Blow, blow, thou winter wind,
    Thou art not so unkind
    As man's ingratitude;
    Thy tooth is not so keen,
    Because thou art not seen,
    Although thy breath be rude.
    Heigh-ho! Sing, heigh-ho! unto the green holly.
    Most friendship is feigning, most loving mere folly.
    Then, heigh-ho, the holly!
    This life is most jolly.
                  *—As You Like It*, act 2, scene 7

When the young actor Charles Bennett sang these lines, he could not anticipate the depth at which Shakespeare's words would strike his soul and shape his life work. Neither has the film industry recognized the degree to which his Shakespearean legacy and psychology shaped twentieth-century film. But recovering these forgotten elements of thriller history is the secondary reason for my publishing his memoir. The primary reason is to recount a career as storied as the stories it created.

Charles Bennett (1899–1995) bracketed a century in which he contributed to every medium of the spoken word. He entertained four generations, penned many film classics, and enjoyed wide name recognition and professional association. Yet, in 1990 when Stuart Birnbaum and William Blaylock arrived at his Coldwater Canyon house in search of film rights to Hitchcock's *Blackmail,* they were surprised to find the nonagenarian alive, writing and humming, upbeat and ironic, and happy to share anecdotes across a drink at his bar. Thanks to their interest, Charles Bennett would be reemployed at ninety-two to draft a remake of his second play (and third film credit), *Blackmail.*

Their knock at the door signaled the curtain call to an illustrious career. Formerly an actor, director, playwright, film and television writer, and novelist, Charles was now applauded as a living archive. From America and Europe film historians and press arrived to interview the oldest film writer employed by a major studio and discuss topics going back to the era of silent film. Charles was queried extensively about his seven stories directed by Sir Alfred Hitchcock. He was named one of *Buzz Magazine*'s "100 Coolest People in LA," was selected as a Telluride Festival and British Academy of Film and Television Arts honoree, and was the recipient of the 1995 Writers Guild of America, West, Laurel Award for Lifetime Achievement.

But why was Bennett *rediscovered?* Why the obscurity? And what had he been doing during his twenty-two-year retirement?

He had been writing, day in and day out, since he completed a final produced TV script, "Terror-Go-Round" for *Land of the Giants,* in 1968. He wrote plays, films, teleplays, treatments, TV series, and novels, publishing his second novel, *Fox on the Run,* in 1987. Ever optimistic, he delivered scripts to agents and studios, and he patiently waited as . . . *nothing happened* . . . nothing but the slow erosion of his fame.

There is no simple reason why he had been forgotten. It is more a conflux of reasons: Charles's disciplines were spread too broadly for most scholars. His multicareer credits did not appear in any single almanac. His activities spanned two continents, and most of the non-Hitchcock British credits were overlooked in Hollywood. The Hitchcock partnership had been obscured. Advancing in age, Charles was out of the immediate studio picture. And in those years before video (apart from second-run and cinema art houses), *out of sight* meant *out of mind.* Sadly, his literary agent of fifty years, H. N. Swanson, could not reverse the decline.

But such anecdotage! The life-crafted stories of a peerless raconteur. Did anyone know Bennett had a childhood crush on Gertrude Lawrence? Could anyone remember that Peggy Ashcroft had starred in his 1927 London play *The Return?* Or that he had starred with John Gielgud in a 1927 all-star production of *Othello* under royal patronage? Or as Aramis in 1928 against Robert Loraine's Cyrano? While some knew that Tallulah Bankhead starred in Bennett's London play *Blackmail* (1928), who could recall the perennial successes of *Blackmail* and *The Last Hour* (1928) on the road with multiple English touring companies? Who knew he had been awarded the Military Medal for Bravery, been a Hollywood spy, written war propaganda in both Hollywood and Britain, snooped alone through Hitler's bunker, or launched a personal crusade to overturn the Hollywood studio formula system? And who would believe that Charles, employed by 20th Century Fox in his nineties, was advocating against ageism in the Writers Guild?

In 1929 Hitchcock filmed Bennett's play *Blackmail* as the first European full-length talking picture. His comedic thriller *The Last Hour* (1930) was the first talkie for Nettlefold Studios.[2] The crime film *Deadlock* (1931) set British box-office records. In 1933 and 1934 Bennett authored ten produced films! *The Secret of the Loch* (1934) was the first film shot on location in Scotland, and it coincided with press hoopla about a sighting of the Loch Ness Monster. Then came the success of his original story *The Man Who Knew Too Much* (1934), followed by four Hitchcock films in quick succession. In 1936 Bennett was credited by London's *Era* magazine as "the most successful film-writer in England." In 1937, anticipating his imminent departure for America, the British film industry offered to double his salary. And his arrivals in New York and Hollywood were announced by the columnists Irene Thirer (*New York Post*), John T. McManus (*New York Times*), Ira Wolfert (*Hartford Courant*), Walter Winchell (*New York Daily Mirror*), Louella Parsons (*Los Angeles Examiner*), and Adward Adolphe (*New York Herald Tribune*)!

Bennett is best known for suspense; he is credited, with Hitchcock, for co-establishing the thriller genre. To quote the film historian Kevin Mace, "Bennett helped create such popular thriller elements as the falsely accused hero, the beautiful and intelligent heroine, the handsome and charming villain, and the climactic, suspenseful chase that depends as much on the heroine's courage as it does the hero for its successful outcome."[3] But if asked what Bennett wrote beyond thrillers, few might name other interests—supernatural, science fiction, travel adventure, history, propaganda, sentimental story, and drama. In script after script Charles Bennett demonstrated remarkable understanding of construction, as well as versatility of style and content—comedy, suspense, and high adventure.

To be clear, Charles has *not* been credited with invention of the cinematic thriller. In 1926 Alfred Hitchcock directed Eliot Stannard's adaptation of *The Lodger,* based on Marie Belloc Lowndes's 1911 story and 1913 novel about Jack the Ripper. That silent film presents a stunning mix of cinematic effect, ambiguity, and suspense—and the *mis*-assignment as the first film about a falsely accused man on the run.

Watching *The Lodger,* one is conscious of its missing sound dimension—mouths flap, silent conversations amuse or concern its players, and the story plods along by visual continuity and an infrequent use of dialogue cards. From our perspective, it appears that Hitch's silent effect had plateaued. Conversely, Charles's classic stage melodrama, built on eighteen years of experience, was recognized in December 1928, six months before the release of Hitchcock's *Blackmail*. By teaming with Bennett, Hitchcock could infuse the talkie's quick-paced sound element with construction and dialogue proven to propel a melodramatic story line.

But the film historians and press did not arrive at Bennett's bar prepared to discuss his previous career. Had this been their intention, they would have been familiar with his early credits. By the time of *The Man Who Knew Too Much*, Bennett had acted for over twenty years and had scripted and directed six stage melodramas, *The Return, Blackmail, The Last Hour, The Danger Line* (1929), *After Midnight* (1929), and *Sensation* (1931). He had written or adapted for the screen at least five, possibly seven, crime talkies, *Midnight* (1931), *Deadlock, Matinee Idol* (1933), *Paris Plane* (1933), and *Warn London* (1934), among a dozen credited films. And, very notably, he routinely provided their directors with stage and camera directions for each scene of every script. By comparison, Hitch had produced three talkies in the crime genre, *Number 17, Murder,* and Bennett's story *Blackmail*. And though the interviewers were uninformed, Hitchcock would have known all this when he was partnered with Bennett at Gaumont British.

As early as 1965, the scholar Robin Wood in *Hitchcock's Films* made an observation both astute and accurate. He observed that Hitchcock's later films compared favorably to Shakespeare's plays. But had Professor Wood studied the British credits and known of Bennett's extensive Shakespearean stage experience, he might have traced the continuity back to the Bard of Avon.

Remembering Bennett primarily for his Hitchcock talkies rereleased on video, the film historians and biographers wrongly credited his success to Hitchcock's direction. And their post hoc error was perpetuated as later scholars focused attention on Hitch to the exclusion of Charles's primacy.

In 1980 a soon-to-be-published Hitchcock scholar wrote to Bennett, asking him to elaborate on his early film credits. Charles sent this reply:

I rather resent your line, "It is chiefly his work for Hitchcock which makes Bennett worth consideration as a screenwriter." I am not suggesting that your line should read, "It is chiefly Hitchcock's work for Bennett which makes Hitchcock worth consideration as a director." This wouldn't be true. Hitch is a great man. But I do think with fifty-four screenplay credits behind me (and many other scripts written but among the missing) I am entitled to more than "worth consideration" due to Hitch. . . . Looking back over a very long screenplay life, I am aware that I would have achieved a certain amount of recognition . . . without Hitch.[4]

Charles hoped to nudge film history in a different direction. Objecting to the scholar's diminishment of his status—"overshadowed by the creative directors with whom he worked"—Bennett gave a deliberate reply: "I only worked with *one* creative director in my life. . . . The director, of course, was Hitch, but I hate to think that my only after-death recognition is due to the fact that I worked with Hitch on six movies. There were others— some quite famous. DeMille (who was entirely dependent on his writers). Sam Wood. John Farrow. James Whale. Edmund Goulding. John Sturges."

The historical damage was irreversible. By 1983, when the *Curse (Night) of the Demon* (1958), with its brooding tone, was compared favorably to Hitchcock's British films, its critic did not recognize that Charles Bennett was the author of them all.[5]

And as Hitchcock's films continued to overshadow Charles's film legacy, so was Bennett overshadowed by the persona of Hitchcock himself. The historians and journalists inevitably turned their line of questioning to how Bennett had contributed to the career of Hitchcock the auteur.[6]

au·teur: A filmmaker whose individual style and *complete control* over all elements of production give a film its personal and unique stamp.[7] (Emphasis added.)

Of course, Charles Bennett acknowledged Alfred Hitchcock as Master of Suspense. But Bennett was talking about Hitchcock the director, not an auteur. He spoke of Hitch as a creator who "could come up with great 'ideas' but he was hopeless on story line. . . . The problem for a writer was incorporating Hitch's ideas without messing up the story progression."

Critical comment was not satisfied at denying Bennett's primacy; it also sought to marginalize his talent. In the aforementioned 1980 letter, the film historian judged Bennett's classic and masterful stage melodrama

*The Last Hour* by its conformance to modern taste. Bennett replied to the inappropriate criticism: "Looking back over fifty-two years to the end of 1928, I still resent your term 'resolving an absurdly complicated plot,' etc. The play was enormously successful and had every right to be. . . . I believe there will be a swing back to *my old type of melodrama* before too long; a vast relief from the psychopathic crap with which we are presently being confronted" (emphasis added). The international success since 2006 of the comedy-melodrama *The 39 Steps* has been a partial vindication of Charles's reply.

As time wore on, Charles became outraged that critics and journalists continued to make him a footnote to Alfred Hitchcock's genius, a director whom he considered his *partner*. He was insulted by press titles such as "Gaining Fame from 'A Little Fat Man.'" He was indignant at interviewers' mislabeling Hitch as a scenarist. Then what he feared might happen after his death did actually occur—his melodramas were analyzed for their "typical Hitchcock scenario."[8]

Critical comment has dismissed Bennett's anger as the rant of a declining author whose glory days had passed. The implicit ageism of this critique was a matter he argued before the Writers Guild. But the criticism actually misses its mark. Though one does not doubt his disappointment at being sidelined in the industry he loved, that was not his principal upset. His anger was directed at writers, directors, and producers who took undeserved credit or rewrote his stories. Coming from "the man who knew too much," this justification could not be grasped by those who knew too little.

Charles loved to write, and in retirement he found the freedom to write what he wanted. He believed he became more skilled as he aged and said as much in his attack on ageism. What he did not disclose was that he had advanced the art of suspense to a new level, recombining *apprehension* with its pre-1929 melodramatic *anxiety*. That would have given a film historian much to write about, had one inquired.

Despite being shunted aside for twenty-five years, it is to Charles's eternal credit that he never gave up hope of selling another script, play, or novel. He said he wanted to live only so long as he could hold a pencil. And he died three months after receiving the 1995 Writers Guild of America, West, Laurel Award.

In July 1995 my wife and I moved into Dad's Coldwater Canyon house. Before long I unearthed a treasury of early manuscripts, novels and stage plays, unpublished films and teleplays. Also among a seventy-year clutter of stories, jottings, letters, and press clippings was an incomplete memoir and forgotten film history. It was a yearlong chore to sort the disarray into twenty-seven large boxes for delivery to the American Film Institute's Margaret Herrick Library. The interested researcher will find there a special collection devoted to Charles Bennett documents—an abbreviated list of those materials is found at the end of this book under the heading "Suggestions for Further Research." A significant number of rare manuscripts, however, are held in my personal Charles Bennett Estate Collection.

Though tempted to promote the sale of his unpublished manuscripts, I was fully determined to complete his memoir. I recognized that its significance was greater than any film I might hope to sell. But to do this, I had to cross-reference the clippings, retype or scan the memoir fragments, and record such anecdotes as I remembered. I read all the interviews that I found in his library (often worded identically to what I had recalled). And, curiously, while I was assembling the memoir, my father's voice seemed to speak from the past (or was it the hereafter?), offering words whose meanings I sometimes did not know.

I direct any scholar inquiring about my contribution to the appearances of my name in the Contents. Those chapters are my thoughts and experiences. The remainder is Charles Bennett's work, supplemented by details and anecdotes as I have recalled them or recovered them from letters and interviews. The reader will understand that when a child hears stories told at the dinner table, and then hears them repeated to houseguests, and (as an adult) hears them retold for another thirty years, those stories become woven into the warp and weft of memory. I have added only objective detail and facts, however, leaving my father's sentiments and characterizations as direct or raw as ever he expressed them.

I have also assiduously avoided reading any books of film history, including Hitchcock biographies, to avoid biasing my account. The exception has been Internet-available content, which is cited in the endnotes. The upside is that Charles Bennett's point of view has been presented as it stood twenty years ago. The downside is that my contributions will not have caught up with current scholarship.

While considering the manuscript for publication, the publisher asked about Charles's life with my mother, Betty. That was an unpleasant assignment. But putting their horror to paper helped me understand his film psyche, in which I discerned a murderous, chivalric, Shakespearean code.

That unexpected insight, presented as "the Avenger" archetype, underlies both his thriller and film noir genres. I hope my deceased mother will recognize in that discussion some vindication of her thirty-eight-year pain and neglect.

Charles originally intended his memoir to be titled *Life Is a Four-Letter Word*, and he had named several chapters to that effect. I dumped the title and changed the chapter headings. To my mind, his title was too cynical and did not acknowledge his genius. I am satisfied with *Hitchcock's Partner in Suspense* for its asserting the truth of their relationship, despite the irony of Hitchcock's name appearing in the title of Charles's memoir.

So, it is with pride for my father's lifetime achievement that I present this memoir. I hope the reader will find its anecdotes entertaining, characterizations revealing, history authentic, insights revelatory, and suggestions tantalizing.

There are two people I wish to thank. For her many years of patience, encouragement, and editorial assistance, I extend my love and gratitude to my wife, Frances. But there is one person who deserves my father's personal gratitude. He is the University of Kentucky Film Classics series editor and consummate cinema biographer, Patrick McGilligan. Where other Hitchcock biographers made only passing reference to Bennett—or worse, only listed his name among Hitch's film credits—Patrick mentioned him repeatedly in *Alfred Hitchcock: A Life in Darkness and Light* (2003). Also, his *Backstory* interview (1986) of my father was of inestimable value. And none of this would have been printed off my hard drive were it not for Patrick's persistence in bringing this memoir to publication.

John Charles Bennett

# Sowing the Wind

I used to be young. It didn't last. In fact, without noticing, I seem to have drifted into what Rupert Brooke called "that unhoped for serene,/That men call age."[9] I'm not complaining. A product of August 2, 1899, I've learned that age has its compensations—like being able to put one's feet up without worrying about the gas bill or where the next vodka tonic will come from. I've been lucky. I like my home in Beverly Hills, and although I've eaten by writing for nearly seventy years, I still like putting words together, perhaps as some enjoy figuring out crossword puzzles.

Also, I like the film industry. But it might be better described as an opportunist's paradise, a nesting place from which the guy on the right spot at the right time has a chance to spread his wings and soar—usually over severed heads—into a world of multitudinous millions. Quite a few times in my life I've been the right guy on the right spot at the right time. The opportunities have been there, but I've never known when to grab the stairway to the stars. No matter. I've enjoyed a very great deal of my long life in filmdom, and thanks to the variance of it, I can't remember ever being bored.

As Jacques says in Shakespeare's *As You Like It,* "Each man in his time plays many parts." I can say that when it comes to the creative rather than the physical side of the industry, I've played all except cinematographer. This has included work as a film editor (but only of footage that I directed), and as an associate producer of Eddie Small's TV series *The New Adventures of Charlie Chan* (1957). I have been a director of both feature films and TV shows, an occupation that has taken me nearly halfway around the world. And my name has appeared as writer on more than sixty produced feature movies, ten propaganda newsreels, and at least sixty, perhaps well over one hundred, teleplays.

But here's the stickler. Although I've spent considerably more than half my life in filmdom, I'll admit that theater remains my true love—maybe because I was born into it. During my toothless years, my mother, Lilian Langrishe Bennett (1863–1930), wildly stage-struck, was fast being separated from her inheritance by a theatrical con man, Arthur Skelton. For fifteen months, after March 1900, they toured four plays as the Miss Lilian Bennett Repertoire Company. Two of these were revivals—F. C. Philip's comedy, *The Dean's Daughter,* which probed the tortured soul of the wife of an unfaithful socialite, and *An Unequal Match* by Tom Taylor, a Victorian dramatist.

Also offered was Sydney Grundy's controversial play *Sowing the Wind,* which tells the story of an illegitimate girl, Rosa, who is neck-deep in shame.

> BRABAZON: I did not say there was a fault, Miss Athelstane . . . but you must see that it makes marriage with Ned Annesley impossible.
> ROSA: I see, I see! (*Rises.*) It's not the leper's fault that he's a leper, but he must be shunned. Oh yes! Oh yes! . . . What will become of me? . . . What am I to do? . . . I am in everybody's way and in my own. If I were wicked I should be of service. The world would want me then? But I can't be! . . . I can't be! (*Flings herself upon the sofa striking it.*)
> (*Sowing the Wind,* act 3)

Between August 1900 and June 1901, Skelton toured another dreadful four-act melodrama, *The Children of the Night,* which played theaters in Ventnor, Stalybridge, Stratford, and small towns in the North. By the end of the tour, I was one year old; Eric, my older brother, was five; Vere would be born eight months later. In return for her financial backing, Skelton— piling up new shirts while my mother was coming near to losing her last chemise—permitted his sucker to play a character named "Baby Bellamy," a part that I'm afraid hardly matched up to Lady Macbeth or Portia. Mother was happy. She was appearing on the boards, speaking drivel before an actual audience, thus achieving her proud ambition to become what in those ancient days was known as a *pro.*

In act 4 of *Sowing the Wind,* Brabazon admits to Rosa that he is her father, so things work out well enough for her. But not so for Mother. She reaped the whirlwind of her family's displeasure at her stage career and her reputation for being "a bit frisky." She was cruelly cast aside, contact with her family limited to our receipt at Christmas of a barrel of Newfoundland cod—always appreciated by my starving family.

Mother told me that Father was named Charles Bennett, a London civil engineer killed in a boiler explosion—though this scenario appears lifted from *The Children of the Night.* My wife Betty suggested Father was Kyrle Bellew (1855–1911), an international stage actor and matinee idol, gold miner and playwright. Betty's conjecture is supported by multiple tangible bits of evidence and our similar appearance. I'll accept this, since it explains Mother's interest in my following a stage career and has me directly descended from the Plantagenet monarch King Edward III.[10]

Mother's performance as Baby Bellamy did not set England ablaze. And after *The Children of the Night* were allowed to rest their gore-bespattered heads, she never spoke a line on any actual stage again. Now, thanks to Arthur Skelton, the Bennett family—minus any papa—was flat broke and eventually starving in the open fields around Greenford, west of London.

Looking back, I am inclined to believe that, given a real chance, Mother might have been a good actress. I say this because, in her struggle to provide sustenance to her offspring, she got away with many superb performances in a score of nontheatrical roles—from teaching French, of which she knew little beyond "Où est la plume de ma tante?" to being an alleged nurse in charge of a baby incubator sideshow at the Crystal Palace.

There came a glorious though short period when, thanks to recognition by a failing fashion house, her very real talent as a dress designer came into its own. I display on my dining room wall her dress designs—including a brilliantly conceived bridal gown that would be as fashionable today as when she drew it ninety years ago. But with fashions changing with the seasons, and her employers going out of business, the yapping of three hungry kids forced her to switch professions.

Always imaginative, gaudily attired, and seated before an equally gaudy kiosk, she became "Gypsy Lee," reading sweaty palms at sixpence a throw on the Cockney-beloved South Shore beach at Southend-on-Sea. Lilian Langrishe Bennett was as much a palmist as she was a gypsy, but she taught herself palmistry's four major lines. And while summer lasted, the sixpences rolled in. Her clientele, mainly postpubescent couples, eagerly swallowed the wisdom falling from her tzigane lips. Never out of character, Gypsy Lee defined the certainties implicit in the palm, starting with a line of fortune that, she announced, was firm and full of promise. Better still the head line, denoting unusual intelligence. The life line, reassuringly lengthy, would follow. But the topper was the ravishingly portentous heart line, fraught with wedding bells and a lifetime of happiness. In other words, Gypsy Lee never failed to deliver readings that guaranteed glorious togetherness. And all for a sixpence. Well, *two* sixpences. It was a con, but nobody complained of readings so consistently encouraging. And while it lasted, that wonderful summer had us Bennetts eating voraciously, like bears filling their stomachs before winter.

Nothing lasts. Gypsy Lee didn't. As far as memory serves, I think her palm-reading days began and ended in 1912. In the following year the poor dear was so broke that purchasing a South Shore pitch was dream department. Come chilly October, she put paid to the South Shore's giant roller-coaster, its coconut shies, its shooting galleries, and of course its cos-termongers, with their cheery cries of "Cockles and mussels, all alive! Oh!" Also put paid was Gypsy Lee, waving her offspring back to London, through the rain, to its pawnshops and bidding a heartrending farewell to what was left of her never-to-be-redeemed onetime finery. It was all very sad, and a very long time ago, but hard to forget.

Also hard to forget—in fact my earliest recollection—are the brokers' men. Happily, their breed became extinct soon after the turn of the century, and I am probably one of the few alive today who remembers any personal contact with the subspecies. Assigned by the government, these homeless gents lived with us to make sure we didn't shoot the moon (skip out on the rent). Mother lodged and fed them while they spied on us. But their loathsome presence didn't prevent her escape. Mother—with children in tow—was often on the run across London, to Plymouth, or Bristol, or somewhere else—a condition that fueled my fascination with the ideas of spies, chase, and the wrong man accused.

I have said that I was born into the theater. That's not strictly true. I drew my first breath in a theater railway coach, not en route from anyplace to anywhere, but plunked down on the pebbly beach of Shoreham-by-Sea, Sussex. Our derelict carriage must have been among the very first of the habitations known as Bungalow Town. My birth achieved a certain noto-riety reported in London's *Daily Mirror* as the "First Baby Born in Bungalow Town," with, I'm sure, a stomach-turning photo of me in swaddling clothes.

My grandfather Charles Thomas ("C.T.") Bennett (1830–1900) of Clifton was a rich man, a Newfoundland mine owner and shipping mag-nate who owned a score or more of Bristol-based vessels transporting salted cod from Newfoundland to England. Mother said, perhaps erroneously, that C.T. had owned the steamer *Terra Nova,* which carried Robert Falcon Scott to his death in Antarctica. Family history tells that, before 1897, C. T. Bennett was invited to become a founding partner in Shell Oil Company but—preferring to hold on to his cod-shipping interests—retorted, "There's no future in oil!" My great-grandfather Thomas Bennett (1790–1872) of Shaftesbury, Dorset, had been magistrate of St. John's, Newfoundland, at the time my great uncle Charles James Fox Bennett (1792–1883) was premier. The brothers owned the Bank of Newfoundland, over a million square miles of Newfoundland territories, and numerous mines. It was said they toasted their loss of a million pounds sterling one afternoon in a bank crash.

Grandpa Bennett was an exciting and active character, particularly between the sheets. Known as "The Chief," he never ceased to behave as such, conceiving a brood of nine, five sons and four daughters. The sons, with the exception of Hugh, who died in infancy, went to Clifton College and then on to Oxford University. Not that this running start to life paid off. In the long run not one of them did a damn thing to justify such beginnings, except perhaps for Uncle Harold, who, ending up as a very drunken ship's doctor, at least seems to have emerged as the best of the bunch.

So my uncles received the form of education that I'm sure they considered their birthright. But as Mother so frequently shot the moon, there was no time for my schooling. I acquired my three R's from her. She had me reading the Bible from an early age. My favorite writer was H. Rider Haggard, who wrote *King Solomon's Mines, Allan Quatermain,* things like that. My second favorite writer was H. G. Wells, author of *The War of the Worlds.* I read everything Jules Verne had come up with and loved it all.

I've always wondered whether writers are born or made. With me the former is the case. Mother taught me the craft as I composed stories and plays and wrote letters about fictitious situations. I attempted to write my first play, *The Mill Mystery* (1907), at the age of eight:

Act 1. Scene 1. *Inside a Mill. Darkness. Enter the Duchess.*
Duchess: This morning I had a letter. Who wrote it? I know not. Ah!
    Here it is. It says, "Meet me at 6:30 tonight at the mill. If you
    don't . . . death. Signed, Robert Allers." Yes, it's a long time since I
    saw Robert . . .

I kept a journal from the age of seven and was always writing stories or poetry, titles like *The Man of Basing* (1910), *The Moon God's Secret* (1911), *The Steam Hammer* (1912), *Black Dick* (1913), *Under False Pretenses* (1914), *The Room of Death* (1915), *The Mysterious Mr. X* (1916?), and *The Penalty* (1917). I wrote my first three-act play at the age of thirteen, *The Druid's Treasure*. My only formal education was at fourteen, when I spent nearly eighteen months at St. Mark's College School, Chelsea, and edited the *St. Mark's Gazette*. Bewilderingly, I was the top student and received the book award, *Masterman Ready* by Captain Marryat. But as for further education, I guess having to earn one's living is the best teacher of all.

The beginnings of my stage career came when I tumbled into a job as a child chorister in Max Reinhart's production of Charles Cochran's *The Miracle* at London's Olympia in 1911. During the run I believe I showed an early spark of good taste with regard to the opposite sex, a spark I hope I've never lost. I was eleven; and during the first week I found myself eyeing a little girl of my own age among the twenty or so kids who were a part of the mise-en-scène. We children had to dance and sing pipingly together when the great gates of Max Reinhart's cathedral opened, revealing us on a fairy-tale hillside. If ever an eleven-year-old can fall in love, I did—hook, line, and sinker—with an adorably elfin female dancer-cum-chorister. So deeply entranced was I that I spent an entire penny of the tuppence Mother allowed me for lunch to buy an apple for my beloved. Whether my love was reciprocated I wouldn't know, but I remember my adored was grateful; she even took my hand for about five seconds, held out the apple and said, like Eve, "Would you like a bite?" We finished the apple between us.

Tragically, time moved on. I lost my love, apple core and all; but life being what it is, we were to meet again in 1948 when I was directing *Madness of the Heart* for Arthur Rank, staying at Fountain House in Park Lane. I ran into her, almost literally, in the foyer. I must have been conscious of a flash of recognition—even after thirty-seven years. Something prompted me to ask this beautiful but unintroduced lady if she happened to remember a little boy who'd once given her an apple and with whom she'd exchanged apple bites. To my delight and surprise she responded warmly, saying she'd never forgotten the apple—or the little boy. We became immediate friends and a week later she invited me to a cocktail party in her Fountain House apartment. But by that time I was shooting my movie in the south of France and never saw her again. Her name was Gertrude Lawrence.

In 1913 I entered film, starring as the younger John Halifax in a very early G. B. Samuelson silent film, *John Halifax, Gentleman* (1915), based on Dinah Craik's classic novel. I played an orphan who, through hard work apprenticing to a Quaker tanner, eventually succeeds in love and business.

The interesting thing is that Samuelson must have been one of the very first British producers to send a production unit to a distant location. Under dear George Pearson's direction ("Honest George Pearson," as he was later known in the industry), we went to Tewkesbury, Gloucestershire, at the confluence of the Severn and the Avon rivers, a lovely old town, and stayed at the famous Bell Inn. But it was raining—a normal proceeding for a location trip even today. So there we were stuck. Weirdly enough, the sun actually came out on a Sunday morning. Perfect weather for shooting. We set up our camera at the gates of the glorious old Norman abbey. No way. The good old people of Tewkesbury—highly religious—turned out en masse. How *dare* these Londoners come up here and desecrate their Sunday morning? Honest George Pearson tried to argue, "We weren't doing any harm." Useless! There were people with pitchforks, shovels, other means of attack, telling us in no mean words that if we desecrated the Sabbath, we would be desecrated beyond measure. It's so long ago, I can't remember how it worked out; but I do know that eventually we returned to Worton Hall with enough film in the box to make some early feature film at least showable.

The film was quickly forgotten, as was my excursion into stardom. I must have been so bad that nobody ever asked me to play in a picture again. Missing the early boat, I had to start from scratch—and in a way it worked out. I became a film extra, and then achieved some importance in 1917 as an assistant to Adrian Brunel by directing at Hampstead an exterior night-time sequence of a silent film, *The Cost of a Kiss.*

In theater, as in film, I can claim to have covered the entire gamut as callboy, chorus boy, assistant stage manager, actor, and director. After *The Miracle,* I played child roles in *Alice in Wonderland* (1913) at the Savoy Theatre and *The Marriage Market* (1915) with George Edwards. As my jobs took me all over England, I became very familiar with the rail system—an element that figured into many later films.

One memory stands out. At fifteen, I was the front legs of a donkey in a Christmas pantomime called *Goody Two Shoes* at the Lewisham Hippodrome. A young gentleman of my own age named Rodney Barrie played the back legs. It was a thankless part, consisting of his crouching in the pitch dark in the donkey's rear end with his nose directly pinned to my backside. Meanwhile, I was in the happy position of peeping ahead through the donkey's eyes and pulling strings to open and shut its mouth. My part also entailed emitting asinine brays and neighs, a role that hardly demanded any dramatic training. Sad to relate, when the pantomime's run finished, and Rodney Barrie and I finally emerged from the donkey hide, our very intimate relationship came to an end. Rodney's two legs went one way, my two legs the other. Perhaps sadder was that Rodney, later a London actor, never spoke to me again.

When Germany invaded France in August 1914, I was speaking one line in Sir Herbert Tree's production of *Drake* at His Majesty's Theatre in London. The distant war inspired me to write short stories with titles such as *The Great Invasion* and *The Siege of London*, about British troops staving off German soldiers. Soon the actual war was hitting closer to home. In February 1915 my brother Eric was killed in the trenches. Then came the great German zeppelins dropping death for the first time in the history of man's inhumanity. When the airships glided over our Chelsea digs, we'd go lower in the building to escape the bombardment—and hear the antiaircraft fire. Early British flyers found a means to shoot down the monsters and the attacks ceased, but not the war.

Meanwhile, I graduated into *actual* acting in 1916, both speaking my first lines in the Horsefield and Woodward touring company's production of Conan Doyle's *The Speckled Band* and playing my first real role as Edgar in Sir Herbert Tree's production of *King Lear.* Therein brother Edmund voiced my own unseemly question:

EDMUND: Why bastard. Wherefore base?
When my dimensions are as well compact,
My mind as generous, and my shape as true,
As honest madam's issue?
As to the legitimate: fine word,—legitimate!
Well, my legitimate, if this letter speed,
And my invention thrive, Edmund the base
Shall top the legitimate. I grow; I prosper;
Now, gods, stand up for bastards!
(act 1, scene 2)

Offstage, I realized "If not by birth," I would "have lands by wit:/All with me's meet that I can fashion fit." But epiphany does not put food on the table! And now my dilemma was how best to grow and prosper.

Though I was really a bad young actor, I seemed to get employment in productions such as Gerald Alexander's *Raffles* (1917); and I continued to act through much of the World War. But acting was not enough, and like so many patriots of my generation, at seventeen I felt the call to duty.

# 2

# Duty, Honour, Country

HECT.: The brave man holds honour far more precious-dear than
life.

—*Troilus and Cressida*, act 5, scene 3

In 1917 I joined the Royal Fusiliers. I didn't wait to get conscripted—I was
underage. In those days you said, "This is my job, to join." It was all duty,
honor, country. I applied for the Royal Air Force—but the spin test made
me giddy. The RAF turned me down, thank God, because in 1918 the
casualty rate of pilots in France was 100 percent *dead*. So, before long, I
was on the Marlborough Downs, learning to be a soldier. Actually, learning how *not* to be. The camp was very big—known as Chiseldon Camp,
south of the village between Chiseldon and Ogbourne St. George. It was
high country and, in that winter of 1917, snow-covered. Sons of bitches—
they'd get us up at six-thirty in the morning, icy cold and still dark, and
soon enough they would have us out in the snow, marching up and down
and obeying idiotic orders like "Move to the right in fours, form platoon!"
Very useful, I suppose, if parading outside Buckingham Palace, but about
as useful when it came to killing Germans as carrying a rabbit's foot. Just
as well. There are probably Germans still alive whom I might have killed,
had I been more successfully instructed. I never saw a gas mask until I was
forced to use one while bringing up rations to the front line trenches facing
Albert, a town on the river Somme.

My entire war was spent on the Somme, in front of a village, Amiens.
The first night we struggled into the front line. A German shell burst right
in front of me. It came so fast I couldn't hear it coming, and the explosion
went over me. I thought that was a lucky start. Then I saw on my left a
German lying on his back—dead—with a rifle and bayonet in his body.
That was a normal proceeding. I got used to it after a while.

The Germans' March 1918 offensive was simply horrible! We retreated for about thirty or forty miles. There was thick fog. We never knew where the Germans were—whether they were behind us or on our right or left. The British front held them in front of Amiens.

I proved such a good shot that I was immediately given the title of First Class Shot, which was second to Marksman. That was dangerous. It meant that when I got to France, they made me a sniper—the most dangerous position in the world. The moment the Germans said, "There's a sniper over there," they would concentrate their guns. The life of a sniper was very short. After six weeks as a sniper on the front line, I transferred to machine gunner.

In July 1918 the Germans attacked at Château-Thierry, aiming directly at Paris. My division was thrown into support, but we never came into action, thank God. The Germans were held back. Already smashed up in the March retreat, we held the trenches near Albert, gazing down on its shattered basilique. Hot summer days passed in stuffy dugouts, the German shells shrieking overhead. Vivid moonlit nights were spent on desperately dangerous patrol through high-standing corn.

My first time "over the top" was at dawn on August 8, 1918—in the fog. With a roar that must have shaken the whole of northern France, the British front attacked from Albert to Montdidier, and my 3rd Londoners were in the first wave. There were two or three hundred tanks. And instead of helping us, the tanks became a fearful danger. A British tank would come through the fog, collecting all the barbed wire along the front line, dead and dying men in the wire. So any time we heard a tank, we'd go any other possible way through the fog. But the attack was an enormous success. The Germans were thrown back along parts of the front for ten miles; in fact, their generals were taken prisoner the following morning. I remember coming through the fog and suddenly seeing twenty to thirty Germans who had been captured; I was shocked to find they were as young as I was—I felt so sorry for them. I went over the top thirteen times. The next morning, August 9, August 10, and so on. I got used to it.

My greatest experience of the war was September 1, 1918. I was a *full* corporal by that time, which gave me great importance. I felt I was the leader. We went over the top, and I remember an awful thing—a British shell came over, and blew to pieces a German who was running for his life—and we all laughed, the funniest thing we ever saw in our lives. Then we went on, and got in advance of the battalion. The battalion had stopped at a given point, but we were about a hundred yards ahead, in an area that was nothing but shell holes and ruined trenches. We were stuck there, about twenty-five of us. The Germans knew we were there, but the battalion behind us didn't, and they kept on shelling and we were catching the shells. Our Captain Knight—a terribly nice guy—sent a soldier back across no-man's-land to try to find the battalion—but he got killed on the way.

I was in a shell hole with four or five other men, and one of them was badly wounded. We were trying to help him, but there was nothing we could do. We could hear a guy dying in a shell hole about six yards away—I couldn't take it. Eventually I got out of my shell hole and went across to his, and there he was, with his face down in the mud. I pulled him up and tried to get him out. At which point I was visible to the Germans, who were only a couple of hundred yards away.

And Captain Knight, who was in a shell hole about ten yards back, said, "Bennett, get back to your shell hole."

I said, "Sir, I want to help this man."

He yelled, "No! You're drawing fire."

Which I was—the Germans could see me moving, and they were shelling us for all they were worth, and the machine guns were opening up.

He commanded, "You're killing us. Get back to your shell hole!" He drew his gun on me, saying, "Either you get back or I shoot you right now—you are endangering our lives."

So I got back to my shell hole. That night we had hell; and eventually Captain Knight was wounded going back to tell the battalion that we were in front of it.

There's an amazing sequel. Two or three weeks later, we were ten miles or so behind the line, near a lovely little village, and everything was happy—drinking wine in the village. I was platoon corporal, and it was my job to serve out the rum ration every night.

There was a soldier, who was a cobbler, and he accused me, saying, "Corporal! You're stealing our rum! Depriving us . . ."

I replied, "I'm doing nothing of the sort!"

The next night I went into the village with a sergeant and another corporal, and we got very drunk on the red wine. We came back, staggering. This was enough for the cobbler to say, "This proves my point! You drink our rum. I'm going to report you."

So next morning, a guy came across and said, "You're wanted at company headquarters." I thought, *Oh, God! He has reported me, and now I'm really in trouble. How will I prove I didn't steal the man's rum?* So I went across to the company headquarters, and there was our new captain, a bright and delightful person. And I came in shuddering.

He said, "Oh, Bennett, yes. I want to congratulate you."

"On what?" I asked.

"You've been awarded the Military Medal for Bravery in the field."

"Me?"

"Yes, you! Captain Knight said you behaved so bravely in the attack the week before last. You've been awarded the Military Medal."

The Military Medal carries the picture of George V on its front and "For bravery in the field" on its reverse. It's not quite the "For valor" inscribed on the Victoria Cross, but nice to have all the same. I wasn't brave—just too young to know any better. But I admit I'm prouder of it than any of my plays, screenplays, or novels.

In early September I was sent to train at the III Corps Lewis Gun School, which was a welcome relief. Identified as a "keen N.C.O. who will make a good instructor," they put me in command of a nine-man Lewis gun unit. Being a Lewis gunner was a dangerous job too, but safer than being a sniper.

I loved the Lewis gun—a wonderful weapon, much faster and more effective than a Maxim machine gun. A platoon, reduced from fifty to a meager twenty men, had one or two Lewis guns, usually one, holding down about fifty yards of front line. I grew accustomed to the roar of the Lewis gun from behind. It was a very quiet roar compared to the roar of the machine guns facing me when I attacked. That roar was absolutely appalling.

Fortunately, one never knows how many people one kills. Nobody likes being in a war, but it's a job you have to do—so you do it. It never crossed my mind that I might be killed—no apprehension whatever. I don't think fear enters into it in wartime. I don't understand fear.

Firing my Lewis gun, I believe I winged a German aircraft early in November 1918, just days before the Armistice was declared. Battered but pursuing the retreating Germans across the French-Belgian frontier, the remnants of my battalion were spread out along the western banks of a canal near a devastated village. I was with a three-man Lewis gun crew, dug down in a ditchlike shell hole, on guard against any counterattack across the canal.

Seemingly, counterattack was the last thing in the enemy's mind; in fact, his only interest seemed to be in postponing our pursuit. This became evident when a Gotha bomber came over, flying low, dipping even lower as it circled and deposited bombs on the one little bridge that crossed the canal. Having done its job, it scurried back across the German lines, only to reappear minutes later with a new bomb load. By this time our antiaircraft guns were coming into action, but the Gotha pilot wasn't discouraged. He dropped his bombs and retired again, only to pay us a third visit, coming in even lower this time—I'd say at three hundred feet. But to me this seemed too good an opportunity to let pass. I let fly with a burst of bullets streaming up as the ship passed directly over us.

The plane faltered and a wing dipped; a crash seemed inevitable. I was almost sure I'd made a hit. Perhaps I had, but in any case the little Gotha recovered, flew on—although staggeringly. At least we'd achieved *some* success; the craft disappeared across the canal—and took its final bomb load with it. We didn't hear any air crash and weren't to know whether the plane managed to hobble back to an airfield or if the pilot had been wounded. If he was, I do hope it wasn't serious. We had seen the pilot, probably no older than ourselves, take his life into his hands three times in succession: a very brave young man.

Bravery? During months on the front line you have many close calls. I remember an occasion when the Portuguese artillery, shelling the Germans from behind us, got mixed up on their distances and shelled us! The Germans were throwing grenades at us all the time. A wallet in my tunic pocket was singed by the liquid fire of a German flame-thrower. I scouted numerous times at night through no-man's-land—a horrible area of total annihilation—trying to locate the placement of German machine guns. But my closest call came on the last night of the war, when we were pursuing the Germans through Belgium. I caught a chlorine-gas artillery shell, which should have killed me, and passed out when the shell hit. Fortunately, a guy managed to lean over and push my gas mask over my face.

I awoke from a coma, lying on a stretcher at a casualty clearing station half a dozen miles behind the lines. An orderly was bending over me. "The war is over—this minute," he said.

I felt mad. I had been wishing for a "Blighty one" for months. Now I had it—November 10, 1918—and it wasn't of any use to me. I don't remember anything more for about three weeks, until waking in a military hospital on the north coast of France. There was a volunteer nurse holding a lamp above me, like Florence Nightingale.

She looked at me and said, "Little boy? You're awake, little boy?"

I resented being called "little boy"! Only a few weeks before, I had been in command of a battalion of Lewis guns (fifty guns)—I was made a 2nd lieutenant on the field. But hers was the most beautiful face I have ever seen in my life.

I remained in a convalescent hospital in England for quite a long time. The gas had destroyed my throat, and I couldn't speak for six months after the war. There was no treatment, all they could do was just wait. And eventually my voice started to come back. It was very difficult. I came out of the army at the end of 1919, and I had nothing left to do but become an actor. Unfortunately, I couldn't trust my voice at that time. It was way into 1920 before I was quite sure I could use my voice again.

The sacrifices of World War I were immense—probably about ten million combat troops dead on both sides. An entire generation annihilated. But what was it about? Who controlled the North Sea? A stupid war—it could have been worked out politically. But from my point of view, maybe it was a good thing. It arrested a lousy acting career. And my first produced play, *The Return* (1927), was about the war, so in that sense it did me a lot of good.

❧ ❧ ❧

## Excerpt: *The Return*

### Opening lines from the Prologue

*A shell-hole post somewhere in France, between midnight and dawn. Only the actual shell hole is visible, except perhaps for a vague suggestion of barbed-wire entanglements beyond. The rest of the scene is lost in the darkness and mist of the winter night. The forms of two men are just seen in the gloom—Wilkins and Eric Norcott—both of them privates in the Hampshire Rifles. They are crouching low, gazing out into the darkness that conceals the German lines. For a while there is silence . . . then, far away, is heard the boom of a gun and presently the whine of the shell passing high overhead. Suddenly . . . close at hand . . . shattering the comparative quiet of the night, is heard the sharp clattering rattle of a Vickers machine gun and the roar of the bullets passing over to the German line. The irregular rattle continues for a moment or two, then stops, and the ineffable silence that follows seems, by comparison, unutterably complete. One of the figures—Wilkins—stirs with a low grunt of annoyance. He speaks quietly, with a very decided Cockney accent. A note in his voice reveals a heartfelt grievance.*

Wilkins: Bloody tikes . . . ! [*The rattle of the machine-gun is heard again. It continues for a moment or two, then stops. There is a slight pause before he speaks again.*]

Gord! Why the 'ell they can't keep back in supports beats *me*. Always the same. Front line the bleedin' onion, as usual! Tikes . . . !

[*The other figure—Eric Norcott—speaks. His voice reveals him as little more than a boy, well educated, but not at all affected. At present, decidedly nervous.*]

Eric: Do they often do it?

Wilkins: Often? It's always the same. Puttin' it acrost Jerry's ration roads, they think they are. If it ain't them it's the Tock Emmas. . . .

Eric: What are they?

Wilkins: Trench mortars. Flyin' pigs. Always the same! Always askin' for it. . . .

[*The machine-gun opens up again . . . then suddenly, out of the darkness, comes the shriek and crash of a high-velocity shell, exploding somewhere close at hand. The two men duck down into the hole. The machine gun stops again. There is annoyance, but also a kind of resigned philosophy, in* Wilkins's *voice.*]

There y'are. Jerry's got 'is rag out.

Eric (*nervously*): It's . . . it's that machine gun of ours . . . drawing fire.

Wilkins: Blimey . . . ain't that what I said?

Eric: It wasn't like the other ones.

Wilkins: Whiss-bangs. You can't 'ardly 'ear 'em comin'.

Eric (*a quiver in his voice*): It was too close . . .

Wilkins: Bloody sight too close . . .

[*The machine gun starts again. There is infinite disgust in his voice.*]

Gor' blimey! Ain't they satisfied yet?

[*The machine gun continues firing for a moment or two, then stops.*]

Eric: Will it go on much longer?

Wilkins: No. They'll buzz off back to supports afore long. Always the same. They comes up . . . gets Jerry's rag out . . . then 'ooks it back to dugouts an' leave us to stick it out. Always asking for it, we are, on this front.

Eric (*hopelessly*): Why do they do it?

Wilkins: Why? Look out . . . !

[*The whistle and crash of another shell is heard . . . nearer this time. There is silence for a moment . . . then* Eric *speaks, tensely.*]

Eric: That was nearer.

Wilkins: Um! Gettin' our range. Jerry's fed up. Gord . . . What a life!

# 3

# Shakespearean Actor

Once recovered, I went back to acting. At first I was terrible—I used to get jobs and be fired from them. But gradually I learned to act, playing with the *Brewster's Millions* company (1920), then the Compton Comedy Company, the Lena Ashwell Players, and the Gertrude Elliott Touring Company, among others. I remember roles with the Henry Baynton Company in *Antony and Cleopatra* and *A Midsummer Night's Dream*. I played Lord Fitzheron in *Tancred* (1923) at the Kingsway.

In 1923 I joined the Alexander Marsh Shakespearean Company, probably the most insignificant Shakespearean company that has ever toured the United Kingdom. We traveled through the smallest of the mining towns in the north of England, where I played in *Romeo and Juliet,* sometimes twice nightly, as well as Wednesday and Saturday matinees. I remember a week in Whitehaven, a seacoast mining town in Cumberland where I fell deeply in love with the local vicar's young daughter—a love that didn't last, not with other up-and-coming vicars' daughters along the way. One of my fans—a fair Juliet whose beauty made our vault "a feasting presence full of light"—took my virginity on a cemetery gravestone. We were in the churchyard, and I remember she did not remove her hat.

I also remember going to the Alexandra Theatre in Birmingham for a two-week season. I played Marc Antony with his famous speech in the afternoon, and Romeo twice that evening—for the princely salary of four pounds (twenty dollars) a week. It's then I began facing up to some grim financial facts. Such as: if I earned four pounds a week for playing Romeo—who never stopped talking—how much would I earn when I had to play Romeo's dad, Montague, with only twenty lines? The situation wasn't good, nor was my Romeo, for that matter.

I never had dough for drama school. Looking back at my early career, I was surely the worst young actor around, but I eventually worked myself into being a reasonably good one. After acting in a different play every week and wandering around the British provinces with three Shakespearean companies, frequently filling two roles in two different plays during matinee and evening performances—I really learned to act, developing the ability either to proclaim or play naturally. So by the autumn of 1924 I was acting in the second season of the Bristol Little Theatre doing a play a week, taking most of the important parts.

In January 1925 I became the leading juvenile man with the Ben Greet Repertory. During the first six months of 1925, our repertoire consisted of *Julius Caesar, Romeo and Juliet, The Tempest, The Taming of the Shrew, The Winter's Tale, As You Like It, The Merchant of Venice, Twelfth Night, Macbeth, Othello,* and *A Midsummer Night's Dream.*

Though Ben was a delightful codger, I was ever apprehensive. During my debut as Mark Antony, he interrupted me with a question about my stage makeup, asking, "Who do you think you are? Felix the Cat!?" And once, during our swordplay, he drunkenly tumbled off the front of the stage.

Ben Greet's company traveled to Paris in March 1925 to join with Edward Stirling as The English Players. We performed a Shakespeare play every two weeks, about eight in all, at the Théâtre Albert Premier in Paris. I became quite a hit at the English theater—my name on the marquee, and so on—starring with the twenty-one-year-old Thea Holme. In September our repertoire changed, as Shakespeare was replaced by *The Speckled Band, The Importance of Being Earnest, You Never Can Tell, Pygmalion,* and *School for Scandal.* In September 1925 Sir Arthur Conan Doyle was attending the Paris International Spiritualist Congress, when both he and Lady Doyle came to see *The Speckled Band.* He was delighted, telling Edward Stirling that I was the best Watson he had ever seen. So I must have been a pretty good actor by that time. But I never told this to Nigel Bruce, who played the role so often with Basil Rathbone.

There were in Paris at that time two well-known cafés wildly decorated as heaven and hell—where cocktails were served by lovely angelic or devilish prostitutes whom you could take upstairs. One night following our performance, another actor and I visited heaven, then after a few drinks stumbled across the boulevard to Café Mort (Death). We were seating ourselves at a coffin for drinks when the devil sauntered through the door, exquisitely cloaked and standing about six foot five—certainly the most magnificent-looking creature I have seen in my life. He approached me and spoke in English: "Mr. Bennett, I'm a fan of yours. I've seen you in the theater and I'm so happy to meet you. May I have the honor of buying you a drink?"

I said, "Certainly!" as he proposed a Faustian deal.

"If you agree, Charles, I'll look after you, see that you do very well; you'll be happy and will have enough money. But when you're a hundred, I will take your soul."

I thought about it briefly, then agreed wholeheartedly—it sounded too good to pass up.

My friend asked to get in on the deal, but the devil replied, "No. Sorry. I'm only interested in Mr. Bennett."

Then he smiled wickedly, finished his absinthe, shook my hand, and left—leaving me to pick up the tab. So here I am in my nineties, having second thoughts. But I'm not too concerned, since he owes me—I bought the devil his drink. His character, the suave villain, has remained one of my perennial favorites.

Back in London, in December 1926, I was crowned with laurel as Theseus in a spectacular production of *A Midsummer Night's Dream* at London's Winter Garden Theatre. This was followed in April 1927 by my appearing in a performance of *Othello* at the Apollo to benefit the Shakespeare Memorial Theatre Fund—and accorded royal patronage! Our all-star cast included the luminaries John Gielgud, Robert Loraine, Gertrude Elliott, and Esmond Knight. But I was aware that I was never destined to be a Robert Loraine or John Gielgud.

During his final soliloquy at Dunsinane Castle, Macbeth utters:

MACBETH: Out, out, brief candle!
    Life's but a walking shadow, a poor player
    That struts and frets his hour upon the stage
    And then is heard no more.
(*Macbeth,* act 5, scene 5)

I was about to be "heard no more"—at least on London's West End stage. In December 1927 my career culminated with an acclaimed performance as Aramis in Robert Loraine's *Cyrano de Bergerac* at the Apollo. Then came 1928–29, and events in my life changed with remarkable rapidity as an unexpectedly profitable future as a writer opened for me.

# 4

# Keith Chesterton

## *My Most Unforgettable Character*

I was discontent throughout my early twenties—in the eyes of society I was a struggling young actor. But like Antipholus in *Comedy of Errors,* I had my honor to stand for. Like Arragon of *Merchant of Venice,* I wanted people to choose me for my worth, "to cozen [my] fortune" with their "stamp of merit." I needed an opportunity, a mentor.

Then came the break I had hoped for. I met a prominent woman whose friendship I valued enormously. She helped me find direction and introduced me to London's most creative and successful society. With her help, I would imagine a future.

Mrs. Cecil "Keith" Chesterton—widow of the journalist Cecil Chesterton (G.K.C.'s brother)—had come into my life late in 1923. During a financially depleted looking-for-further-work period at home in London, I attended a Stage Society performance of Anton Chekhov's *The Cherry Orchard* at the St. Martin's Theatre. I had been given a ticket—I hadn't the money to pay for one, anyway. But the evening had completely bewildered me. In the vestibule after the show I was introduced to a very smart, very dazzling, very bright-eyed lady, Mrs. Cecil Chesterton. She asked me how I had enjoyed the performance, and I frankly admitted that I hadn't understood any part of it. The lady's male companion frowned, and—feeling I had got off on the wrong foot—I apologetically added that perhaps I would be able to better understand and appreciate Mr. Chekhov when I was older. The companion, whom I presently realized with deep awe was Hubert Griffiths ("H.G."), one of the two dramatic critics of the London *Sunday Observer,* coldly remarked that he was quite sure that I would *never* be able to understand and appreciate Mr. Chekhov.

Curiously enough, H.G.—whose opinion of my intelligence was so justifiably low—gave a remarkably good *Observer* review of my first play, *The Return,* some three years later. For that matter, so did Mrs. Chesterton in *G.K.'s Weekly*—though she gave a first-class write-up to my every play, good, bad, or indifferent, which suggests that she was more honest as a friend than she was as a critic.

As things worked out, H.G. did me a great service by making me feel rather less than six inches tall. Keith Chesterton, whose middle name should have been compassion, reacted to my obvious discomfiture. In what I conclude was an attempt to alleviate my unhappiness, she then and there invited me to her next Saturday-night party—and that was the beginning of one of my most treasured friendships.

It was also, although I didn't realize it at the time, the beginning of a step up the ladder. At Keith's I met playwrights and novelists and journalists and editors, and I began to realize that there was a world outside the Theatre Royal, Widnes, Lancashire, and the Grand Theatre, Hetton-le-Hole, Durham. Soon I started to write. And out of the supreme kindness of her heart, Mrs. Cecil Chesterton gave me infinitely more than the encouragement that a budding writer needs. She gave me a belief in myself, and what greater gift can there be than that?

Through the late 1920s I used to go up to her flat and read her my plays, act by act as I wrote them. Her advice was always constructive. Later on, when I became caught up in the film industry, I used to read her my screenplays. Here Keith was on less solid ground—the talking picture was a fledgling form of entertainment—but she was never wrong in her fundamental criticism.

Her friends, and they were legion, knew her as Keith. She was a Londoner bred and born. Her flat was on Fleet Street, opposite that big hanging clock at the Law Courts and directly overlooking the original site of the old Temple Bar. To use a cliché, the printer's ink of Fleet Street was in her veins, and at that time she was probably the most successful and most highly paid woman journalist in London. Her frequent two-page feature spread in the *Sunday Express* was always exciting and rewarding reading, and sometimes truly sensational.

Keith was slim and chic and completely charming, and her laughter was spontaneous and tremendously catching. Her personality was so vital, her approach to life and people so vivid and bubbling with interest. On occasion she could be passionately eloquent, and her personal magnetism was such that her parties—those oh-so-frequent parties—drew most of the artistic and literary names of London. Not that names meant a thing to Keith Chesterton. Her all-consuming interest was in people, successful or not—it didn't mean a thing to her, so long as they were lacking in sham.

Her six-story, shallow-fronted building must have been two hundred years old, and its stairs had not been constructed for easy access. At one of Keith's wilder costume parties, those stairs should have been, but weren't, the end of Stacy Aumonier—always to me one of the world's finest short story writers. My wife Maggie—whom I would marry in 1930—and I had appeared at the party as a pantomime horse. Naturally, I had insisted on being the front legs—the head and mouth end—while she, poor girl, stooped and staggered blindly in the buttocks. We had donned the array down below in Fleet Street, then mounted the infinitely narrow stairway slowly and painfully—and from her point of view, complainingly. Our appearance at the party caused a minor sensation, and Stacy Aumonier insisted on taking over as the horse's front legs while I retired to the kitchen for my first drink. With my poor wife still as the obedient buttocks, they mounted those steeply narrowing stairs, up past Weingott's tobacco store-rooms, up past Keith's living room and kitchen, narrowing further as they scaled the heights past the bedrooms, to emerge into the highly atmo-spheric but seemingly quite useless attic beneath the leaded roof. Stacy complained of the heat and shook himself free of the costume. Whether it was the sudden change from dark to light or the effect of some previous whiskey and sodas isn't known, but Stacy promptly fell down those steep and twisting and narrow stairs, three solid flights of them, without even raising a bump.

The party was uproariously successful. Crowded, noisy, ridiculous but fun—full of the greats and the ungreats. Young actors and actresses and would-be dramatists and journalists on the way up mingled with the giants, some of whom were already on the way down. Leading drama crit-ics such as Sydney Carroll and St. John Ervine forgot that they were men of letters and discussed everything from Charlie Chaplin to the general strike while they tippled whiskies and sodas in the kitchen. G. K. Chesterton, perched voluminously in the largest available chair and look-ing like an overflowing Buddha, regaled fascinated listeners with fascinat-ing stories, many of which couldn't be heard because a top Covent Garden opera singer was leading floor-squatting guests in roof-raising sea chanteys out in the front room. And H. G. Wells and Gilbert Frankau and John Galsworthy and Sybil Thorndike chatted and laughed through the small hours. And there was a very young man down from Oxford University, brought to the party by his elder brother, then riding the crest of a successful novel, *Kept: A Story of Post-War London.*

Some time around three in the morning, the bank manager who lived above the bank next door, wearing a nightgown and nightcap, bobbed furiously at his window in a fruitless attempt to still the adjoining uproar. He shouted wild threats to the effect that he would appeal to the policeman on the Fleet Street beat; but as the policeman was naturally an *en passant* guest at the party, the poor bank manager got nowhere with his protests, and presently he took the line of least resistance, abandoning his night attire to come to the party himself.

As for the young man just down from Oxford, nobody missed him until around five o'clock in the morning, when it was realized that he hadn't been seen since soon after his arrival. His novelist brother suggested he might have gone home; parties weren't the youth's cup of tea, anyway. But an alarming element entered the situation when it was learned that he had been seen shortly after midnight ascending the ladder that led from the attic up through the skylight to the roof.

He wasn't on the roof, although many of the guests were, overworked Fleet Street editors and publishers and painters, lolling on mattresses and cushions and exchanging restful pleasantries with this lovely lady or that. As it happens, one of the closest friends of our wonderful hostess was Val St. Cyr, who at that time was among London's leading dress designers, so the parties were never lacking in alluring models. There was also an exquisite young creature named Doris, who had long, golden tresses and lived like Rapunzel at the top of a tower in that immediately adjoining medieval area called the Temple. Doris dearly loved the roof and the companionship she found there, but her report only added to the growing concern. Yes, she had seen the young man, around half past twelve. He had climbed away into the night over a flying buttress that led to heaven knows where.

And just when the confusion was mounting to a crescendo and the local cop was summoning the fire brigade to search, or pick up the pieces, the youth came climbing back to the party, alive and well. He had spent the small hours of the night on the high old rooftops of Fleet Street, climbing from roof to roof—along the street's southern side as far as Bouverie Street and back. Rooftop climbing was his hobby. His name was Evelyn Waugh, who only two or three years later was to startle the world with *Decline and Fall* (1928) and *Vile Bodies* (1930).

Evelyn Waugh survived a nighttime trip across the Fleet Street rooftops; Stacy Aumonier survived a fall that should have broken his neck. I can only believe that some special guardian angel supervised Keith's parties. Keith was an angel herself, but she could hardly have been responsible for either Evelyn's or Stacy's survival. It wasn't until some two years later that a large proportion of the destitute women of London would have been more than willing to bestow the title of guardian angel upon her. Her compassion changed the face of London.

In those days I lived in a strange old flat above an early eighteenth-century church at 26 West Street, Shaftesbury Avenue. The Ambassadors Theatre was on my left, and that teeming slum area of the Seven Dials was directly behind me, the slums stretching away through St. Giles to Drury Lane and looking much the same as they must have looked in the days of *The Beggar's Opera* and Captain Macheath. Charles Wesley (John Wesley's brother) had been rector of the church around 1727. Today the church has been converted into dance and theater rehearsal rooms. So much for what should be a historical monument. Sad.

The church had narrow stone steps at its door. Every night when I came home, whatever the hour and however desperate the winter cold, old women would be sleeping on those steps. There was just room for two of them, huddled together in their stinking rags. To open the door and pass through the church and ascend to my own warm bed, I used to have to step over the poor old souls. Usually they didn't wake; they were too numb with cold and utter weariness. If I had money I would slip it into a fold of their rags in the hope that they would find it when they awoke at dawn.

I remember it all so well: the Gay Twenties, the Roaring Twenties, the Hideous Twenties. The starving, homeless women, contemptuously abraded as besotted and immoral pariahs, found all over London. In the West End one saw them on the steps of St. Martin-in-the-Fields, and under the arches of St. Paul's Church in Covent Garden. The old, broken women huddled in doorways throughout Central London, and when the police moved them on, as they frequently had to—because to sleep in the open through the bitter winter night was frequently to die—they would walk . . . and walk . . . and walk. Usually their frostbitten feet were bleeding because their worn-out boots or shoes had ceased to afford protection. Some tied bundles of newspaper around their flapping, soleless footwear.

Keith was a woman of compassion. But she was also a journalist, a smart one, a top one. Thinking journalistically, she was looking for the story behind the horror that the rest of us accepted as the ordinary face of London. Keith started out to explore, and she was nothing if not thorough. She chose the bitterest months of winter to eye the problem, donned her oldest clothes, and left that easy apartment in Fleet Street. She disappeared out of our lives and into the vastness of what was then the biggest city on earth.

Less than three months after that party at which Evelyn Waugh explored the Fleet Street rooftops, Keith was down-at-heel and ragged, selling matches, sleeping in flophouses and sometimes in the streets, seeking pennies for her next cup of tea or her next piece of bread and margarine—but seeking a future for thousands of agonized souls. I recall the day when Keith returned to Fleet Street—out of the vast anonymity of London—filthy and ragged and more than half-starved. She was pale and thin and strangely beaten. And all the laughter had gone out of her, not because of what she had personally suffered, but because of what she had found and what she had seen.

Keith started to thaw out, and after the passing of a week or two we found that she could still laugh. But there was little time for laughter in her life now. First she wrote a six-part, two-page weekly spread for the *Sunday Express*. In it she stripped the shining peel off London and revealed the rotting core beneath. Next she wrote *In Darkest London*, the full story accompanied by facts and the shame-making figures. Then Keith started in to *do* something about it—and do something she did!

Her immediate object was to create bearably comfortable night shelters, hostels where homeless women could find clean and comfortable beds, hot baths and a hot meal, and the facilities to wash and fumigate their reeking and often verminous rags. Rehabilitation was a part of the plan—but the crying need was for beds where the hopeless and weary could escape the bitter cold and inhospitality of the streets. Keith was a prodigious worker, and she poured her fantastic energy and courage into what was at first a one-woman crusade.

Help was quickly forthcoming. Her book created a furor—the bishop of London preached a sermon on it—and the lord mayor promptly lent the Mansion House for the first fund-raising meeting. Queen Mary—a great humanitarian herself—stepped into the picture, lending her sympathy and her real help. Within a year of Keith's wanderings among the lost, the first Cecil House (named after Keith's husband, Cecil Chesterton) was established in what had been the old Poetry Bookshop in Devonshire Street, Bloomsbury. The queen was there, and her close interest in Keith's great work was ever continuing. Others followed fast: one wonderful woman's dream coming true.

I had the honor and pleasure of seeing the birth pains and triumph of the Cecil Houses. Women who hit the lowest depths regained their pride and hope. And as life without hope is death, Keith Chesterton brought women back from the grave.

The last time I saw Keith was about 1958. If the London *Times* was right about her age, she was then around ninety. She looked like a woman in her sixties, and she still could laugh. I took her to dinner at Le Bon Viveur in Shepherd Market behind Park Lane. We sat beneath the little balcony, and that delightful three-piece Gypsy orchestra played and played and played—for Keith. I doubt if any of the three musicians knew who she was or had even heard of her. But I felt by the way they played that they sensed here was a *living* soul, with laughter and gaiety and an appreciation of life. A friend.

She died on January 20, 1962. At Queen Mary's urging, she had been awarded the O.B.E. (Order of the British Empire ) in 1938. Nellie Denstone Fennelle—a member of the Council of Cecil Houses from their inception—said of Keith in an obituary appreciation: "Ada Elizabeth Chesterton will never be forgotten by any who have sheltered under the roof which has embodied all she wished and worked for. 'Her children arise and call her blessed.' "

And though to the ragged women of London's streets Keith was a saint, her friendship and helpful criticism of my writing was a most wonderful and life-altering gift.

In 1925 I was to learn that to be a friend of Mrs. Cecil Chesterton was to be a member of a sort of international club or brotherhood. I was living in a small, ten-francs-a-night hotel in the Rue de Vaugirard off Montparnasse, but Keith's close pals Jan and Cora Gordon were only just around the corner on the Rue du Cherche Midi. Both painters and writers of great talent, they lived in a small studio in the heart of the Latin Quarter, but they spent more than half of each year wandering across Europe, painting and writing. Their books (with reproductions of their paintings) always sold well. This didn't mean that they were rich, but in the Latin Quarter in the mid-1920s, nobody gave a damn how much money one had.

Through Jan and Cora I saw the Latin Quarter as it really was. I dined at tiny, superb, but cheap restaurants; the Rotonde and the Dome became my local pubs. I met Picasso and Utrillo and Diego Rivera, and dozens of others. I ventured underground, from the brightness of the Latin Quarter's Place Denfert-Rochereau into the accumulating gruesomeness of the Paris catacombs. For a while I was allowed to become a part of the Quarter—but only because, in effect, Keith Chesterton had sponsored me. And the Keith Chesterton club extended far beyond the Latin Quarter of Paris. Armed with Keith's introductions, I met "club members" in Budapest and New York in the 1930s, and later on, in Hollywood. I met up with it again in Berlin in 1946, and in the 1950s in Madrid, and in Toledo, which Keith considered the loveliest of all European medieval cities. I still have friends in Hollywood who come under the heading of the Keith Chesterton brotherhood.

$$\backsim \backsim \backsim$$

## Interlude: Magic in Montmartre

I heard a night wanderer singing an Italian love song in the shadow of Sacré Coeur. Away to the south, far below me, the crimson lights of Pigalle blazed across the sky. The murmur of Paris came to me softly on the breeze. I knew what that murmur meant. The Paris night . . . still young. The noisy throng on the boulevards. Laughter. The glitter and bustle of the crowd. But up here in the narrow, ill-lit streets was peace . . . and an Italian love song!

There was a spell in that song although the singer was invisible to me. And as I listened, I realized that in this modern world of ours, magic is only a matter of luck! Here was I, alone, on the sleeping heights of Montmartre, and here was magic, filling the streets, stirred into being by that song of southern love in the moonlight. Magic memories. The magic of the night. The magic of the enchanter's spell and the sigh of a dreaming princess!

The ancient hag who slept on a doorstep before me, I knew for a witch! Wretched? She? Not a bit of it! With a wave of her crutch, gold would drop on her from the skies, and on many a dark night, at a muttered incantation, her stick would whisk her swiftly away to a Witches' Sabbath in the deepest gorge of Fontainebleau! A cat slunk away from under my feet as the song swelled through the streets. Its eyes gleamed wickedly and, in spite of the warm breeze, I shivered involuntarily. I had stumbled on magic by the purest chance. The Butte, strangely medieval in the dimness, was alive with it. But it was not all white magic!

Several times since, I have tried to recapture the wonder of that night. I have prowled the heights from the Abbesses to the Lapin Agile. In the warm darkness I have wandered through the Rue Ravignan and round by the Jardin des Oliviers, but I have met with no success. But I shall search again a week or so hence, when my friends, the gargoyles of Notre Dame, stand out once more so vividly against the full-moon sky.

I am told that they are comparatively modern but I refuse to believe it. They are as old as Paris itself and they know the wisdom of the ages. In the dim, dim past, the dreadful strains of the Black Mass have hummed about their twisted ears, and for a million mysterious Paris nights they have gazed out over the silently flowing Seine. When the moon is full I will ask them for their secret.

# 5

# Sensation

Acting in Paris off and on during 1925 and 1926, I wrote my first three full-length plays. We were performing and rehearsing a different play every two weeks, and I wrote when I should have been sleeping. *The Return,* my first play, was written in the spring of 1925, inspired by one of several weekend visits to the battlefields where I had fought in the trenches. *Blackmail* and *The Last Hour* were written in Paris later in 1925 and in 1926.

I appeared May 30, 1927, in the opening-night performance of my first produced play, *The Return,* at the Everyman Theatre—without salary. I was the director, and Alexander Field, who had acted with the Ben Greet company, was its producer.

The famous investigator of the paranormal, Sir Oliver Lodge, wrote an endorsement that we quoted on *The Return*'s book jacket: "I hope that the multitudes will gain an opportunity of seeing it. The problem set is of great interest, the climax is ingenious, and the whole play is thoughtful and interesting. The first message of the play, I take it to be, is that normal life furnishes an ideal opportunity which no spirit or anyone else can emulate or replace, and the second is that the consequences of our acts live after us and only by love can be gradually effaced." A very fine credit, for an author's first play.[11] Except—Sir Oliver claimed I was not the actual author! He told me the dead Oscar Wilde had used me as *his* pen.

One thing for certain was that I had a voice in the casting of *The Return,* and I'm proud to say that I gave nineteen-year-old Peggy Ashcroft her first real job in London's professional theater. She was magnificent; the critics acclaimed the young actress, and she never looked back.

When the American impresario Al Woods arrived in London in 1927, he found himself in possession of a theater but in need of a play to replace Frederick Lonsdale's *Foreigners,* which had been abandoned. He advertised for authors to send their manuscripts for review, and to my satisfaction, he chose my play *Blackmail* from among three hundred submissions. The play was based on the experiences of a girl of whom I was once very fond, an adventure she had after attending the Chelsea Arts Ball. *Blackmail* opened at the Globe Theatre on February 28, 1928, produced by Raymond Massey, and starring the lovely Tallulah Bankhead, then in her mid-twenties.

I remember that during the run Tallulah invited me into her dressing room for a drink—she was stark naked. It wasn't an invitation to an affair; it was just the way she was. But the play met a stormy reception, as Tallulah's enthusiasts rushed the gallery stairs and the police were called. There was press notoriety concerning her role, then the play flopped. Critics remarked that if this was the best of several hundred plays, exactly how bad must the others have been? I had to go around apologizing, eventually replying to the criticism in a letter to the *Sunday Express*. When it was mentioned that I was the author, people thought it funny. Fortunately, S. Rossiter Shepherd, film critic for the *Sunday People,* published the truth about the miserable business, revealing how the original play had been hacked about and spoiled by Al Woods. This cleared me, as I could not really say a word in my own defense without repercussions among producers. Later, in Hollywood, Al Woods borrowed a couple of hundred dollars from me, so things wouldn't go well for him.

An interesting side note: I was actually knifed during a June 1928 performance of *Blackmail* at the Regent Theatre, King's Cross. I was playing the artist Peter Hewitt and, during the rape scene, the bread knife slipped from the grasp of the actress Violet Howard and sliced into my left ear. I received treatment at the Royal Free Hospital and then was able to return to the stage, head bandaged, for the curtain call.

When the original version went on tour with multiple touring companies, it proved the success it should have been in London's West End. Thank God. One reviewer wrote kindly of me, "His object is to show the moral murderousness of blackmailers, and he succeeds vividly. He not only shows the tortures of the blackmailed, but lays bare also the state of mind of the blackmailer. The subtlety of alternating drama and psychology demands from the cast an unfaltering accuracy of interpretation."[12]

My third play, *The Last Hour,* was a suspense melodrama, full of surprise and turnabout, with liberal comic relief, and pioneering a bombastic use of stage special effects. It was a spy adventure staged in the bar parlor of the Goat and Compasses, a hostelry located in the lonely Devon fishing village of Coombe Regis. *The Last Hour* featured a cruel and suave, totally unscrupulous foreign agent, Prince Nichola, attempting to steal an all-powerful death ray (laser) out of England while matching wits with two disguised British Secret Service agents. There was a heroine in love with a British agent, whose father was emotionally extorted to assist the ruthless villain. And there was a time limit imposed by the midnight sailing of a ship; suspense built through a convict's escape, a murder, the strangulation of our heroine's love interest, and the glorious before-our-eyes incineration of the villain. Comic relief was provided by a name-bungling constable, often more officious than competent.

*The Last Hour* was enormously successful in London and on tour. The Duke of York—later King George VI—personally congratulated me, after he and his future queen consort saw the show on its third night. I doubt if many people can name-drop like that.

*The Last Hour* cemented my second career as a melodramatist in the classic style. In his review of opening night, December 26, 1928, at the Comedy Theatre, the drama critic of the *Sunday Times* of London compared favorably my work to that of the British dramatist John Webster (1580?–1638?). But most curious was his long adulation of Webster:

Of a playwright long since demoded and his thrillers which many generations have forgotten, a famous critic wrote: "The culmination of these tragedies, setting like stormy suns in blood red clouds, is prepared by gradual approaches and degrees of horror. The materials with which this dramatist builds are sought for in the ruined places of abandoned lives, in the agonies of madness and despair, in the sarcasms of reckless atheism, in slow torture, griefs beyond endurance, the tempests of sin-haunted conscience, the spasms of fratricidal bloodshed, the deaths of frantic hope-deserted criminals. He makes free use of poisoned engines, daggers, pistols, disguised murderers, masques, and nightmares. Yet in his firm grasp upon the essential qualities of diseased and guilty human nature, his profound pity for the innocent who suffer shipwreck in the storm of evil passion not their own, save him, even at his gloomiest and wildest, from the unrealities and extravagances into which less potent artists—Tourneur for example—blundered." The dramatist was Webster and the critic John Addington Symonds.

Webster endowed villains with matchless cunning, a hatred of good for its own sake, and a plentiful lack of conscience.[13] My *Nelson's Encyclopedia* (1940) acknowledges Webster as the *master* of terror and violence second only to Shakespeare! Of course, like the Elizabethan Webster, I had learned my dramatics on the Shakespearean stage. So upon this acceptance as the modern-day Webster, I continued to write thrillers for stage and film, in the Shakespearean tradition.

*The Last Hour* was an overnight hit mainly because I burned two of my main characters to charred embers before the thrilled eyes of my audience—trick stuff beautifully arranged by David Devant of the famous magical and illusionist theater, Maskelyne and Devant. On opening night I had to make a speech following the final curtain, and according to the drama critic of the London *Daily Mail*, "The author was trembling so violently that he obviously feared that his death ray was about to be turned on *him*." But the truth be known, the death ray had already turned on me.

On the evening of August 10, 1928, my younger brother, Vere (full name Thomas Vere Fane Bennett)—stage director for Laddie Cliff's *So This Is Love* at the Winter Garden Theatre—went mad and hanged himself. Vere was the talented one! He was a playwright, and a stage director employed at the St. Martin's Theatre, the Carlton, *and* the Winter Garden. But on that fateful evening he had gone up to bathe and change before going to the theater. Later I found him hanging in a tall portable wardrobe closet. Vere ended his life without warning, and without apparent cause. There had been no trouble, no unhappiness. My mother was delirious with grief. She warned, "Don't go near the closet! It got Vere . . . it will get you too!"

I wrote immediately to a psychic investigator, Hannen Swaffer of London's *Psychic Times* newspaper: "I am in rather a terrible state, and want to talk to you. I feel the end of the world has come. I can bear it, but my mother can't. You will wonder why I inflict this on you, but you once talked to me about Spiritualism, and you were sincere. I must find comfort for Mother. I hope you don't think me an ass. I will phone you about five, and ask if you can see me."

Swaffer told me there would be a séance that night in his flat with a nonprofessional medium named Noel Jaquin, and he suggested that I come along. At the séance the spirit, a Scottish schoolmaster named Macdonald, acknowledged, "There is somebody here in trouble," then proceeded to explain.

Generations ago, the spirit explained, one of my forebears had murdered someone, and the victim had been seeking vengeance ever since. "When your brother went up to bathe," the guide told me, "the door of the wardrobe was open. And when your brother hung up his clothes, the evil entity took advantage of the semidarkness to bring about in his mind a condition which caused his suicide. Tell your mother that Vere is in no way to blame. It will ease her mind. We have dealt with the entity, and he has been taken where he can do no more harm."

I had had no particular previous experience with spiritualism—though there was a time in the trenches when I sensed a presence on the battlefield, and which I wrote into my play *The Return*. So this Macdonald experience had me bewildered. "You don't believe me, do you?" the spirit guide went on. "Well, I will try to prove it to you. Will you believe me if I come to your rooms tonight and knock on the wall?"

"Yes," I agreed, skeptically.

"Well, at two o'clock I will knock on your wall at home," Macdonald promised.

"What sort of a knock?" I asked, for this hardly seemed credible.

"I will knock twice like this" was the reply, and the medium's hand rapped on the chair.

Soon after, the séance ended and I returned home. At two o'clock, I was still up with my mother and a cousin in the sitting room. I had not told Mother anything about the séance, as I did not believe anything would happen; and neither did I want to disturb her. Then we heard it, like Poe's raven: "Suddenly there came a tapping, as of someone gently rapping, rapping at my chamber door."

The rapping from the outside hall was very like what I had been told to expect. Mother heard it also and wondered what it was. It was not until the next day that I told her of the extraordinary prophecy and how it had been fulfilled. My flat was in a building, all alone. Nobody could have rapped outside, because no one was living or working there. I was staggered by that confirmation happening in the early hours of the morning.

A day or so later I had the closet burned. Then I visited the secondhand dealer who had sold it to Vere. He disclosed that there had been a previous suicide in it, which is how it came to him. There was talk of black magic. Was it coincidence? Retaliation? Malevolence? Almost seventy years have passed; when asked today, I invariably claim the séance and rapping were somehow fraudulent. But Vere's suicide actually convinced me that at death everything isn't quite over. And to this day, I will not allow rope in my house.

Soon after *The Last Hour,* I adapted a Hazel May Marshall story, *Ten Minutes to Twelve,* as a play titled *The Danger Line.* It was produced in September 1929 by the Chamberlain Brown Players in association with the impresario Lee Shubert at the Greenwich Theatre, Greenwich, Connecticut. *The Danger Line* was not memorable, but, never mind—with two plays already produced in London's West End in less than one year, and not yet out of my twenties, I was being mentioned as one of the most promising of the younger British dramatists.

In 1929 I bought my first car, a Buick Century that I dubbed the Prince Nichola. I was stupidly considering myself to be on top of the heap, and I was surely strutting. Dancing, too! For the first time, I could afford to take this or that lovely young lady to the Café de Paris after we had dined at the Savoy Grill. Among these was Margaret "Maggie" Riddick, an actress who starred in *The Last Hour* with the North Touring Company. I had chosen not to marry, had decided to take care of Mother in her old age. But Mother died unexpectedly on June 30, 1930—and less than a month later I married Maggie after a much-publicized one-week romance.

Now, with an immense amount of money pouring in from the West End, from multiple companies touring *Blackmail* and *The Last Hour,* and from the sale of a *Blackmail* novel—which the author Ruth Alexander wrote from the film (and which I never bothered to read)—my future seemed assured.

Maggie and I spent our first eighteen months living over a butcher's shop on Finchley Road. But as soon as our lease ran out, Maggie found a delightful flat at 4 West Halkin Street, adjacent to ultraposh Belgrave Square. Our life together was fun—theater, cocktail parties, sports, travel. *Blackmail* and *The Last Hour* were touring successfully, and both of their film versions played the cinemas. The director George King was churning out my stories in film. I was contracted to British International Pictures, and then Gaumont British. There was talk of the Shubert brothers producing my plays *Sensation* and *Masquerade* in New York.

Except—for the ancient truism of mice and men—came the crash! It had nothing to do with stock markets. Suddenly *theater,* along with circuses and other regalements, had fallen to pieces. The reason? The coming of talkies! In just months the onslaught from Hollywood spelled the end of what hundreds of generations had known as a pleasurable diversion. All over the world the live playhouses were tumbling like ninepins, either closing down completely or grabbing at the talkie bonanza and converting into cinemas. In 1929–30 there were six touring companies performing plays of mine around Britain. By 1931 only two remained; in 1932, none. This was because there weren't enough theaters left in which to present live shows. Oh, a few places stuck it out—in Manchester, Birmingham, Glasgow. But taken as a whole, the great cities suffered as much as did the littler ones, and London was no exception.

Up until the day Warner Bros. somersaulted the film industry by having Al Jolson warble "Mammy," Leicester Square alone had had two revue houses, the Empire and the Alhambra, and two musical comedy theaters, Daly's and the Leicester Square. Only yards away was the London Hippodrome, where I had seen bevies of beauties belting out Gershwin's "Swanee! How I love you." All these theaters went. The lovely Alhambra was replaced by the far-from-attractive Odeon Cinema, this being perhaps the greatest tragedy of all because the Alhambra, birthplace of such songs as "If You Were the Only Girl in the World," to which hundreds of thousands of young men had sung their way into France's front-line trenches in 1914–18, should have been preserved as a monument to a million of them dead.

Time has marched on, and although talkies still have the theater down for the count, the chances of the oldest entertainment species in the world surviving seem to be improving. But I'm digressing. In Frank Loesser's wonderful musical *Guys and Dolls,* the Damon Runyan characters—all hot-shot devotees of Nathan Detroit's "Oldest established floating crap game in New York"—are exhorted by a Salvation Army lass, Sarah Brown, to "put down the bottle and stray no more." I don't promise to put down the bottle, but I do promise to "stray no more"—well, no more than I can help.

So back to the irony at hand. I continued to write for the stage at the rate of a play a year until 1936. I directed my next melodrama, *Sensation,* at the Lyceum Theatre, London, on October 15, 1931. The press called it "lurid and exaggerated," "raving," a "melodramatic thriller," "a guileless orgy of gore." It tells of an innocent journalist who discovers a corpse on the Southampton boat-train, then allows himself to be arrested for the murder so his paper would get a scoop. There is an endangered heroine (the lovely actress Eve Gray), a chase scene, diamond smugglers, secret passageways—lots of nonsense—and a courtroom drama ending with the shooting of a witness.

By modern standards, *Sensation* should have been a great success; but melodrama was out of vogue. Denis Dunn, theater critic for the *Daily Express,* had written a lousy review of opening night. And I remember Maggie's father saying, "From what I hear, the theater can't *give* the seats away." But I would have my revenge. I sent Dunn a courteous invitation to come backstage during a later performance and "play with the works." I fiendishly timed his arrival to coincide with the stagehands' preparing the train for the thrilling scene of the first murder. "Would you care to see inside one of the carriages?" I asked Dunn. He assented, as two stagehands lifted him into a carriage to seat him with two members of the cast. Immediately, I sent up the curtains—and Dunn was a player, facing the packed Lyceum audience. A porter served him neat whiskey. Then the murder occurred, with all its ensuing chaos and pandemonium, and a horror-struck Dunn nearly fell into the euphonium. The audience howled with laughter, and I escorted him out to the open air with "Well, cheerio. Pop in again some time when we have a part for you. Bye-bye!" Happily, on November 2, Dunn was sufficiently recovered to publish a favorable account of his sensational experience with the caption "The Nitwit in the Train—When the Gun Went Off—Revenge!"

In February 1932 my play *Big Business* premiered at the Beaux Arts Theatre, Monte Carlo, with Edward Stirling and his English Players. I acted and directed, joined by my actress wife, Maggie. It tells the story of a ruthless financier trying to take over a profitable scheme from an entrepreneur sent abroad, only to find himself in a battle of wits with the entrepreneur's intuitive wife. The play was reviewed for the *London Referee* as "the most interesting event of the Monte Carlo season . . . an exceedingly clever play which sparkles with amusing dialogue from beginning to end and is tense with dramatic moments." The *Monte Carlo Life* described it as "comedy drama at its best with an excellent and well knit plot, sentiment, and humour, all blended in the right proportions to make an excellent evening's entertainment." Shortly after, it played in London at the Comedy Theatre. And in 1934 I adapted *Big Business* for the screen, starring Eve Gray in place of Maggie.

*Heart's Desire,* a play I wrote in 1934, was undoubtedly the best play I have written, and my only play I *really* loved. It is a love story built around early aviation themes, telling of a female pilot waiting at lonely Pendine Sands, South Wales, hoping to attempt the first woman's solo east-west Atlantic flight. I came close to staging it in London in 1939, but the West End producer Hugh "Binkie" Beaumont double-crossed me when Fay Compton wanted to play it, so it never achieved production. Later, I rewrote it under the title *Who Was Jenny?* It's beautiful, awfully good. I plan to dust it off and try to promote it again. God willing, I may sell it yet. A good story never dies!

But not so the king of England.

In January 1936 my play *Page from a Diary* (also known as *Masquerade*) opened at the Garrick Theatre, starring Greer Garson. It came to a sticky end as King George V died four days later. All theaters closed for two weeks of mourning, and we were never reviewed. The cast rallied; but without a house to pay salaries, that was the end. My play died, like the king.

All together, eight of the fifteen or so plays I have written have been produced—*The Return, Blackmail, The Last Hour, After Midnight* (1929; one act), *The Danger Line, Sensation, Big Business,* and *Page from a Diary.* But it was the second of these that would catapult me into a third career in an industry of which I'm still a part. Again quoting Shakespeare's *As You Like It,* "it was upon this fashion" that I came into film.

## Excerpt: *Blackmail* (the play)

Censorship required that much of the "attempted rape and knife murder" scene of Hitchcock's *Blackmail* (1929) be left to the viewer's imagination. But the stage edition, published by Rich and Cowan in 1934, portrays the shocking attempted rape of the innocent Alice Jarvis by the painter Peter Hewitt. The published edition is also notable for meticulous and vivid stage directions, an expertise that Bennett brought to the Hitchcock partnership.

ALICE: This door is locked.
PETER [*dully*]: Is it?
ALICE: You know it is. You locked it.

PETER [*morosely*]: Well?

ALICE: When?

PETER: In the dark . . . before I switched on the light.

ALICE: Why?

PETER: Oh, I don't know. I didn't want us to be disturbed by my landlady
. . . that was all.

ALICE: Give me the key.

PETER: But look here . . .

ALICE: Give me the key.

PETER: You're really going then?

ALICE: Yes. Give me the key.

[*They are facing each other. Peter stares at her for a moment, then gives in
and lowers his eyes. He slowly puts his hand to his pocket and takes out
the key. He sinks onto the end of the bed couch . . . looks at her again
. . . then throws the key onto the ground at his feet. He speaks sullenly.*]

PETER: Oh, blast you then . . . take it.

[*Alice looks at him disdainfully for a moment, comes down to pick up the
key. Peter watches her resentfully. He is breathing in quick gasps—
evidently not master of himself again yet. He has intended to let her go
but her defiant carriage and steady eyes are too much for him. His lips
curl into a twisted smile—desire and bitterness warring—then,
suddenly, as she stoops to pick up the key, he covers it with his foot. His
voice is quiet but hoarse with passion.*]

No. Why should I let you go?

ALICE [*taken aback*]: What?

PETER [*his eyes fixed on her*]: You knew what you were coming to when
you came in here tonight . . .

ALICE [*frightened*]: What do you mean? Give me that key . . .

[*She makes a dart for it but Peter's hand shoots out and seizes her wrist.
She writhes as he twists it and her coat slips from her shoulders and
falls to the ground.*]

PETER: You knew . . .

ALICE [*in agony*]: Let me go . . .

PETER: A girl knows what to expect when she comes into a man's room at
night.

ALICE: Let me go.

PETER: I'm damned if I do.

ALICE: Let me go, I say . . .

PETER: No. You've been playing me up . . . It's my turn now.

ALICE: Oh . . . !

[*Thoroughly frightened, she is struggling desperately by this time. Suddenly she stoops forward and bites his hand. He lets go her wrist with an exclamation of disgust.*]

PETER: God! You cat!

[*Alice, free for a moment, darts away across the room . . . but Peter is just behind her. He seizes her frock at the neck but it tears right down, revealing pretty "cami-knickers" beneath. Having lost her momentarily, he sways drunkenly, almost falling . . . evidently the result of intense emotional excitement . . . and Alice, seizing her opportunity, reaches the table and turns on him with her back to it. But Peter is after her again . . .* ]

ALICE: Keep away from me . . .

PETER: What . . .

ALICE: Keep away. I'll shout for help.

PETER [*closing with her*]: No you won't . . . you damned little cheat.

ALICE [*fighting desperately*]: You . . . You . . . Help!!

PETER [*thrusting his hand over her mouth*]: Shut up . . . Blast you . . .

[*Alice tries to scream but can't. For a moment they are struggling fiercely . . . then Peter has her in his arms and is kissing her wildly. Alice is gasping for breath, but Peter is forcing her farther and farther back onto the table. He is obviously carried away by his passion and doesn't know what he is doing. SUDDENLY Alice's right hand is disengaged, and somehow THE BREAD KNIFE IS IN IT! Peter tries to seize her hand, but it is too late. The knife whips through the air and a moment later Peter is reeling back with an ugly wound in his throat. Alice drops the knife and staggers away from the table. Peter is writhing horribly—one hand to his neck—another to his heart. He falls but rises again. Alice watches him—horror-stricken. He falls across the bed and for a moment is writhing in his death agony . . . then he lies quite still. Alice stares at the form on the bed for a while—her eyes wide with terror. Presently she speaks . . . intense fear in her voice.*]

ALICE: What's the matter? What's the matter with you? You're trying to frighten me . . . aren't you? [*She draws a little nearer—speaking very appealingly.*] Aren't you . . . ? [*She draws nearer still and her eyes dilate. She leans over, and putting out her hand, touches the dead man's face, but snatches it back again with a stifled scream as she comes in*

43

*contact with blood. She shrinks away from the bed . . . agony in her voice.*] Oh . . . I didn't mean to do it. You shouldn't have . . . You shouldn't have tried to . . .

[*Her voice is shaking with fright and emotion and she tails off weakly. For a while she stands gazing at the silent form . . . obviously in a quandary as to what to do next. Presently she goes to the window and looks out furtively . . . then she comes back to the bed again. She stands there for a moment—still undecided . . . then, suddenly, she makes up her mind. She picks up her coat quickly and draws it about her . . . gets the key . . . crosses to the reading lamp and switches it off. . . . goes to the door and opens it stealthily . . . looks round once more . . . then passes out into the blackness of the passage, closing the door behind her. . . .* ]

# 6

# Alfred Hitchcock and
# My Early Talkies

I have five dictionaries. The best of them is an ancient publication by some gentlemen named Ogilvie and Annandale, circa 1912. It gives six definitions of the word *suspense,* but the definition dearest to my heart is: "State of doubt with some apprehension or anxiety." (The best my *New Oxford Concise Dictionary* can come up with is "State of usu. anxious uncertainty or waiting for information.")

The Ogilvie and Annandale definition fits directly into the type of plays and movies that I have spent nearly seventy years writing. Some of these have been quite dreadful; but I am sure that suspense played a main part in maybe fifty of these. Sometime around 1930 I wrote a story-screenplay called *Warn London*—a quickie known as a pound-a-footer. I haven't the faintest idea what it was about, but the title speaks for itself. Suspense.

Alfred Hitchcock, quite rightly, is known as the Master of Suspense, but as *suspense* has been my middle name, and, being a somewhat conceited individual, I like to believe that I contributed in no small way to Hitch's reputation. In fact, I know that it was my sense of suspense—"state of doubt with some apprehension or anxiety"—that moved Hitch to enlist me as his regular writer for six of his sound movies, already having released my *Blackmail* (1929) as the "first super talkie" for British International Pictures (BIP).

We were the same age. I was born on August the 2, 1899, and Hitch on August 13. Both of us were Leos—maybe a factor that was conducive to a relationship that started in 1929 and lasted as a close friendship until his death.

His film was adapted from my second play, *Blackmail,* which during its London run caught the fancy of the rotund but highly talented young director. Hitch loved the story—his kind of stuff (and mine). Attempted seduction. Murder. The young innocent murderess being blackmailed. The switch in which the blackmailer himself becomes the suspect of the murder. Suspense.

Anyway, in 1928 Hitchcock had BIP lease the film rights to *Blackmail*. He adapted the play to the screen; it would be the first talking picture shot in Europe.

The film was made in two versions. The first was a silent picture starring Anny Ondra, a Czech actress who could hardly speak English; the second had the sound added, and Anny's voice was dubbed. The voice belonged to Joan Barry, and she actually did have a tinny little voice. When I was twenty and just out of the army, I toured in a play called *Brewster's Millions*. Joan was our leading lady, aged nineteen. She was the loveliest thing I had ever seen in my life, and one day while we were playing in Cambridge I took her out in a canoe on the river Cam. This was in 1920 and I was deeply in love with her.

Some mile or so out of Cambridge some wretched young actor from our *Brewster's* cast—also in love with Joan—came alongside in a punt and said, "Charles, you don't know how to paddle a canoe. Let me show you." Joan, obviously happy to have two young men fighting about her, said, "Oh, yes, Charles, do let Jack show you." I got out on to the riverbank. My rival got into my canoe, started to paddle. The canoe tipped, catapulting the young man's head deep in the mud of the river and his two feet sticking up just above water level. Meanwhile, Joan was screaming in the still rocking canoe. Realizing it was my job to save my rival's life, I started to undress as slowly as I could on the riverbank. Right then a punt came along, and its occupant pulled the young man out of the watery depths. It was my moment of triumph. The young rival—who happened to be the nephew of the theater impresario Sir Abraham Walter de Frece—had demonstrated how *not* to paddle a canoe.

A strangely unexpected moment came during the filming of *Blackmail*. Hitch said at one day's end, "Well, let's go up to the Plough and have a drink." The Plough was and still is an ancient wayside pub in the old village of Elstree. We were having our drink at the little bar, and there, somewhere close, was that tinny little voice. Hitch said, "Oh, Charles, do you know Joan, who is dubbing Anny Ondra's voice in *Blackmail*?"

Joan looked at me. "My God!" she must have said to herself, "This is that awful young touring actor I knew way back." And she looked at me as though I had crawled out of the woodwork.

I asked, "Don't you remember me, Joan?"

She said, "I don't think so."

Hitch said, "Oh, for Christ's sake, Joan, this is Charles Bennett, who wrote *Blackmail*."

Joan gasped. "Oh, how wonderful," she said, and embraced me. It was an entirely new ballgame.

*Blackmail* was released June 21, 1929. It was a gigantic success, and it is still shown as a classic. But more immediately important to me was that its success gave me a footing in the film industry. Now, in addition to my writing for the stage, I started on eight years of London-based screenplay writing.

On April 15, 1929, two months before the opening of Hitchcock's film *Blackmail*, Archibald Nettlefold (who controlled the Comedy Theatre) optioned the film rights to *The Last Hour*. Nettlefold had a film company in his own name that produced *The Last Hour*, directed by Walter Forde. This was the first talkie for Nettlefold Studios. I think Hitch would have gone for its death ray, spies, international intrigue, and MacGuffin (the midnight smuggling of a weapon) in a big way. Unfortunately, the film was completely ruined by advice from some lousy scenarist named Harry Fowler Mear. All the gloriously possible special effects stuff, so easy from a film point of view, was cut out in favor of a single use of the death ray against an extremely phony-looking dirigible. I was disgusted, and I'm sure the movie, left with only lots of dialogue (probably not very good anyway), was a ghastly flop.

In September 1931 I signed a slightly crazy contract with BIP, agreeing to deliver three film stories a year for two years.[14] More important, it was at BIP that I was reintroduced to Alfred Hitchcock. Walter Mycroft, the story editor at BIP and incidentally a hunchback—of whom Hitch with his perverted humor said, "If you break his back you'll find chocolates inside, poisoned"—suggested that Hitch and I get together on a subject they dearly loved but for which they had no story. BIP owned the rights to the famous "Bulldog Drummond" character, so I was asked to write a story based on his character, not any specific story theme. What emerged was a story of my own, not a dramatization of anybody else's tale. Hitch, also under contract, was assigned to direct the movie, to be called *Bulldog Drummond's Baby*.

I rejoined Hitch and came up with a story that wasn't too bad. As the prospective director, Hitch joined me and we worked together on its development. The tale was pure suspense. Bulldog, in Switzerland with his wife, inadvertently learns a terrible assassination will take place very shortly in London. But the heavies know he is aware of the plan, with the result that Drummond's five-year-old daughter is kidnapped. She will die unless Drummond holds his tongue. Meanwhile, the story stalks toward the assassination—at a certain time and place.

It was the almost perfect formula—lacking only the idiot interference of the police—but regarding its production, rather horrifying. Though *Blackmail* put BIP on top, Hitch's next couple of movies had been flops. John Maxwell, head of BIP, became nervous about the cost of *Bulldog Drummond's Baby* because the movie entailed some location shooting at St. Moritz, Switzerland. Soon enough Hitch and John Maxwell (whom Hitch regarded with his usual "fear of the boss") parted company. I worked out my contract while Hitch entered into an agreement with Alexander Korda, from which nothing emerged. With Hitch's departure from BIP, our association ended.

During the early 1930s I wrote or contributed to at least thirty British films, the names and stories of many of which elude me after over half a century, and many of which were filmed by the "boy wonder" and world's worst director, George King. It is through George King that I met the publicist and story writer Billie Bristow, with whom I collaborated on eight films. Often these played to the public's fascination for new technologies. *Midnight* (1931), running eight weeks at the Tivoli, London, had the lovely Eve Gray help a man recover secret technical plans from spies. *Number, Please* (1931) involved a telephone switchboard operator flirting with a crook. *Matinee Idol* (1933) was staged against the Brooklands automobile racetrack.

In those days passenger flight was in its infancy. England boasted Imperial Airways, whose "fleet" consisted of two lumbering fifteen- to twenty-seat biplanes called Hercules and Heracles. Their jobs were to hop back and forth across the Channel between an inconspicuous grass airfield at Croydon, south of London, and an equally uninviting field on the outskirts of Paris. My *Paris Plane* (1933), featuring the directorial debut of twenty-three-year-old John Paddy Carstairs, had a Scotland Yard detective chasing a murderer aboard a Paris-bound Heracles. The detective did not know the murderer by sight, so every passenger was a suspect.

*Deadlock* (1931) showed a murder on a very early sound stage. An actor—involved in an off-stage love triangle—is wrongly accused of the crime and faces imminent conviction in court. Film footage, discovered in a camera that had slipped from its platform during filming, was found to have filmed the murderer! I was pleased with *Deadlock* for its setting new box-office records.

But trains were my perennial favorite element because of my frequent travel as a young actor. My stage play *Sensation,* which began aboard a train, was adapted for the screen in 1931. *Night Mail* (1935) features a correspondent who thwarts an attempt to kill a judge aboard the "Aberdonian" Express and a climactic chase on the coal scuttle. More familiar was the nonstop Flying Scotsman of *The 39 Steps* (1935), the railway disaster of *The Clairvoyant* (1935), and the train-yard finale to *Curse of the Demon* (1958). Recently I wrote the Flying Scotsman into my novel *Fox on the Run* (1987), and the Super Chief into a screenplay and novel, *Thunderbird* (1990, not produced).

Not every script involved crime or suspense. *Hawley's of High Street* (1933) was a comedy about a henpecked draper and a butcher who were rivals in a council election; I don't know how the hell I wrote it—I'm not a comedy writer. But I must have been somewhat versatile, what with *Partners Please* (1932, comedy), *Mannequin* (1933, a romance about a boxer), *Big Business* (1934, comedy—adapted from my play), and *Blue Smoke* (1935, about gypsy boxers).

Several were adventures. *The Secret of the Loch* (1934) was a suspense–love story in which the juvenile lead is very nearly killed by the Loch Ness Monster during a "hard-hat" dive. The Loch Ness Monster was just starting to hit the London newspapers, and I decided that there might be a film in it. That was midwinter 1933. I got my car out and drove to the highlands of Scotland. I'll never forget the pass of Glen Coe, a very wild pass in the highlands, with this great drop on one side and the car skidding all over the place! Anyway, I got to Loch Ness, to Fort Augustus, where the monks were reporting that they had seen the monster. I got hold of the head of the monastery and said to him, "I understand you saw the monster."

"Oh, yes, yes, yes, it was here this morning."

"Oh fine," I said. "Where is it *now*?"

"It's gone up the loch. Go up there," he said.

So I drove up the loch about fifteen miles to Urquhart and found the pier master of this broken-down pier. He was an old gentleman with a split beard. I asked, "Well, where's the monster? I understand it's around here."

The old gentleman said, "Oh, yes, yes, yes, it was here this morning. But it's gone back to see the monks down there!"

So I couldn't find the monster. I was struck by the utter loneliness of the loch—not a soul anywhere. I decided to go along the road on the south side of the loch, a narrow road with weird little bridges. I followed it around, not finding the monster—but I found a pub, and inside were about ten news reporters from Glasgow and Edinburgh, and even a few from London.

But it was worth the trip, as I found the most beautiful Scotch in the world! So beautiful, that when I came to California years later, I used to import the whiskey.

Back in London, I wrote *The Secret of the Loch*, a story of a reporter falling in love with the daughter of a professor who built his career researching the monster. Ultimately, the monster is unimportant, a device to propel the love interest. The climax is fraught with claustrophobia, a professor gone mad, apprehension for the reporter's safety, anxiety about the professor's daughter, and the terror of the monster itself. But the monster was disappointing, laughable, looking more like a salamander than what I had envisioned. I have learned that it is preferable often not to display the object of terror—better to leave it to the imagination. As I routinely wrote camera directions into my scripts, *Secret* did pose difficulties of filming underwater, which were solved by the use of a large water tank interposed between the camera and the action. My *Secret of the Loch* was the first film about the Loch Ness Monster, and the first talkie filmed in Scotland.

I remember collaborating with my dear pal, the late and sadly lamented Sidney Gilliat, on an adventure film, *King of the Damned* (1935), for the actor Conrad Veidt, a not bad if forgotten movie about the mutiny of convicts on Devil's Island. And *King Solomon's Mines* (1937) had British explorers searching for the fabled diamond mines in the remote interior of Africa. It was crammed with wild adventure, romance, and thrills; but it was also crammed with writers—there were five on the project—which resulted in its being overwritten and tedious. But I was pleased with the suspense delivered in its final scenes. My good friend Sir Cedric Hardwicke starred as the lead adventurer, Anna Lee as his love interest, and the American bass Paul Robeson as an African tribal chief.

I was pleased by *King Solomon's* beauty, Anna Lee, whose life has intertwined with mine over more than sixty years. Born as Joan Boniface Winnifrith, Anna Lee began her stage career at the age of fifteen as an understudy to the innkeeper's daughter in my South Touring Company's performances of *The Last Hour.* Three years later "Boniface" had her first film job costarring with Maggie in my *Mannequin*—the story of a boxer who leaves his true love for a society lady but eventually returns to her. After Anna Lee married Robert Stevenson, director of *King Solomon's Mines,* both were invited to the States at my suggestion to David Selznick. Anna had a great career starring with such luminaries as John Wayne, but she outlasted them all as the immortal matriarch on the TV soap opera *General Hospital.* Our friendship goes way back, and I adored her second husband, the great poet and novelist Robert Nathan.

One of my favorite pictures was *The Clairvoyant,* a psychic suspense story starring Fay Wray and the brilliant and delightfully human Claude Rains. I remember that Gainsborough Pictures said they'd got Claude Rains coming over to do a picture for them, and they could also get the *King Kong* woman, Fay Wray. They had a lot of writers trying to come up with ideas, and I came up with an original idea that they used. A clairvoyant makes predictions, but the events happened only *because* the guy had prophesied them. I was told to go ahead and write the story and screenplay, so I did. According to the credits, it was based on a novel by Ernst Lothar, but I'd never read it—I'd never *heard* of it! But that sometimes happened—studios would put the name of an author to a novel after the screenplay was finished, after the picture was finished!

*The Clairvoyant* was based on a series of experiences I had during and after World War I. For some years I had the faculty to cause things to happen in my presence. Mind you, none of them was of my actual doing. I just happened to be passing by or to have walked into the room. But it seems the person next to me was either dropping dead or jumping off a building or contemplating suicide. I became very superstitious. My imagination started working, and soon I was turning out melodramas for the London stage.

Returning to Hitchcock in 1933 and my story *Bulldog Drummond's Baby:* though down for the count at BIP, it was not out. Hitch, in his very early twenties, had started his film career in various capacities—cutter, set designer, and the like—and he eventually rose to silent film director, all under Michael Balcon (later Sir Michael Balcon). By the 1930s Mick had become production head of Gaumont British (GB) and Gainsborough Pictures. He was a delightful man, very encouraging to writers, some of whom he would bring across from Hollywood. On one occasion Mick introduced Sidney Gilliat, Frank Launder, and me to Haworth Bromley, who instructed us on how to make our British movies more salable in the States. We ended up playing Monopoly, very drunk at Haworth's flat; and I emerged about twenty-five pounds richer, which I somehow took home at three o'clock in the morning and poured in pound-note fashion over Maggie's pillow, much to her delight. We were a close group of friends, Michael Hogan, Victor Saville, Sidney, Frank, and I. On one occasion, Sidney and Frank guided me, paralytically drunk, home from the Chelsea Arts Ball.

Now Hitch returned to Mick at GB's Shepherd's Bush studio, and he immediately asked to be allowed to buy and make my Bulldog Drummond story. The purchase deal was made with BIP, and it went into production—naturally with Hitch directing. The title was changed to *The Man Who Knew Too Much,* and I received the original story credit.

My story remained fundamentally the same, but the characters got new names. The picture starred Leslie Banks and Edna Best; young Nova Pilbeam played the child, and the recently discovered Peter Lorre, the star of Fritz Lang's *M* (1931), was the chief heavy. Quite frankly, I wasn't worried about losing a BIP credit; in fact, I was happy at the thought of gaining a GB credit—a much more prestigious organization than the rather cheap British International.

I suppose I was the best-known constructionist, scenarist, scenario writer in the world at that time. I'm not being conceited, but I was awfully bloody good, and Hitch recognized this in me. The fundamental thing—and Hitch always used to say it—is that you've got to get the story line first. By *construction* I mean architecture—knowing the ending before you know your beginning, then working up to that ending. When you build a house, the architecture has to be perfect. And once the architecture is right, the house can be built. But if the architecture is wrong, you haven't a hope. It's from construction you know what your characters are about. They build the story. Hitch would say that when the screenplay is finished, the picture is finished, that "putting it before the cameras, putting it on the screen, is nothing."

After construction and the development of character comes the matter of dialogue, and perhaps the necessity of collaboration. It is a fact that some writers are better at certain forms of dialogue writing than others. But the dialogue must develop the story, or—and both Hitch and I agreed on this—it should not be included.

But collaboration can lead to complications with the film credits. A peculiar example is the case of D. B. Wyndham Lewis, credited in *The Man Who Knew Too Much*. "Bevan"—the name by which we all knew him when he was writing a *London Daily Express* column under the title of "Beachcomber"—was a personal friend of mine called in during the very earliest development of the script to provide some dialogue. His dialogue was never used, but as some sort of compliment he was given a story credit, which he hadn't earned. In those early days the allocation of credits was up to the producer, and things got awfully messed up when a "name" writer who had done practically nothing got the main credit—whereas the guy who really had done the job but was less well known got practically nothing. Along this line, Alma Hitchcock received credits she did not deserve.

So at Hitch's request, I joined GB in 1933 and began dramatizing John Buchan's book *The Thirty-Nine Steps*. No easy task, as it wasn't really a filmable story. The story contained just one good basic plot point—the double chase—an innocent man accused of murder, on the run with both the police and the "heavies" out to get him. But the book lacked incident, it hadn't a woman in it—neither the Madeleine Carroll character nor Peggy Ashcroft's character as the crofter's wife. And practically every twist of events was based on an unlikely coincidence. By the end of my work at it, the entire construction was mine, with a lot of wonderful dialogue written by Ian Hay, a British playwright who later became the director of public relations at the British War Office.

The script of *The 39 Steps* was coming along fine—almost ready to go—until C. M. Woolf opposed us on *The Man Who Knew Too Much*. His rejection created a personal suspense that had nothing to do with murder, robbery, rape, or blackmail—just the matter of whether Hitch and Charles Bennett were to emerge important, or be wiped out, easily forgotten.

C. M. Woolf, the vastly powerful managing director of British and Dominions Pictures Corporation and of General Film Distributors (GFD), was the prime executive at Gaumont British—without whose consent hardly any film was ever shown. In the 1930s and 1940s to have described C. M. as a power in the film industry would have been the understatement of all time. So omnipotent was he that hardly a picture—British, foreign, or the product of Hollywood itself—could be shown in the United Kingdom without his stamp of approval. From the early 1930s on, for two decades or more, there wasn't a film organization in the world entirely exempt from GFD affiliation. C. M. saw the first cut and raged, said the picture was appalling, and flatly moved against distributing it unless it was rewritten, reshot by another director, and recast.

His choice of director was Maurice Elvey, a delightful character and a friend of mine, but in no sense a great director. I used to visit Maurice's home on the Pilgrim's Way in Kent, where he had the greatest array of toy soldiers I've ever seen, vastly displayed on a huge table. I am inclined to say that Maurice played toy soldiers with the advertising mogul and MP Sir Charles Higham, the father of Errol Flynn's biographer Charles Higham.

Our personal suspense—Hitch's and mine—went on for days. At one point Hitch said to me, "Charles, forget working on *The 39 Steps*. If we lose on *The Man Who Knew Too Much*, our *Steps* will never be made." Since the power of C. M. Woolf was immense, it seemed we were likely to lose and, in effect, be confined to the garbage can. *Suspense?*

For the moment I gave up working on *The 39 Steps* and devoted my time to a cheap original I knew would pay for the milk. But Hitch went practically on his knees to Mick Balcon, begging him, as head of GB film production, to defy Woolf and allow the picture to be put out—as shot.

Somehow—although in awe of Woolf—Mick Balcon summoned up all his courage, and the picture was released, as written and shot. Hitch won. It was a smash! The picture opened at the New Gallery in Regent Street with fantastically good reviews and was a sensational success, running—I seem to remember—for thirty-one weeks. So *The 39 Steps* was allowed to proceed.

Getting back to actual suspense—"state of doubt with . . . anxiety": expressed very simply, suspense means that something anxiety-producing is going to take place. The horror of such a happening has to be averted, but in the meanwhile the dramatists have to keep the audience on the edge of its seat. Will the bad guys win out? Or will the audience go home happy because the good guys won? This disastrous happening is the MacGuffin—a plot device that motivates the characters but becomes less important to the unfolding story. In *The 39 Steps* the MacGuffin was the smuggling of a secret out of England, very similar to the smuggling of the laser weapon that had motivated *The Last Hour*. But the story was really about what happened to the relationship between Robert Donat and Madeleine Carroll.

Hitch used to say the MacGuffin doesn't matter. It's just a destination to reemerge at the climax. The audience, however, needs to accept its inevitability and go along with it.

Suspense is the most important thing you can get into a story. It may be played against incidental subplots and romantic interludes, but the secret of successful melodrama lies in the last ten minutes of your story. If your action causes an audience to tingle during this period, the story is a hit. But if you let them down at the climax, no matter how much terror you've built earlier in the plot, the battle is lost.

There are naturally variations on this theme. The first and often most important is, I believe, the "double chase" element, as exploited in *The 39 Steps.* This is a simple formula. Something disastrous is going to happen at a certain time. A time limit is always vital in this type of story. Our hero sets off to try to find out the dreaded secret behind the up-and-coming catastrophe to avert its culmination. But our hero has, in effect, been himself mislabeled as the heavy, so he is now fighting a double battle. The true heavies must stop him. And the police will stop him in any way possible, thus inadvertently allowing the heavies to win.

Adding to the suspense is the mystery element. What exactly *is* going to happen? This is something our hero has to ascertain along the way, while dodging the attacks both of the heavies, who are against him, and of the police, who *should* be on his side. John Buchan, the author of the short novel *The Thirty-Nine Steps,* did not invent this formula. His novel, good as it is, only edges on the fundamental formula, and I am inclined to think that Hitch and I developed the pattern, which has been used so often by others. Anyway, with the release of *The 39 Steps,* Hitch was truly on top. Playing to full houses in New York City, it secured his and my international reputations; and thus our long association took shape.

When I was writing for Hitch, suspense had to be the element that we were persistently seeking; but, strangely enough, suspense can sometimes harm rather than help. Take, for instance, our Gaumont British movie *Sabotage* (1936), starring Sylvia Sidney and Oskar Homolka. The film was based on Conrad's novel *Secret Agent,* but since Hitch and I had already used this title in our immediately preceding film based on the Somerset Maugham character Ashenden, we had to find another title.

Conrad's tale is of a cheaply paid anarchist who is given a murderous assignment. To carry out his job, the anarchist, Verloc, finds it necessary to make a bomb courier of his wife's younger brother. The young boy is killed.

And the wife, in turn (not without reason for revenge), kills Verloc. A very good story.

But we, Hitch and I, had to dramatize it, had to visually develop the tale for its suspense value—the possible up-and-coming death of the boy who was carrying a packaged time bomb set to explode. Using the best suspense formulas, Hitch and I planned a sequence in which the bomb was to detonate at a given minute, even second, right in the heart of the traffic of Piccadilly Circus.

This suspense built up beautifully, playing against the time limit of the bomb ticking away toward explosion. The audience members were on the edge of their seats! Would the situation be saved before the bomb exploded in Piccadilly Circus, and the boy, unaware of his danger, died? Unfortunately, film audiences, when put through the suspense mangle, expect things to end happily. In this case it didn't. I remember a cocktail party after the press showing of the film—this must have been around 1936. C. A. Lejeune, a famous critic for the *London Sunday Observer,* was furious, her ire directed at *me.* She protested, over a strong drink, that I had manipulated the audience by a crescendo of suspense, only to disappoint by not having the marines to the rescue.

Joseph Conrad's story (which of course has nothing to do with a bomb blowing up in Piccadilly Circus) does dictate that the bomb, carried by the wife's young brother, explodes and its young carrier dies. We were making Conrad's *Secret Agent,* so there was nothing we could do about it; there was no possible way of writing a happy ending. I pointed out to her that this was Joseph Conrad's story shape, and that all we, Hitch and I, had done was build up the story suspense to the bomb blast. No good. Lejeune gave us a horrible review, and maybe many members of the audience shared her attitude. If you spell out suspense, the suspense sufferers have to be rewarded—not by the opposite of their hopes and expectations. Our *39 Steps* fulfilled the audience demand. *Sabotage* didn't.

I was happy during my years with Gaumont British, but at the same time I was always conscious of regret at having finally put my play-acting days behind me. It was as if a chunk of my life had gone. And I suppose it had. I doubt if anybody who has ever known the smell of greasepaint can ever quite shake off the sense of nostalgia. None of the radiance of a lighted film set can ever erase the glitter of footlights. And except for eighteen months of British army service in World War I—*theater* had been my life.

But the curtain dropped. In January 1936, the same month as the opening of my stillborn play *Page from a Diary*—and four months before *Secret Agent* was released—*The Era* film magazine identified me as Britain's "Most Successful Screen-Story Writer." The next month I addressed the Film Society on the subject of "The Story in the Film." Believe me, by now I *really* considered myself on top of the heap.

❦ ❦ ❦

## Excerpt: *The Secret of the Loch*

*The Secret of the Loch* was a film and original screenplay released in 1934, the same year as *The Man Who Knew Too Much*. This excerpt from the "climax and knife" scene, from a draft titled "Sinister Deeps," gives the detailed stage and camera direction routinely provided in Bennett's screenplays. The scene finds Jimmy, a journalist, on a hard-hat dive, terrified by the approach of the Loch Ness Monster. Above, on the deck of the *Black Hawk*, Heggie, a zoologist, maneuvers to murder Jimmy; and Angela, Heggie's granddaughter and Jimmy's love interest, is overcome by terror. The abbreviations C.S., L.S., and so on are camera directions (close shot, long shot; the meanings of others have been lost among the acronyms of film history).

CUT TO: C.S.
*446 Underwater—(Tank)*
*Jimmy's face seen through glass of diver's helmet.* Dramatic music.
Jimmy is looking down—as if at bones—amazement in his eyes. His face is reflected by the light from the lamp. He looks up—looking straight toward the camera. Suddenly he starts violently. His eyes almost start out of his head. His face is alight with vivid and urgent terror (an almost exact replica of the situation when Jock was in the cave). He is staring straight at the camera. He has evidently seen something more than disturbing.

CUT TO: S.L.S.
*Underwater—(Tank)*
*The cave seen through the fixture.* Dramatic music.
(As Jimmy sees it.)
Now we are seeing through Jimmy's eyes just what Jock saw earlier. The

beam of light is thrown into the black depths of the cavern. The effect is weird in the extreme—a world of strange shapes, festooned weeds, and deep shadows, the whole distorted by the glass and the oily water. The weeds are stirring, parting slowly. There is a disturbance in the waters—bubbles are rising. The great weirdly shaped festoons are being thrust aside . . . and suddenly a hideous, leathery face is seen—the face of a creature of nightmare. A gray flat head is, for a moment, enshrined by the weeds, then it is free of them, a horrible serpentine neck reaching out, swaying. The mouth is seen now—distorted by the water—vast—slobbery—utterly loathsome . . .

CUT TO: S.C.S.
*Underwater—(Tank)*
Jimmy—head and shoulders down to his belt. He is staring ahead, half crazed with fear. His hand goes to his knife, jerking it free. But he remembers what he has come for. For one moment he raises the underwater camera, touching the lever, then he is jerking wildly at the lifeline.

CUT TO: S.C.S.
*Deck of* Black Hawk
Angus, Burwood, the deckhands beyond at the pump. The air line is jerking. All are conscious of the urgency of the summons from below.
BURWOOD: What's that?
ANGUS: Danger! Haul away, quick.

CUT TO: S.C.S.
*Deck of* Black Hawk
Heggie, standing with gun raised as if facing Angus and crew. His face is illuminated as if from light from the bulkhead and he strikes an awesome and crazy spectacle. He has evidently managed to creep forward on the boat, unseen. The waters of the Loch are beyond him.
HEGGIE: Leave those lines alone.

CUT TO: S.C.S.
*Deck of* Black Hawk
Angus, Burwood, and deckhands, big heads in foreground. Heggie, a

wild figure beyond. All have turned, facing Heggie, with gasps of surprise.

HEGGIE: Leave them, I say!

ANGUS: Professorrr, for Heaven's sake . . .

CUT TO: S.C.S.

*Rock on foreshore by* Black Hawk, *night.*

Angela, center of the reporters—Hector, Hargreaves, Marks, and Smith. All are staring forward, very disturbed. There is terror in Angela's eyes.

MARKS: What's going on . . . ?

ANGELA (*terrified*): It's Grand'pa . . . Grand'pa.

She runs forward past camera as if to go aboard.

HECTOR (*after her*): Miss Heggie . . .

CUT TO: S.C.S.

*Deck of* Black Hawk

Angus, Burwood and deckhands, big heads in foreground. Heggie, a mad spectacle beyond, the gun leveled at them. Angus is desperately protesting.

ANGUS: Professorrr . . . Ye must see . . .

Angela comes into picture in foreground, speaking desperately.

ANGELA: Grand'pa!

Heggie's eyes light up wildly.

HEGGIE: Ah—you *too. You're* against me too!

He points out of picture as if toward reporters (*forward past camera*).

HEGGIE: And those men on the bank . . . If they come aboard I'll shoot!

Angela (*to Angus*): Who's below?

ANGUS: It's Jimmie.

Angela's eyes are alight with terror.

ANGELA (*desperately*): Jimmy! Grand'pa . . . For *my* sake . . .

CUT TO: C.S.

*Heggie on deck of* Black Hawk

Heggie, looking entirely maniacal in the light of the bulkhead light, gun leveled forward.

HEGGIE: No . . . I've had enough! You've all gone back on me! Even *you,* Angus!

CUT TO: S.C.S.

*Deck of* Black Hawk

Heggie beyond, Angus, Burwood, Angela, and deckhands, big heads in foreground.

HEGGIE: You've let this young whippersnapper of a pressman in on it, have you? He's to find the monster . . . *He's* to get all the credit while I'm forgotten!

ANGUS (*desperate*): You're wrrrong! He's doing it forrr *you!*

CUT TO: C.S.

*Heggie on deck of* Black Hawk

Heggie with gun leveled.

HEGGIE: For *me!*

[*He peals off into maniacal laughter.*]

What'd he do for *me?*

CUT TO: S.C.S.

*Deck of* Black Hawk

Professor with back to camera. Angus, Burwood, Angela, deckhands beyond. The rope is jerking.

ANGUS: The rope again! Professorrr . . . he's in dangerrr . . . For Heaven's sake!

HEGGIE (*wildly*): Keep back! Leave those ropes alone . . .

CUT TO: C.S.

*Underwater—(Tank).* Dramatic music.

*Jimmy's face seen through the glass of the helmet.*

He is staring straight ahead, utter terror in his eyes. He backs slowly away from the camera till he is in S.C.S. We see the knife raised in his hand; he is backing onto a rock.

CUT TO: S.L.S.

*Underwater—(Tank)*

*The cave seen through the fixture.* Dramatic music.

(As Jimmy sees it.)

The terrible head among the weeds. It is moving slowly from left to right, coming forward, swimmingly, its very movement churning the turbid waters, further distorting the vision, giving the entire scene the weird, indefinite quality of nightmare. The head is coming forward toward right of shot, growing in enormous proportion as it comes into S.C.S.

*Camera pans*—as if Jimmy's eyes are following the terrible head. For a moment it looks as if the horror will pass, then the great bulging nightmare eyes turn, directly facing the camera (Jimmy).

CUT TO: S.C.S.

*Deck of* Black Hawk *(studio)*. Dramatic music.

The professor still holding up the others. A deckhand is trying to edge around one way, Angus round the other. Heggie jerks the gun, edging away himself, so that he has them all covered again.

HEGGIE (*madly*): I'll shoot, I tell you.

ANGUS: Professorrr!—ye must see . . .

ANGELA: Grand'pa!

HEGGIE: Back—all of ye.

CUT TO: S.C.S.

*Underwater—(Tank)*

*The cave seen through the fixture*. Dramatic music.

(As Jimmy sees it.)

The terrible head again as seen by Jimmy, distorted, horrible. It is evidently facing Jimmy, and it is as if the creature has seen him. The great head on the reptilian neck moves from side to side, then recedes, the motion of a serpent before it strikes. Suddenly it is shooting forward into vast close-up.

CUT TO: C.S.

*454 Underwater—(Tank)*. Dramatic music.

*Jimmy's face seen through the helmet front.*

He is gasping for breath. There is utter terror in his eyes. Shot goes down to his shoulders. We see him raise his knife to strike. He strikes again and again—knife going out of shot.

CUT TO: S.C.S.

*455 Underwater—(Tank)*

*The cave seen through the fixture*. Dramatic music.

(As Jimmy sees it.)

A huge eye—bulging—frightful—fills the screen. Jimmy's knife is buried in it. The knife withdraws and a thick, filthy liquid floods from the gouged eye, misting the seawater.

CUT TO: C.S.

*456 Underwater—(Tank).* Dramatic music.

*Jimmy's face seen through the helmet front.*

He is gasping for breath and yelling now, his eyes mad with fear, staring to the right. Suddenly the water swirls. Jimmy's eyes jerk to the left— as if the creature has passed him, Jimmy's terrified gaze following it. The sea water is thick, oozy.

*Camera tracks back.*

So that Jimmy is in S.C.S. staring out of shot as if after the creature. A great wash of thick, swirling water sweeps across the shot. Jimmy is jerking violently at his lines. The water seems to be darkening, thick with the filthy liquid from the gouged eye.

CUT TO: S.C.S.

*Deck of* Black Hawk (studio). Dramatic music.

Burwood in foreground at lines, deckhands beside him. Angela is beyond, gazing in terror at Heggie, who stands in the light of the bulkhead, still with the rifle raised. Angus is not in the picture. Suddenly Burwood is conscious of the movement of the lines again.

BURWOOD: The lines! He's still alive!

HEGGIE (*wildly*): Don't touch those lines!

CUT TO: S.C.S.

*Deck of* Black Hawk (studio). Dramatic music.

Heggie, staring ahead, the rifle raised. Suddenly Angus appears from behind him, looming up swiftly almost from under his feet, seizing the old man round the waist, forcing the rifle out of his hands. Heggie is taken completely by surprise.

HEGGIE: (*Gasps*)

ANGUS: Haul in! Quick—Haul!

# 7

# Alfred Hitchcock

## *A Strange and Bewildering Character*

As the top writer, constructionist, and story author of Hitch's early talking films, I knew him extremely well. In our nearly fifty-year association, I became closely acquainted with his brilliance, idiosyncrasies and weaknesses, jealousies and fears, and politically calculating mind regarding his own career. I was also familiar with his sense of humor, which, all too often, was lacking, perverted or misplaced, and verging on sadism. Having known him so, I write not of the world-famous director, but of the man himself—a very strange and bewildering character.

There were so many sometimes contradictory facets attached to this man. Genius, of course. Tremendous ambition. Vast inventiveness. Curiously enough, an overwhelming fear of authority. There was also impatience—Hitch hated to wait for anything or anybody—except for me when I used to pick him up outside his Cromwell Road apartment on our way to the Gaumont British studio. He could be the kindest guy in the world. He could bend over backward to be kind. He could bend over backward to be sadistic and horrible. I suspect he was only kind because it made him feel how wonderful he was. Actually, he was a bully.

I'm not saying anything I would not say to his face. I remember the evening he showed me *Psycho*—we were drinking at his house, and I said, "Hitch, you're a sadist."

"Sadist? How could you possibly say that?" he asked.

"Because only a sadist could have filmed that bathroom scene."

"What do you mean?" he inquired.

I replied, "It was horrible, sickening." I pointed out the obvious, the harrowing knife murder of Janet Leigh, the blood flowing down the drain, and so on.

Hitch only grinned and answered, "Charles, you've lost your sense of humor. I directed that scene for laughs."

Laughs? I've seen the picture twice, but don't remember any member of the audience falling in the aisle out of mirth.

Then there were Hitch's practical jokes, often cruel rather than funny. He bet his favorite property man that he couldn't spend the entire weekend with his hands handcuffed behind his back. The man was delighted, jumped at the thought of five pounds, so the handcuffs were applied. What the poor man didn't know was that Hitch had arranged a drink for him up at the local pub, laced with a very strong laxative. The result was obvious. Pity the man's poor wife, having to tend to a husband who suffered a call of nature every few minutes but, with his hands locked behind his back, could do nothing to help himself.

To Hitch this was hilarious, only encouraging further, often vicious sadism. But strangely enough, the people he seemed to enjoy hurting most were those whom he had every reason to be fond of and respect. I remember instances of his joking treatment of his favorite assistant director, Richard "Dicky" Beville.

Dicky was a delightful guy. He'd been a turret gunnery officer who survived the ghastly World War I Battle of Jutland, even though his battle cruiser had been sunk and the British lost 6,274 crewmembers. But for Dicky, surviving Hitch's droll tricks was another matter. There was the occasion when he had booked seats for the opening of the Covent Garden opera season, in those days a full-evening-dress affair—for Dicky, white tie and tails, and for Molly, his lovely, young wife, a specially designed evening gown.

Leaving the BIP Elstree Studio after the day's shooting, Hitch offered to run Dicky into town, so that he would have plenty of time to prepare for the important evening. He accepted gratefully and boarded Hitch's huge, chauffeur-driven Minerva, which—since Hitch loathed fresh air—had closed and hermetically sealed windows. The journey proceeded, but along the way Dicky realized that the car seemed to be skirting London rather than driving into it. He pointed this out.

But Hitch shrugged it off, saying, "This chauffeur likes to pursue his own shortcut routes. He knows his job."

And the chauffeur did his job, exactly as Hitch had ordered. The car ended up at Shamley Green, Hitch's country home, some twenty miles or more out of London. Dicky and Molly never made it to the opera season opening.

Not all Hitch's humorous excursions were vicious. Dicky and Molly had moved into a tiny but elegant West End flat. Hitch sent them two presents, carted up by burly delivery men. A huge but practically worn-out grand piano—almost as big as their entire living room—and a large, old-fashioned, rusting iron clothes mangle.

In those days I gave a birthday party at my lovely flat overlooking Belgrave Square. There were way over a hundred guests. Hitch arrived with gifts, five hundred pairs of kippers and one brush and crumb tray. This was funny, except I had a tough time disposing of a thousand kippers to my guests. To another party he delivered a crate containing bottles of a most wonderful Champagne—all empty!

And there was the St. James's Theatre event. Sir Gerald du Maurier spoke the line "I haven't got a horse." So while Gerald was on the stage, Hitch had a large cart horse led into the actor's dressing room. Gerald left the stage, entered his dressing room, confronted the horse, and said casually, "Oh, hello, old fellow." Hitch and others listening had expected a big shock reaction. A disappointment for Hitch.

He derived immense satisfaction from his pranks, provided others were the butts. When these backfired, however, he was far from amused. I remember two dinners at which Hitch was hoisted by his own petard.

There was a play, *Young England,* produced at the Victoria Palace in 1934. The Reverend Walter Reynolds wrote it as a deadly serious, patriotic glorification of British high society and its younger sprouts. The "hero" was a master of Boy Scouts, shorts and all. The show was a huge success, a riot, but not the kind of riot its author had hoped to achieve. London flocked to the Victoria Palace for 278 performances to laugh and roll in the aisles. Central to this unexpected hilarity was the Scout mistress, "Lady Mary," a personification of English upper-class breeding. She was played by what appeared to be a simpering young idiot. Her uplifting lines were appalling, her mincing manner adding to the audience's rapturous amusement.

Hitch and I went to see *Young England* four times, laughing ourselves sick. We joined with others speaking her line "I must go and attend to my girls' water." And eventually Hitch announced to me, and his dear wife, Alma, that he had fallen in love with Lady Mary and just had to meet her.

Alma and I both knew this was Hitchcock's humor at work again. He wanted to take the young actress out, mock her, and enjoy laughing at her simpering stupidity. I knew a member of the cast, whom I contacted, and arranged a foursome supper party, Hitch and Lady Mary, me and my date. My wife, Maggie, made other plans.

Hitch insisted on a spectacular evening. He rented a magnificent Daimler, the kind seldom driven by anybody except members of the Royal Family. Hitch and I donned white tie and tails, silk top hats, everything in style. We waited at the theater's stage door, just like the stage-door Johnnies who used to cluster at the Gaiety or Daly's Theatre, awaiting the lovely ladies of the chorus. Our two ladies emerged. Chauffeur-driven to the Savoy Grill, we were seated at one of the very best tables. Everything seemed in order, except it wasn't. Nothing worked out—not Hitch's way. Soon Hitch started his insidious mockery, sadistically enjoying what he concluded would have the simpering Lady Mary dancing to his amusement. But—shock! The true personage behind Lady Mary came out of her closet, proving to be a bitingly bright Londoner whose wit and repartee could outmatch Hitch at every turn of the conversation. I had never seen Hitch more unhappy. The biter was *bit*.

On another occasion, in Hollywood, Hitch was discomfited at a dinner party arranged for twelve guests in the garden of Chasen's restaurant. A thirteenth guest arrived, an elderly lady whom none of us knew. This was a gag, designed to embarrass the guests bewildered by the presence of this stranger. Knowing him as I did, I spotted the whole thing as a practical joke. The woman was a film extra employed for the evening. Throughout the meal she sat silent and smiling. But again, the biter was *bit*. She got gloriously drunk and mocked her host with a good, earthy wit. Poor Hitch. He hated that dinner party.

Since Hitch didn't drive, for a long time I drove from Belgrave Square to pick him up at about ten o'clock every morning. We'd proceed to the Gaumont British studio in Shepherd's Bush, where we'd chat for a while and I'd present my latest thoughts and ideas. During this time he'd usually have a barber shave him, and then at one o'clock we'd lunch at the May Fair Hotel. Then, back at the studio, Hitch slept while I did some genuine work in my office. After an hour or so, he would wake and say, "What are we doing now, Charles?"

So we'd talk a little more until the studio day ended at five o'clock. Then we'd repair to Hitch's flat for cocktails. Our cocktail hour frequently proved the most productive time of day, when we could discuss our thoughts and battle ideas.

Hitch was not a writer—he had flashes of ideas, many of them very good, unlike most directors I've met. But all too often the ideas had no relation to the story. As we agreed on the primary importance of story construction, my problem was how the hell to get his ideas into the picture, or tell him to forget it. This was often a bewildering task calling for extreme ingenuity. Samuel Taylor, cowriter of *Vertigo* (1958), said Hitch had in his mind a mosaic of vignettes, but "if he didn't have a good writer, there were pieces missing in that mosaic."[15] The writers Sidney Gilliat and Frank Launder, collaborators on *The Lady Vanishes* and *Jamaica Inn,* said the same thing. This was a problem experienced by all writers who worked with Hitch.

But Hitch would not acknowledge any writer. It was a very ungenerous character flaw, actually, as Hitch was totally incapable of creating or developing a story. Without me, there would not have been any story. Hitchcock was never a constructionist, never a storyteller. I would take a story and turn it into something good. After that, Hitch and I would turn it into a screenplay. As I always wrote my own dialogue, the picture was mine—though sometimes he'd call in dialogue writers after I'd left the picture. I've never worked with anyone else in quite that way. We were a *writer-director partnership*—but his vanity could not credit me. He credited no one but himself.

There were other sides to Hitch's character, which I knew better than anybody, excluding his wife, Alma. As both of us were fascinated by anything unusual, we loved to explore. There was the time when we went into the generations-closed Princess's Theatre on Oxford Street, the London base of Charles Kean, who had produced his plays there in the 1840s and 1850s. That was a somewhat uncanny experience: the great, shadowy theater had been turned into a furniture repository. The two of us stood onstage, viewed what had once been a great auditorium, and sensed the presence of century-back audiences, bombastic actors, thrills, and applause—now as dead as Kean himself.

Or once, as usual, I was driving Hitch from GB Shepherd's Bush to his flat for our nightly cocktails. We passed over a railroad bridge, beneath which was a derelict, long-abandoned railway station, a sort of ghost train habitat. A door was open, leading down a flight of steps. We descended onto the empty platform. It was interesting, until I heard scuffling, running feet. I turned, and there was tubby little Mr. Hitchcock high-bolting it for his life, back up the stairs to the safety of the car. I shouted to him, "What's the matter?"

He answered over his shoulder, puffing, shuddering, "There's a man!"

There was. A completely harmless caretaker who couldn't have been less interested in two passersby. But when I got back to the car, Hitch was shuddering with fear. It took a strong drink at Cromwell Road to pull him together.

Why was one of the greatest directors of this century a scared man— fearful of authority, his bosses, and other elements? Gaumont British was owned by the Ostrer brothers, Isidore and Maurice. I never met Isidore in spite of the fact that my pen provided his company with some of its best successes. But I did meet Maurice—a stupidly rude man, full of conceit, whom I disliked on sight. But Hitch's relation to Maurice wasn't dislike—it was downright fear of his boss. For three years Hitch and I used to sit opposite Maurice when we lunched at the May Fair Hotel. Hitch never spoke to Maurice. I believe it was because he felt it would be disrespectful unless his employer condescended to speak first.

Until the time of his death in 1980, owning something like 30 percent of MCA/Universal Pictures, Hitch still remained in awe of Universal Studio's chairman, Lew Wasserman. Lew was the boss, and Hitch the employee. In honor of Hitch, Universal built a magnificent cinema theater on the lot named the Alfred Hitchcock Theatre. I would like to think that Hitch knows this and has at last realized his own vast importance, so much greater than that of anybody for whom he had worked.

Hitch and I loved to travel. He adored the Palace Hotel at St. Moritz, where we went for four consecutive years in the mid-1930s, and always at Christmas and New Year's. His wife, Alma, Maggie, and I would ski (or tumble in the snow), while Hitch would plant his tubbiness in the Palace Hotel bar lounge. Some work would get done, usually over a casual predinner drink. And when preparing to make *Secret Agent,* we spent time at Kandersteg in Switzerland, up the glorious Lauterbrunnen Valley. Those were amusing days, searching for ideas and locations.

At the Three Kings Hotel in Basel, Hitch and I had bedrooms separated by a shared bathroom. I was awakened one morning by Hitch, dressed as a hotel servant, as he politely announced, "Your bath is ready, sir."

And it was. He'd prepared it. Of course, this was only one of the many instances I remember of Alfred Hitchcock, the performer. As shown by his comedy appearances in his *Alfred Hitchcock Presents* (1955–65), this great director secretly craved to be an actor. It was part of his vast success. He *was* an actor. There was no part in any of his movies which he could not have played. And he demonstrated this by showing his actors, male and female, exactly what he wanted.

Once we drove down to the depths of Cornwall—an idea and location trip made memorable by Hitch's climbing a hillside to stand in a testicle of the Cerne Abbas Giant. Somewhere near Land's End, we entered a delightfully warm little pub. As we drank at the bar, we heard gramophone recordings of the great night club entertainer Sophie Tucker playing in the next room. Drawn to the music, we went in. A gramophone? Certainly not. There was the famous, fat "Red Hot Momma" singing blithely to herself, all alone, with pure enjoyment. Recognizing us, she continued to sing—a beautiful one-woman performance before an audience of two.

Then there is the question of sports. I remember only two forms of sport that Hitch liked. However deep we were in a story's development, we always had to go to the center court at Wimbledon to watch the championship tennis finals. Hitch had a beautiful tennis court of his own at Shamley Green, and he would play sometimes with Joan Harrison, his secretary, in his court, and Alma and me in the other. But I never once saw Hitch go after a ball. The tubby little man would just stand there and stolidly wait until the ball came directly to him. It never made for a very good game.

The other sport he appreciated, if one can call it such, was all-in wrestling at the ring in Blackfriars. The murderous "Black Panther" versus "Mr. Mayfair"—a gentleman who would dispose of his white tie, tails, and monocle to his obsequious valet in order to face the villainous Panther. Of course, both Hitch and I knew that the whole exhibition was phony, each match carefully rehearsed in advance, the winner already chosen before entering the ring. But the shows were amusing and Hitch loved them.

Supposedly Hitch was a great music lover. I say supposedly because I was never quite sure. In the early days at Cromwell Road he had a sincere adoration of Hungarian Gypsy jazz music, such as "Play, Gypsy, Play," which he'd listen to indefinitely. But though he booked seats for prime opera occasions at Covent Garden, his appreciation was open to question.

I remember our going to a superb performance of *Die Meistersinger*, both of us in full dress. The night was sensational. But the famous German opera star staggered everybody, orchestra and all, by breaking down and forgetting both libretto and music in the middle of her famous aria. The only person who wasn't staggered was Hitch, who slept and snored comfortably through the entire performance. Perhaps he had made a change in his habits and had decided that he didn't care for music any more.

This was possible. Hitch could change his habits, just as he could change his techniques. He once decided that the only way to shoot an entire movie was in one take—no cuts whatever. He experimented with this new thought in *Rope*. It was an utter disaster. Also, after thirty years, he changed his personal attitude toward fresh air. I once drove him from Los Angeles up to his lovely forest home near Santa Cruz, California. We drove the distance in my beautiful Chrysler New Yorker convertible, with the top down, at speeds between seventy and eighty miles per hour. But Hitch kept on urging me to drive faster because he loved the rush of fresh air on his chubby face. I must have set a speed record for those four hundred miles.

Upon arrival, he told me, "This is a business-recreation trip, Charles. Let's talk business!"

We never talked business at all!

In 1956 Hitch remade *The Man Who Knew Too Much*. In spite of Technicolor and heavy expenditure, I found the remake to be a muddled mishmash of what had once been a good film. Star-studded though it was, it came out as a pathetic shadow of the original. Hitchcock shared my view. In 1958 he said to me, "Redoing that film was the greatest error of my life, but I learned my lesson—never remake a classic." Hitch stuck by his resolve. He never remade *Rebecca, The Lady Vanishes,* my *Blackmail,* or anything else. Incidentally, *The 39 Steps* was remade twice, but not by Hitch. I did not see either of them, and both remakes flopped.

One thing I never liked about Hitch was his toadying to the newspaper and radio critics. They were all warmly welcome at Cromwell Road and his country home at Shamley Green. To the contrary, I've always shunned critics rather than trying to buy their friendship and consequent friendly reviews.

Hitch wasn't always adored by his actors—his "cattle," as he called them. After completing *Secret Agent,* John Gielgud complained bitterly that Hitch ignored him, throwing all the good scenes and best camera angles to Madeleine Carroll. This may have been true. Madeleine Carroll was the type who interested Hitch, perhaps physically. The cold type with a hint of fire beneath. Grace Kelly. Tippi Hedren.

But Hitch's obvious preference for the cold, mysterious type didn't always work. In February 1936 Hitch handed me a rough story line titled "Notes and Original Story for Sylvia Sidney Subject." These plot ideas were soon abandoned, but Sylvia was cast in our upcoming movie *Sabotage*. Hitch called Sylvia three or four times by radiotelephone while she crossed the Atlantic (we didn't fly in those days), welcoming her. She was happy. But when they personally met, it was a different matter. Sylvia just wasn't Hitch's type—although she gave a beautiful performance, she was continually resenting his treatment of her.

In his "Notes" Hitch had hoped she would suffer every torture, and then react with arresting and explosive assertiveness. He wrote, "I have encountered several people who definitely enjoy the masochistic Sidney, and would have her no other way. I am all for preserving *some* of this . . . but we might play her in a pseudo-lighthearted way as a cloak for her real feelings." Pseudo-lighthearted masochism? No doubt the same humor that he intended in the *Psycho* shower scene. Vintage Hitch! Some years later, over lunch at The Cock and Bull in Hollywood, Sylvia told me how much she had hated Hitch and never wanted to see him again.

I believe Hitch's married life was a happy one—until a second woman became a disruptive part of it. She was a lady whose for-a-while sensational film career was built on nothing more than Hitch's sexual interest in her. Most of us in Hollywood know who she was and a lot of us know the inside story, but how far that story can be told is a matter for consideration. Although seventy-nine or eighty now, and I believe sick, the fact remains that she is still alive.[16] Its revelation could sell books like hotcakes, but none of us wants to be sued off the face of the earth for telling the truth. My long-dead mother used to say, "The greater the truth, the greater the libel."

At a cocktail party celebrating my forty-seventh birthday, Hitch wrote a facetious remark into my party book, "You owe *everything* to me, including your love life!" My wife, five months pregnant, questioned his remark. I believe Hitch possessed strong sexual desires and suffered personal discomfort, jealousy, even hate because his huge bulk rendered him unattractive to women. And I think he hated one and all, but he occasionally found that he had need of them. Gruesome.

Hitch objected to the fact that I'd been so successful and such a part of his beginnings. His resentment was really a part of him. And since I had written seven of his top movies, for a while he resented me, and then, oddly enough, he became my friend again.

We talked frequently on the telephone; he offered helpful criticism of some of my later story ideas. For years he remained my friend and my enemy. Hitch was like that. One day he could write a wonderful letter saying, "My love to you always," and the next letter might be signed, "Yours very truly."

I could visit his house, or meet him at a party, where he might hardly talk to me. Once, the actor Brian Aherne gave a beautiful beach party where I chatted with Hitch for almost an hour. The next day I received a case of expensive Champagne with a note, "From that stupid man, Hitchcock." So I phoned to thank him for the Champagne, and asked why the "stupid man"?

And he said, "That's what you called me. Isn't that what you said to everybody—there's that stupid man?"

Needless to say, I was shocked! "When could I have said that?" I asked. "We were talking for an hour."

"No, we didn't talk!"

Hitch couldn't remember a thing. But he imagined I'd called him *stupid*.

I could have written for his series *Alfred Hitchcock Presents,* but I never wanted to. I preferred to remain a great friend, instead of getting mixed up with that particular show. This was partly because the producer, Joan Harrison, had been our secretary for so long. I couldn't bear the thought of working under my own secretary. But she wanted to produce a few of my stories, "The Power of Babel," "The Thirteenth Hour," and "The Hunter and the Hunted." But "Babel" was too similar to something they already had produced. "The Thirteenth Hour" died because Hitch suddenly turned against me and wouldn't consider it. And by the time Joan got around to "Hunted," the program was going off the air.

I occasionally lunched with Hitch at Universal, in his own building, or visited for private screenings. In 1972 Hitch ran his film *Frenzy* for me. I didn't like it. Puzzled about why I didn't, I went to the Directors Guild showing a week later and loved the picture!—which suggests that one's reaction to reading a script or seeing a movie can be a matter of immediate mood.

I won't go on any further. There is no need to dwell on Hitch's eventual downhill plunge. His gradual loss of talent. His hopeless final addiction to alcohol, which had him sneaking drinks rather than consuming them socially. His chasing secretaries in his own office building. And on and on.

Hitch was first and foremost a great showman, and his showmanship took the form of scaring the daylights out of his audience. Some are critical of this, accusing him of being a monster. But he was practicing his profession, making the most of a genre of which he was the master. What of it? The great lawyer whose brilliant line of rhetoric condemns a suspect to death row isn't necessarily a heavy. Hitch, the great bully, could also be very kind, a happy, comfortable homebody who loved animals.

Hanging in my home bar is a glossy photograph of Hitch and me, snapped at a Los Angeles County Museum of Art reception shortly before he died. When the photograph came into his hands, Hitch gave it to me. Written across his bald head is the epithet, "To my first and beloved writer. Love Hitch." Below his name he had drawn his famous profile; practically a signature in itself.

I am proud of the picture—a valued memento and in a way a final curtain to a fifty-year-old relationship. I was and am flattered by Hitch's last message. But was there any feeling, any heart behind Hitch's mind when he described me as his "first and beloved writer"? He had nothing to gain by making such a kindly statement.

❧ ❧ ❧

# Interlude: A Study of the Bennett-Hitchcock Partnership

John Charles Bennett

What was the Bennett-Hitchcock partnership? Imagine both at Gaumont British studio in 1936, head-to-head like the two faces of Janus. Charles is speaking left across a stage; Hitchcock is looking right through a camera. By now they have a practiced synergy of voice and sight, scenario and direction, experience and invention, authenticity and effect. They are creative alter egos exploring both sides of a story. Charles acts through scenes, and Hitchcock studies their direction. Charles is advocate and Hitchcock is devil's advocate. Their discussion brings them to agreement on matters of direction, scenario, and characterization. And in consequence, Charles attributes to Hitchcock the remark "When the screenplay is finished, the picture is finished."

To illustrate, let us consider their fifth film, *Sabotage*. Alfred Hitchcock, in "My Own Methods"—a 1937 essay contemporary with the film's release—offers this description of his thoughts while directing the knife murder scenes: "So you gradually build up the psychological situation, piece by piece, using the camera to emphasise first one detail, then another. The point is to draw the audience right inside the situation instead of leaving them to watch it from outside, from a distance. And you can do this only by breaking the action up into details and cutting from one to the other, so that each detail is forced in turn on the attention of the audience and reveals its psychological meaning."[17]

Bennett insists the plan was drafted before shooting began. A draft screenplay of *Sabotage*, in the possession of the Bennett Estate, has the name of the associate producer Ivor Montagu at the top of the script. Its knife murder scene consists of twenty-three shots with direction interspersed by sixteen words of dialogue. Typed by Bennett, the scenarist, its stage and camera direction (C.U., S.C.U., S.L.S.) establish beyond all doubt that Bennett and Hitchcock together crafted the direction so each detail "reveals its psychological meaning."

441. S.C.U.
Sylvia has finished carving. She glances at him and then down at her
  hands.

442. C.U.
She finds herself carving potatoes with a carving knife.

443. S.C.U.
She puts the knife down and deliberately changes over to a tablespoon,
  with which she finishes heaping the potatoes and begins serving the
  greenstuff.

444. S.C.U.
Verloc continues in the same strain as before—
Verloc: I don't think I want any cabbage. Can't we send next door for
  some . . .
He looks across and sees—

445. S.C.U.
The place and small chair laid for Stevie.

446. S.C.U.

Verloc realizes his error and stops short. He looks up to Sylvia. But all he
can see is—

447. S.C.U.

Sylvia solemnly carving.

448. C.U.

Sylvia's hand starts again to put vegetables and things on the plate with
the carving knife.

449. S.C.U.

Again we see her realization that the knife is in her hand. She puts it
down deliberately.

450. C.U.

Her breathing is heavy. Her eyes stare across at Verloc.

451. C.U.

Verloc's eyes are glued to the knife she has just discarded. He slowly looks
up at her, and then down again at her hand.

452. C.U.

Sylvia's hand again takes hold of the knife and then thrusts it down.

453. C.U.

Sylvia's face shows the battle that is going on within her.

454. S.L.S.

Verloc, now fully aware of what is in her mind, and appreciating the fight that
is going on, rises in alarm. He makes his way slowly round the table.

455. S.C.U.

Sylvia recoils at his approach.

456. S.C.U.

Equally frightened, Verloc comes round the table, his eyes glued
downwards.

457. C.U.

Sylvia's hand hovering above the carving knife, not wanting to take it.

458. S.L.S.

Verloc's hands rise upwards, going towards her throat. She lifts up the knife.

459. S.C.U.

Verloc—his hands are about to close on her throat in what seems to be some desperate measure of self-defence.

460. C.U.

Sylvia's hand closes on the knife.

461. C.U.

The two heads breathing heavily against each other. Suddenly on Verloc's face a contorted look. He drops down out of the picture.

462. S.C.U.

Sylvia stares down and with the fingers of her left hand scrubs hard at the palm of her right in a wild movement.

463. C.U.

A big head of Sylvia. She looks about with a frightened expression. She starts to call in a small voice:

Sylvia: Stevie! Stevie!

One might also ask how Hitchcock's visual sense was compatible with Bennett's practiced experience of how to commit murder with a knife. The following juxtaposes Hitch's directorial comments from "My Own Methods" with Bennett's stage direction for *Blackmail*, in italics.

"But the sympathy of the audience has to be kept with Sylvia Sidney; it must be clear that Verloc's death, finally, is an accident."

*Peter is forcing her farther and farther back onto the table. He is obviously carried away by his passion and doesn't know what he is doing.*

76

"So, as she serves at the table, you see her unconsciously serving vegetables with the carving knife, as though her hand were keeping hold of the knife of its own accord. The camera cuts from her hand to her eyes and back to her hand; then back to her eyes as she suddenly becomes aware of the knife, making its error."

*Suddenly Alice's right hand is disengaged, and somehow the bread knife is in it!*

"Now the camera moves again to Verloc—back to the knife—back again to his face. You see him seeing the knife, realising its implication. The tension between the two is built up with the knife as its focus."

*Peter tries to seize her hand, but it is too late.*

"In an older style of acting Sylvia would have had to show the audience what was passing in her mind by exaggerated facial expression. But people today in real life often don't show their feelings in their faces: so the film treatment showed the audience her mind through her hand, through its unconscious grasp on the knife."

*Alice drops the knife and staggers away from the table. . . . Alice stares at the form on the bed for a while—her eyes wide with terror.*

It is clear that their mutual sense of direction was consistent, though Hitchcock could add camera close-ups not possible before a stage audience.

And now consider the degree to which their murder scenario is different from that in Conrad's novel *The Secret Agent*. Here is the scene from the novel:

She remained thus mysteriously still and suddenly collected till Mr. Verloc was heard with an accent of marital authority, and moving slightly to make room for her to sit on the edge of the sofa.

"Come here," he said in a peculiar tone, which might have been the tone of brutality, but was intimately known to Mrs. Verloc as the note of wooing.

She started forward at once. . . . Her right hand skimmed

slightly the end of the table, and when she had passed on towards the sofa the carving knife had vanished without the slightest sound from the side of the dish. . . . But Mr. Verloc did not see that. He was lying on his back and staring upwards. He saw partly on the ceiling and partly on the wall the moving shadow of an arm with a clenched hand holding a carving knife. It flickered up and down. Its movements were leisurely. They were leisurely enough for Mr. Verloc to recognize the limb and the weapon.

They were leisurely enough for him to take in the full meaning of the portent and to taste the flavour of death rising in his gorge. His wife had gone raving mad—murdering mad. . . . They were leisurely enough for Mr. Verloc to elaborate a plan of defence, involving a dash behind the table, and a felling of the woman to the ground with a heavy wooden chair. But they were not leisurely enough to allow Mr. Verloc the time to move either hand or foot. The knife was already planted in his breast. . . . Mr. Verloc, the Secret Agent, turning slightly on his side with the force of the blow, expired without stirring a limb, in the muttered sound of the word "Don't" by way of protest.

The dissimilarity of film and novel provides additional prima facie evidence of the extensive collaboration between Hitchcock and Bennett. Comparing to the screenplay, one finds in the novel:

- The murder was no "accident."
- Mr. Verloc was not in the kitchen "unconcernedly eating." He was lying on a sofa, and he did not "make his way slowly around the table."
- The novel offers little "tension between the two" with "the knife as its focus."
- There was no "desperate measure of self-defence," and no "heavy breathing." Mr. Verloc does not move.

So Bennett's murder scenario presents a complete rewrite of Conrad's scene. And the knifing is only one of numerous substantive changes he made to the novel:

- The terrorism in the film's opening scenes is absent from the novel.

- Verloc's lodging is not connected to a cinema.
- Conrad's inspector was not endearing toward Mrs. Verloc.
- There was no comic relief in the novel.

But the most unexpected change was the rewrite of Conrad's ending. After her murder of Verloc, the novel brings the desperately unhappy, guilt-ridden murderess to the apartment of an anarchist coconspirator, a Mr. Ossipon. This heartless villain, judging her an easy mark, says he will help her escape across the Channel—but she is to bring her savings. Instead, she commits suicide.

But Bennett replaced Conrad's denouement with a different story line. The detective coerces Mrs. Verloc's love interest by withholding evidence. As they walk off together, it seems the detective will have his way with the traumatized woman. And that is Hitch's film version of *Blackmail,* retold!

Examination of *Sabotage* corroborates Bennett's statement that they were a writer-director partnership, who planned plot, direction, characterization, camera angle, and staging before the filming began. This is supported by comparison of novel and script, and by comparison of *Blackmail* stage direction to Hitchcock's "My Own Methods."

It is instructive to look at an earlier paragraph of Hitchcock's essay:

Imagine an example of a standard plot—let us say a conflict between love and duty. This idea was the origin of my first talkie, "Blackmail." The hazy pattern one saw beforehand was duty-love-love versus duty—and finally either duty or love, one or the other. The whole middle section was built up on the theme of love versus duty, after duty and love had been introduced separately in turn. So I had first to put on the screen an episode expressing duty.

And further down:

But to get back to the early work on a film. With the help of my wife, who does the technical continuity, I plan out a script very carefully, hoping to follow it exactly, all the way through, when shooting starts. In fact, this working on the script is the real making of the film, for me. When I've done it, the film is finished already in my mind. Usually, too, I don't find it necessary to do more than supervise the editing myself.

Settings, of course, come into the preliminary plan, and usually I have fairly clear ideas about them; I was an art student before I took up with films. Sometimes I even think of backgrounds first. "The Man Who Knew Too Much" started like that; I looked in my mind's eye at snowy Alps and dingy London alleys, and threw my characters into the middle of the contrast.

Oh, really? A standard plot of *Blackmail,* whose "hazy pattern" was the origin of "my first talkie." What *standard plot*—Duty versus Love? This is not what Bennett intended—I know from personal experience Charles would not consider concealment of evidence to be either loving or dutiful. And though Hitch saw it differently, the original *Blackmail* play was not about the detective's state of mind. As I discuss in chapter 18, "The Avenger," Hitch's film is about his manipulation of Alice, whereas Charles's preferred version of *Blackmail* seeks to exonerate Alice. She escapes her family's manipulation by wooing the detective.

And what is this about *The Man Who Knew Too Much* starting in Hitch's mind in the Alps? Perhaps Hitchcock did visualize an opening scene while honeymooning with Alma in 1927. But the statement is an oversimplification. Bennett drafted *The Man Who Knew Too Much* as *Bulldog Drummond's Baby* in 1933, and the Alps opening scene was one of several locations discussed with Bennett. The handwritten manuscript is in my possession.

In a 1980 essay, "Working with Hitchcock," Associate Producer Ivor Montagu says Hitch returned to the Gaumont British studio at the "height of his powers" to work the "genre he made his own." There is no ambiguity here, as he refers to Charles's stories *The Man Who Knew Too Much, The 39 Steps, The Secret Agent,* and *Sabotage.* With these films, Montagu remarks, Hitchcock added technical mastery to his preestablished excellence of narration, artistry, and observation.[18]

But might it be that Charles's actor's perspective and playwright's narration and directions underlay Hitch's *technical* mastery? Unfortunately, Montagu does not mention Bennett. But his essay does explain that Montagu, Alma, Hitchcock, and the "scenario editor" Angus MacPhail—who is not credited—sat around Hitch's flat, fishing for story ideas from *Plotto,* an indexed master book of over three thousand standard plots, published in 1928. So here is Hitchcock's meaning of *standard plot*—a category assigned after the play *Blackmail* was purchased and the film produced. I wonder if Hitch's authors—Buchan, Conrad, Maugham, and Bennett—all agreed that their stories were *standard plots*?

Montagu also states that their foursome conferenced to detail the scripts. He reassures us this method was successful, as the story was "elaborated with suggestions from all of us. . . . The scripts were by consensus; the only special privilege their *credited authors* had was to write them down" (emphasis added). That exaggeration is supported by Montagu's *Sabotage* draft, found in Charles's possession. But among its 116 pages, the only comments on the script pertain to direction on page 67, and a slight alteration of dialogue on pages 77 and 78. But at least Montagu's account is more forthcoming than was Hitchcock's essay "My Own Methods"—which credited only Alma's assistance.

So the deeper question becomes: "Why did Hitch not mention Charles Bennett?" As Bennett tells it, "For a great many years, Hitch objected to the fact that I'd been so successful and such a part of his beginnings, and he loathed anybody getting any credit whatsoever." And with contemporary opinion already naming Bennett as Britain's "Most Successful Screen-Story Writer"[19] and calling for his opinion on "The Story in Film,"[20] perhaps Hitchcock was secretly relieved to see the celebrated actor-playwright-director-screenwriter sail for Hollywood. Perhaps the jealous Hitchcock feared that Bennett's success might eventually disclose his own considerable reliance on the "typical Bennett scenario."

# 8

# Cause for Alarm

Without question, Maggie's life and mine in England was a happy one, even though, except for our bed-shared hours, we were seldom together. During the days I wrote at the studios. During the evenings Maggie (stage name Faith Bennett) performed at this or that theater, on some occasions appearing (and three times *starring*) in films out at Elstree or Twickenham or Walton-on-Thames, any of which called for very early rising and pretty late homecoming. But in spite of long periods of such bisection, we were close. We loved each other and remained bosom pals up till her death—in spite of the eventual breakup of our marriage, which bore no relationship to our transplantation to Hollywood, the city where the Eleventh Commandment has long seemed to be "Thou shalt not commit matrimony *in perpetuity.*"

We would go out to the Brooklands Race Track, where we knew the "Bentley Boys" racers, Jack Dunfee and his brother Clive. In September 1932 we were attending a race with Clive's wife, the actress Jane Baxter, watching from the stands, when Clive's "Speed Six" cartwheeled over the top of the great curve, hurtling Clive to his death at around 140 miles an hour. Grim. A couple of years later Jane costarred with Claude Rains and Fay Wray in my film *The Clairvoyant.* I wish I had foreseen the crash and warned Jane of this tragedy.

Though my acting days had come to an end, not so the itchiness in my feet or my wanderlust with Maggie. With money coming in plentifully from my plays and screenwriting, we grabbed every opportunity to take our car across the Channel and explore any reachable spot on the European Continent. First, of course, came the great cities, although thanks to my time at the Théâtre Albert Premier, I already knew Paris better than other cities. But other capitals needed inspection—Rome, Vienna, Budapest, and so on—and got it. More often than not, we wandered off the beaten track, from ancient villages on the slopes of France's Alpes Maritimes to the horse-herding witchery of the Hortobágy—the Gypsy-music-haunted Great Plain of Hungary.

Until 1937 our vagabond affliction had been limited to the eastern side of the Atlantic. But while working on *Young and Innocent* (1937) with Hitch—we were in St. Moritz at the Palace Hotel—there came a telegram, sudden and unexpected, that rewarded our wanderlust with an eight-thousand-mile leap to Hollywood. It was the turning point of our lives— an offer from Universal Pictures to come over as a writer-director-producer to what then was the truly filmic *big time!*

Universal's offer was better than good, more money than I'd previously heard of. A term contract at a king's ransom salary, first-class transportation across the Atlantic with my wife and cat Nibbs, a luxury suite at New York's Waldorf Astoria, and initially rewarding comfort at the Hollywood end—all we needed at the company's expense until we'd had time to settle in. Mick Balcon, the respected head of production at my beloved Gaumont British, said, "Charles, just write [them] one screenplay, and you'll be the top writer in Hollywood at any price you want." He offered to double what I was earning in England if I'd stay; but the British film industry could in no way combat the Hollywood dollar, so filthy lucre won out as I became the first major British screenwriter to be signed by Hollywood.[21]

We bade farewell to the adorable flat in West Halkin Street and to our three- or four-hundred-year-old weekend cottage, Leatherwagon, on the lovely loneliness of Cliff End, near Fairlight in Sussex. I lost my sense of smell forty years ago, but not the memory of the summertime fragrance that clung to that cottage: the scent of rambler roses clambering affectionately here, there, and everywhere, and on warm evenings the intoxicating odor of night-blooming jasmine. Hitchcock threw a large bon voyage party for me, and then Maggie and I boarded the boat. In May 1937 De Reszke Minors cigarettes ran an ad on the back cover of *News Review* featuring Maggie and me. The photo showed us smoking in a theater lobby, waiting for the curtain to rise. The ad read, "10 Minutes to Wait." It should have read, "Already Sailed," as by that time we were long gone.

March 1937. The wide Atlantic loomed, as did the further three-thousand-mile pilgrimage across the United States. We crossed at record speed on the French Line's S.S. *Normandie,* surely the most beautiful ship that ever put to sea, arriving in New York on March 16. Then, after a much-publicized tour of New York City, we bought a Packard convertible and devoted three weeks to driving and sightseeing across the States.

During the trip I penned a romance melodrama titled *Love Goes West*. The menacing adventure led from excitement at New York's docks to violent murder on the 20th Century Limited train—from crazy hazards in the Carlsbad Caverns to touch-and-go with death amid the cobwebs of a mining ghost-town opera house. It was a three-thousand-mile race against time and obstacle, which commenced in Manhattan and finished in Hollywood.

As did I (finish up in Hollywood). And immediately I experienced a keen sense of disappointment—not at our welcome but at my first glance at fabulous filmdom. We pulled in on a warm April evening, having spent the previous day and night in Nevada's desolate Death Valley. No complaints. Universal had booked us into an elegant suite at the top luxury hotel, the Château Elysée, with a fine pool and tennis court, and within shouting distance of the mountain wilderness of Griffith Park, with its magnificent view over the Los Angeles Basin. Most memorable was the nightly croaking of bullfrogs in the hotel ponds. I had never before heard their throaty cacophony, and I have heard it again only at the Bel Air Hotel, poised beside a stream that runs into Brentwood from the Santa Monica Mountains.

So much for the immediate plusses; disappointment was to come that first evening. Having settled in, I left Maggie and wandered on foot down to where I had been told I would find fabulous Hollywood Boulevard. I found it—and sustained a shock. Somehow I had visualized Hollywood as a sort of glory-days Baghdad, dominated by some half-dozen Caliph Haroun al-Raschid types, the great moguls of movieland. To quote Prospero, I was ready to be awe-struck by "the cloud capp'd towers, the gorgeous palaces." I wasn't!

There were none such to be found on the boulevard, though their absence did not mean the film world lacked them or, for that matter, the modern-day caliphs. It seemed the moguls, along with the film stars, had long since abandoned filmdom's birthplace and taken to the hills—Beverly of that ilk—and the slopes of the Santa Monica Mountains known as Bel Air. Only Cecil B. DeMille, occupying a large lake-encompassing estate close to Griffith Park, had remained in touch with Hollywood itself. Because of the perpetual mate-switching that has for so long delighted the hearts of Hollywood columnists, movie stars' homes are frequently hard to pin down. The heart-throb names are often gone tomorrow as much in abode as in memory.

Although he was reputedly vicious, I have always suspected that the legendary Caliph Haroun al-Raschid of Baghdad possessed elegance and charm. And I've always found that if the studio boss is a decent fellow, life for the writer can be decent, too. Unfortunately, one can run into the reverse; and I'm sad to state I've seldom found elegance or charm among the Hollywood caliphs.

I have to qualify this statement. Remembering the deserved prominence of MGM in its prime, I will say that Louis B. Mayer has to go down in entertainment history as "Mr. Film." David Selznick not only could take no for an answer, but would demonstrate intelligence and even gracefulness—the latter sometimes dangerous, but never absent. I admired Darryl Zanuck's ability: a fine producer who it was said could have been an equally fine writer if he had cared to pursue the craft. I knew Zanuck as a good horseman—and polo's a great game so long as one can survive without a broken neck. Sam Goldwyn, although sometimes inadvertently amusing with such language classics as "Gentlemen, include me out," had immense taste when it came to choosing the right stories, writers, directors, and actors. And I regarded Walt Disney as more an artist than a mogul.

But what with foul-mouthed Harry Cohn of Columbia, and Jack Warner—a very nice guy to meet at a cocktail party but not a writer's dream when writing at Warner Bros.—I'm inclined to dismiss most of the past moguls as born-lucky morons. With filthy language, and their often take-for-granted belief that every lovely young lady in town would willingly tumble into the hay at the nodded invitation of such a divinity, these are about as much like Haroun al-Raschid as were Laurel and Hardy.

Anyway, it was reasonably late that first evening when I emerged onto famous Hollywood Boulevard. Very few people were walking about. The glaring Californian sun, which might have lent warmth and glamour to the scene, had long since sunk in the Pacific. The street lighting was dismal. Maybe it was the unimpressive illumination that was responsible for my immediate reaction, my swift decision that this was no Champs Elysées, no Fifth Avenue or Piccadilly. During the previous week Maggie and I had been driving through a thousand miles of ramshackle cow towns—the Old West. Now before me was what appeared to be another Old West relic. I had known Hollywood to be the breeding ground of cowboy films, and my first thought was that somehow I had strayed on to a standing film set. Wrong! This was Hollywood Boulevard itself, and I had to face the sad fact that one of the most famous streets on earth seemed to represent little more than the background to a Tom Mix movie set. There were a handful of buildings that actually loomed above two stories, such as Grauman's Chinese and the Hollywood Roosevelt, but the immediate impression was of shabby tawdriness and deterioration.

Pathetically, in over fifty years, the boulevard hasn't changed that much. I'm lying. It has—*for the worse.* At some unheralded point the City Council, or whoever is responsible for such "uplifting" enterprises, arranged for the sidewalks to be studded with stars, each implanted in the pavement and carrying the names of in most cases deceased film luminaries. Mary Pickford is there. Douglas Fairbanks, Clark Gable, Charles Chaplin. I'm not sure about Greta Garbo, who made a practice of saying, "I t'ank I go home now." But tourists still visit the boulevard in swarms, carefully circumnavigating the underfoot star symbols and viewing the film celebrity footprints in the court of what was once Grauman's Chinese Theatre but is now Mann's.[22] But to view any of these sacred relics, the tourists have to elbow their way past derelicts, panhandlers, purse snatchers, and the like.

As I believe is reasonably well known, it was in 1911 that Cecil B. DeMille made the first full-length feature film, *The Squaw Man,* in a rented barn at the corner of Hollywood and Vine—and by doing so created world recognition of Hollywood as a place. In the process of writing four films for DeMille, I came to know him very well, and I have a feeling that were he alive today, he would be horrified at the mess that seems to have evolved from his search for a quiet corner in which to shoot something more than a two-reeler. I do hope that, somewhere "up there," C. B. isn't blaming himself for turning a peaceful orange grove–surrounded adjunct of Los Angeles into an odious tourist trap. For years there has been talk of the restoration of Hollywood. Restoration to what? A grandeur that never existed? Sorry. To quote Jonathan Swift, "You can't make a silk purse out of a sow's ear."

Even back in 1937 Hollywood had long ceased to be the center of film production. Almost all the studios had moved to the suburbs of ever-growing Los Angeles. Perhaps from the beginning, Universal Pictures sprouted beyond the Hollywood Hills, way over the Cahuenga Pass. Then Paramount, RKO, and the United Artists lot gave Hollywood Boulevard a wide berth, being at the periphery of the legendary movie town. The famous lion, which for so many golden years had roared out the introduction of a Metro-Goldwyn-Mayer film, was relishing its den on the vast MGM lot in Culver City. And 20th Century Fox, the back lot of which is now Century City, had acquired huge acreage in West Los Angeles. Warner Bros. was already shifting facilities from Sunset Boulevard into the in-those-days spaciousness of Burbank and the San Fernando Valley.

For a while—I think into the fifties—Columbia Pictures alone remained within a stone's throw of DeMille's barn-studio site, hanging on in what was known as Gower Gulch, so named because of the hordes of cowboy soap operas that had emanated from this hallowed street. But even Columbia wasn't to keep its Hollywood flag flying. Like Warners, it shifted to the valley. It's all very disappointing, particularly for tourists hoping to enthrall folks at home with peep tales of the "dream city's" studios—and who were then, and still are, forced to forage thither and yon.

In that first 1937 evening in Hollywood I knew less than nothing about the vicinity of the studios. Least of all did I know where the film stars and moguls parked their carcasses. But as I strayed along that poorly lit boulevard I was conscious that my mood was changing. Maggie and I had arrived in town only hours earlier, full of optimism, interest, and assurance. Now I was aware that a creeping sense of depression was stealing up on me, and with it apprehension. I tried to shake it off, but I couldn't.

And soon enough I realized why I couldn't. Serious thought about my Hollywood future had been conveniently shelved during the hectic weeks following the reception of Universal's offer. But here I was, finally in the heart of the fantasy factory . . . and in hours, strange employers would be breathing down my neck, hands reaching out for the filmic marvels that I would be expected to deliver in exchange for the goodly sums paid my way.

Pausing on the corner of what I was presently to know as Hollywood and Vine, I found myself wondering if by accepting the Universal offer I hadn't bitten off more than I could chew. Self-doubt was creeping up on me. What if Louis B. Mayer, Adolph Zukor, Darryl Zanuck, or my employer, Carl Laemmle, failed to share Mick Balcon's and the Gaumont British's enthusiasm for what I had to offer? Worse—what if I really wasn't as good a writer as I'd believed? Harry Ham, the American representative in London of the then all-powerful Myron Selznick Agency, had set up my Universal deal. Was it possible that Harry Ham, pursuing the usual agency practice of overselling, had passed a piece of goods that wouldn't bear inspection?

Increasing my discomfiture was the growing realization, till now ignored, that within weeks, perhaps even days, the Hollywood film industry might be measuring my abilities against the pinnacles of screenwriting talent. Would my work begin to match up with that of Robert Sherwood, Lillian Hellman, Dudley Nichols, Robert Riskin, Ben Hecht, and the like? What if at the contract's expiration date Universal Pictures should say: "Sorry, Mr. Bennett, it didn't quite work out, did it? 'Fraid we're terminating our agreement."

Harking back to Shakespeare, recollecting the end of the previously quoted Prospero speech didn't cheer me. "We are such stuff as dreams are made on, and our little life is rounded with a sleep." Sleep! Call it another word for falling down on the job, necessitating a humiliating retreat to London, my less friendly contemporaries saying, "Oh, Charles is back. He must have flopped over there." It was a sentiment made worse by my already having stated in a *New York Post* interview my belief that Hollywood had more story vision than Britain and presented films more daring and ambitious.

It was now nearing midnight. My stroll along Hollywood Boulevard hadn't been exactly elevating. I headed back to the Château Elysée, where Maggie asked, "What's it like out there?" I replied without embellishment, "It may take a bit of getting used to." I slept, and I think those croaking bullfrogs helped lift my spirits. "Don't worry," they seemed to croak, "Never worry! Croak, croak, croak . . ."

The happy denouement was that I had no cause for worry. The next morning I reported to the Selznick office and was royally lunched at the famous Brown Derby before being escorted out to Universal City, where the red carpet was down. With the passing of the next days and weeks, things were falling into place, although I was met by a surprising twist at the outset. As it happened, in April 1937 money at Universal Pictures wasn't in abundance. Since entering into the contract with me, the studio had suffered three flops in a row, and since my salary was large (at $1,500 per week, I believe I was getting more money than any other writer at the studio), they couldn't afford to pay me, and within days I found myself "loaned out" to Samuel Goldwyn—naturally at a profit to my contractual employers, which irritated me immensely.

I found myself out on the open lot with Dorothy Parker on my left, Lillian Hellman on my right, and Dudley Nichols across the way. They all descended on me, immediately, and said that I'd *got* to join this comparatively new organization of writers trying to get together to help each other. I'd been brought over by Myron Selznick, my agent and the biggest agent in town at that time. And he said to me, "Charles I want to give you some good advice. You're new to this town. You can, if you like, join this new organization; or you can join the Screen Playwrights—which is much bigger at MGM. But it is complete suicide to join either of these organizations. This will be absolutely the end of you." Anyway, I *did* commit suicide. I joined the very small Writers Guild, and I'm deeply grateful that I did. That was nearly sixty years ago and I've never regretted one moment of it.

At Goldwyn I was put in a room next to some guy who kept pounding at a piano—it was impossible to concentrate—so I asked the office manager to move me. He replied, "That won't be necessary, Mr. Bennett. Mr. [George] Gershwin died yesterday in brain surgery." Shock! That was July 12, 1937. So I kept the office and pounded at my typewriter on two Gary Cooper films—a picture written by Robert E. Sherwood, *The Adventures of Marco Polo* (1938), and *The Real Glory* (1939). I was lost! I was supposed to improve on Sherwood's material, but his writing was so good I could do nothing to better it.

British cinema in those days told stories as they should be told. People talked the way they should talk. But everybody in America believed that the story didn't mean a damned thing; the only thing that mattered was sound—dialogue, dialogue, dialogue. The result was that in Hollywood at that time, every line was supposed to be a wisecrack. Every damned line! Like someone would say, "I won't forget you," and someone else would reply, "I've forgotten you already." That was so bloody revolting, I couldn't stand it. I have said that Hitch and I believed dialogue should support the story; but that sort of dialogue had nothing to do with development, and I was totally incapable of writing it. I was lost.

I remember being confronted by one of Goldwyn's top management people. "What the hell are you doing?" he said. "You've written a scene here for Gary Cooper that he couldn't speak in a million years."

I said, "You mean I should stick to 'yep' and 'nope'?"

He said, "Exactly." Not exactly "yep" and "nope," but short dialogue.

You were really up against it with Gary Cooper. He wasn't a great actor. He was a personality. I suppose I worked on it for about four weeks. So I was rather a flop with Goldwyn. But I amused myself writing a little scene titled *Mr. Shakespeare Comes to Hollywood*, which characterized the imbecility of the whole Goldwyn situation.

There was something else I didn't at all like about Hollywood when I first arrived. I remember our going to a party at the home of Joe Mankiewicz. It was a huge party and, to my horror, hundreds of newspaper photographers were flashing celebrities. It was all for publicity. Disgusting! In England, a party was for fun, not to put your name in the columns.

Then I went back to Universal. I was one of the top drama and suspense writers in England, but they put me on a stupid comedy, *Good Girls Go to Paris* (1939), about some poor French girl. I couldn't do a damned thing with it—I didn't have the faintest idea what to do with it! So after about six months, Universal dropped my contract. I said to Myron Selznick, "What the hell do I do next?" He put me on to David Selznick (Myron's brother), where I wrote a very good Janet Gaynor picture, a sentimental comedy called *The Young in Heart* (1938). I should have got full credit—because I constructed the whole damned thing—but Selznick brought in a wonderful writer named Paul Osborn, who wrote the necessary form of dialogue superbly. He couldn't have built the characters as I could, but he could write dialogue like a dream. Anyway, he got the credit and I got the adaptation credit.

David Selznick was a strange character, and bewildering to work for— horrible to work for. You could spend all day working on the screenplay, and then he'd say, "Oh, Charles, I'd like to have a little chat after dinner. I'll have some food sent in from the Brown Derby."

So you'd come back and eat some food from the Brown Derby, and then you'd have your chat—along with the production associate Bill Wright and a lot of Selznick's top directors, including Lewis "Millie" Milestone. All his "team" would be sitting around all night. I'd come home at dawn, dead tired. And as I was leaving, he'd say, "By the way, Charles, do you think we could have what we were talking about on paper by the time I come in at noon tomorrow?"

Incredible. Impossible. But I liked him very much. I found him extremely intelligent, very productive, very creative. And a wonderful person. As for working for him, I never wanted it again.

In a minor way I was in part responsible for Hitch's coming to Hollywood. During one of those ghastly, practically all-night conferences—I suppose it was at two in the morning—David said, "Charles, it's been suggested that I bring over one of either two British directors— Robert Stevenson or Alfred Hitchcock. You've worked with both of them; which would you recommend?"

I replied, "Bring both over. They're better than most of the directors I've met here."

"Do you really think so, Charles?" he asked.

"Yes," I said, "they are both tremendously good."

"Fine," he said.

So David took me at my word and brought both over. I should have got 10 percent of Hitchcock. My God!

Following this, my literary agent, H. N. Swanson, sold me to Larry Weingarten, a top producer at MGM who was married to Irving Thalberg's sister—always a help. In those days the writer was the lowest form of life—considered rather less than the grip. At MGM, for example, you could get a studio producer who was usually the cousin of the mogul's present mistress, or something like that. He would be paid much less than the writer, and the writer had to do what the damned producer told him—a very peculiar situation. Writers were just factory workers, beneath the notice of their bosses, Louis B. Mayer and his number two man, Eddie Mannix. That was so different from the really good old days under Michael Balcon at Gaumont British.

Larry Weingarten put me to work on a spy story, *Cause for Alarm,* a 1938 novel by Eric Ambler. I loved Eric, but it was a very bad story. What interested Larry was the first four pages, but after that there was no particular story, and I was supposed to provide a new story. I struggled at it for about four weeks in the spring of 1939, and for too long a time felt I was making no progress. This made me unhappy because I knew if I failed on this, and Larry Weingarten and I parted company, it wouldn't do me any good in Hollywood.

*Cause for Alarm* was my type of story, a chase melodrama played against the gathering clouds of war. The MacGuffin found two British art thieves attempting to steal a Leonardo da Vinci masterpiece from a wealthy Milanese collector. One thief poses as a salesman for a British firm selling armaments to Italy. Their theft is foiled by a German secret agent, who frames the British firm with a plot to sabotage an Italian troop train. One thief is murdered by spies; but the other escapes with the assistance of a female American journalist. In the climactic chase, our art thief–turned–hero leads police to thwart the sabotage and kill the German secret agent. All the final scenes were to be filmed aboard trains, which added to the drama.

One day Larry sent me a small scene—about five or six pages—and asked me if I could do anything with it. He said they had thirty writers working on it, and no one had been able to come up with anything. This was *Balalaika* (1939)— a popular London stage musical by one of my closest, oldest friends, Eric Maschwitz. So I read the scene, and I sat down and wrote my own version, which I thought was pretty good. Then I went into Larry's office with these five or six pages and said, "Here's the scene you asked for."

Larry said, "Very interesting, let's have a look at it." So he started to read the scene; but after about three pages, he threw it aside and said, "I don't understand what this is about at all. I don't understand what you're aiming at," and he threw it on the floor.

At which point I saw a guy who was lying on a couch in the corner, also reading a copy. I said, "Wait a minute! Let's see what this fellow has to say." He was Reinhold Schünzel, a German director at MGM, there to direct *Balalaika*.

Presently, very slowly—even though Larry kept saying, "What are you waiting for? What are you waiting for?"—Reinhold said, "Zis is a scene."

Larry said, "What?"

He said, "Zis is a scene. Zis is the first scene I have been presented with for the direction of zis movie."

I said to Larry, "Read it again." So Larry picked it up and read it again and said, "This is a scene." But he had to be told it was a scene. Except for Schünzel, I would probably have been finished in Hollywood. The result was that I was immediately transferred off *Cause for Alarm* and put on *Balalaika,* which I worked on very successfully and got a credit.

By the time I left *Cause,* I had shaped it into a pretty good screenplay. Larry was pleased with it, but then he brought on Herman Mankiewicz to make one or two alterations. And as Herman was a contract writer who wanted his name on it, my script was torn to pieces. This was the way it was at Metro at that time, full of writers—I should think about 160 of them under contract—all desperate for the next credit they could get, in order to ensure that they got their options taken up. Most of them went around with daggers behind their backs trying to stab any writer who got in their way. It was a fight to the finish. So by the time everyone had finished with *Cause for Alarm,* my screenplay was nonexistent. Eventually they'd spent three-quarters of a million dollars in script development, using a succession of writers destroying each other's scripts.

Metro eventually released a film titled *Cause for Alarm!* (1951), but that had nothing to do with me. My script became irrelevant when Italy allied itself with Germany—no Brit would sell arms to Italy during World War II. But I was off *Cause* and onto *Balalaika;* and much to my relief with this change of fortune, my Hollywood apprehension and cause for alarm were gone with the finality of a script's fade-out.

Another reason for not worrying was my realization that Hollywood, with eight major studios churning out around four or five hundred movies a year, had room to spare for anybody who could do little better than write his or her name. It didn't take me long to recognize that for every good writer in Hollywood there were maybe thirty or so hacks who scraped a better-than-deserved living by turning out the trash that the double-bill programs of the period entailed.

And as for the top writers whose names had imbued me with foreboding, again I had nothing to fear. My type of movie—suspense, adventure, pursuit—just wasn't theirs, which meant that they went their way and I went mine. Actually, some of the elite became close friends—such as Lillian Hellman who, on our arrival, went out of her way to introduce Maggie and me to the right people, and even put her home and swimming pool at our disposal.

Meanwhile, I'm sure many of the other greats never even recognized my existence, a circumstance that didn't bother me in the least. I was enjoying myself, living high on the hog, never having to count the coins. Looking back, the greater part of my early Hollywood existence seems to have consisted of writing at the studios by day, and living things up by night. Somehow I managed time to write a short novel titled *War in His Pocket,* published in the November 1939 issue of *Bluebook* magazine, which would later become the basis for an unpublished novel and a TV series idea, *Mr. Hero* (1966). During those halcyon days I earned and got rid of an immense amount of money, but I don't regret tossing away a penny of it. One gets what one wants, and I got mine.

⤳ ⤳ ⤳

## Interlude: *Mr. Shakespeare Comes to Hollywood*

[*Telephone buzzer rings. Background of switchboard sounds. Voice of a female operator heard.*]

FEMALE OPERATOR: Hello? This is the Grunion Film Corporation of

Hollywood. Who? Oh, William Shakespeare! Just a moment, please! (*Sound of bell.*)

OPERATOR: Mr. Grunion's office? Mr. William Shakespeare for Mr. Grunion . . . by appointment.

GRUNION'S SECRETARY: Has he brought the lions?

OPERATOR: They didn't say.

SECRETARY: Send him right in, please.

OPERATOR (*as if to Shakespeare*): Go right in, please.

BOY'S VOICE: This way, Mr. Shakespeare.

[*Sound of door buzzer control; pair of footsteps proceeding along corridor. Shakespeare's voice is heard mumbling sepulchrally . . .*]

SHAKESPEARE: To be or not to be, that is the question . . .

BOY: That's what I always say, Mr. Shakespeare.

[*Sound of rap on Grunion's door.*]

BOY: Mr. Shakespeare to see Mr. Grunion—

SECRETARY: Come in, Mr. Shakespeare. Did you bring the lions?

SHAKESPEARE: Lions, fair mistress?

SECRETARY: Don't say you've let Mr. Grunion down?

SHAKESPEARE: It pleases you, fair mistress, thus to jest,
    With one who humbly offers but his best.

SECRETARY (*realizing*): I know—you're a writer.

SHAKESPEARE: Full thirty times hath Phoebus' cart gone round,
    Neptune's salt wash and Tellus' orbed ground,
    Since I to contract large affixed my seal,
    To write for Mr. Grunion, well or weal.

SECRETARY (*with understanding*): Now I get you. You're the three thousand bucks a week the Front Office's been squawking about. Better wait—I think Mr. Grunion wants to fire you.

[*Knocks on door. Roar of arguing voices from within as she opens door and enters. She speaks through roar.*]

SECRETARY: Mr. Shakespeare to see you, Mr. Grunion.

GRUNION: Has he brought the lions?

SECRETARY: He's a writer, Mr. Grunion.

GRUNION: Never heard of him.

SECRETARY: You're paying him three thousand dollars a week.

GRUNION (*plaintively*): Gosh—Why doesn't somebody tell me these things?

MR. BOOMER (Grunion's "Yes-man"): Mr. Grunion's absolutely right.

GRUNION: Have him come in.

SECRETARY: Yes, Mr. Grunion.

[*Opens door—roar of conference, everyone talking at once, resumes again. Secretary addresses Shakespeare.*]

SECRETARY: This way, Mr. Shakespeare.

SHAKESPEARE (*through uproar*): What roar of battle is't assails mine ears?

SECRETARY: Battle?—That's a story conference. (*Announcing*) Mr. Shakespeare!

VOICES OF WRITERS (*together in uproar*): But Boss—I'm telling you, if this dame were to say to this guy. . . . He's wrong, Louis. Being the dame she is she'd . . .

GRUNION: Boys, Boys! Come in, Mr. Shakespeare. Sit down, Mr. Shakespeare. You know my ace writing team, Mr. Shakespeare? Mr. Bean and Mr. Coon. Mr. Shakespeare! My manager, Mr. Boomer—Mr. Shakespeare!

VOICES: Glad to know you, Mr. Shakespeare. How'ya, Mr. Shakespeare!

GRUNION (*ruffling papers*): Now about the lions? No. Of course—you're a writer. Look—Will your story fit the Marx brothers?

SECRETARY (*as door clicks*): The lions are here, Mr. Grunion!

[*We hear the woofing, snapping, and growling of lions in the outer office.*]

GRUNION: Have 'em wait!

SECRETARY: And Mr. Goldwyn's calling from New York.

GRUNION: Tell him to hang on! Shoot the works, Mr. Shakespeare.

SHAKESPEARE: 'Tis called the tragic and lamentable historie of Romeo and Juliet.

GRUNION: Title's too long—

BOOMER: Mr. Grunion's absolutely right!

GRUNION: We can always cut it—go ahead!

SHAKESPEARE (*rolling it out*): 'Tis a story of great tragedy, in sooth.
    Two households, both alike in dignity,
    In fair Verona, where we lay our scene—

GRUNION: Verona, New York, or Verona, Maine?

SHAKESPEARE: Verona, Italy, fair sir.

GRUNION: Italy's not so hot right now.

BOOMER: Mr. Grunion's absolutely right!

MR. BEAN (the writer): We can change the background, Mr. Grunion.

GRUNION: You're right, Bean! Go on, Mr. Shakespeare.

SHAKESPEARE: Two families noble, to ancient grudge forsworn!

From forth the fatal loins of these fell foes,
A pair of star-crossed lovers take their life.

GRUNION: What's he talking about?—We gotta have laughs, Mr. Shakespeare.

SHAKESPEARE: Born to great love, but born to part in death,
Yet with their deaths bury their parents' strife.

GRUNION: I don't get it!

MR. BOOMER: We'll have it synopsized later, Mr. Grunion.

GRUNION: Go ahead, Shakespeare.

SHAKESPEARE: But that is the argument, my masters.

GRUNION (*with feeling*): It stinks!

BOOMER: Mr. Grunion's absolutely right!

MR. COON (the other writer): You're wrong, Mr. Grunion!

GRUNION: Huh?

COON: For my dough, I think Bill Shakespeare here's got somepin'. Sure, it wants work on it—but I'm tellin' you—there's a sequence under a balcony, Bill told me of. Boy, is it hot? Boy meets girl—you know, the old baloney, but sure box-office every time.

BEAN (*taking it up*): Coon's right, Mr. Grunion. We build a big set, see? Knock out the wall between stage twelve an' thirteen and spend some real dough. All right! This Juliet dame's on the balcony. There's a full moon. Trees. Swans on the lake—

COON: We can shoot the works on that.

BEAN: She's lookin' off, and then this Romeo guy comes—and, oh boy! You know how Gable looks in tights!

COON: With maybe a feather in his hat and a guitar!

GRUNION (*tensely*): Go on!

COON: And this guy climbs up to the balcony—and this skirt's waitin' for him—and the Hay's Office can't kick 'cos they got married right after. And he sings at her and she sings at him. And it's . . .

BEAN: It's in color—

COON: It's exotic—

BEAN: It's neurotic—

GRUNION: It's terrific!

BOOMER: Mr. Grunion's absolutely right!

SECRETARY (*through woof of lions outside*): The lions are still waiting, Mr. Grunion!

COON: After that it's just a matter o' treatment. As it's laid in Old Vienna—

SHAKESPEARE: Verona, sir!

COON (*going straight on*): We can work in the Blue Danube some place. An' then—if like Bill says, they're married—why we can rewrite the finish—cut out the cemet'ry and give 'em a kid! A little toddler—blue eyes—fair hair—Shirley Temple herself!

GRUNION: That's great!

BOOMER: Mr. Grunion's absolutely—

GRUNION: And now all we need's a title.

SHAKESPEARE (*desperately*): The title, sirs, is "Romeo and Juliet!"

GRUNION: No class!

BEAN (*triumphantly*): The title, Mr. Grunion, is "Old Vienna!"

GRUNION: Tremendous!

SHAKESPEARE (*wildly*): But 'tis not my title!—'tis not my play!

GRUNION: You're too modest, Mr. Shakespeare. (*Generally*) Okay, boys, hash it up! Bean, do the construction—Coon, get ahead with the dialogue—

SECRETARY (*from door, through woof of lions*): What about these lions, Mr. Grunion?

GRUNION: And get Charlie Chaplin for some gags—

SECRETARY: And Mr. Goldwyn's still calling from New York—

GRUNION: Gee—Why didn't ya tell me! (*Grabbing phone*) Hello, Sam! (*To others*) All right, boys, wait outside—

SHAKESPEARE (*as door opens and lions roar*): But, sirrah!—Sirrah!—What do I do?

GRUNION: You get the credit, Mr. Shakespeare!

BOOMER: This way, Mr. Shakespeare—

GRUNION (*into phone as door slams*): Sorry to keep you waiting, Sam. Yeah—we gotta story, and, boy, is it big? Gable, Shearer, Garbo, Shirley Temple—all co-starring together. An' the title—wait till ya hear it! "Old Vienna!" How's zat, Sam? Okay! (*Rings off, shouts*) All right, boys, come right in!

[*The lions are roaring.*]

GRUNION (*shouting*): Boys . . . Boys . . . Where are you . . . (as door clicks) Why, Mr. Shakespeare—say, where're the others?

SHAKESPEARE (*with sepulchral triumph as lions roar without*): The lions were still waiting, Mr. Grunion!

# 9

# The British Film Colony and Errol Flynn

I've been a member of scores of clubs. Tennis. Equestrian. Flying. Golf. I'm still a proud member of two London clubs—the Savage and the Green Room—and am an affiliate member of the Players and the Lotus in New York, also the Masquers Club in Hollywood. But in Beverly Hills I am now clubless. Like so many pleasant haunts in the LA district, from the famous Garden of Allah to the elegant nightclubs Ciro's, the Mocambo, the Trocadero, my deeply beloved Cock 'n Bull pub on Sunset Boulevard—all went the way of progress.

But back in 1937 I found the famous Hollywood British film colony in its heyday. It was an expatriate group embellished with many who were major box-office bulwarks of the industry: Ronald Colman, Cary Grant, Charles Laughton, the late Sir Guy Standing, David Niven, Vivien Leigh, sisters Joan Fontaine and Olivia de Havilland, Ray Milland, Sir Cedric Hardwicke, Claude Rains, Roland Young, Basil Rathbone, and Nigel Bruce. Not to speak of Aubrey Smith, Boris Karloff, Edmund Gwenn, Brian Aherne, Greer Garson, the wonderful Dame May Whitty, and the soon-to-arrive Gladys Cooper.

Not that the British film colony designated itself a club, but surely any organization whose membership depends on an accepted nomination has to fall into that category. So *club* it was, and I was a member—and now probably the only living survivor.

When it came to exclusivity, for twenty-five years or more the colony presented a formidable wall of dis-fellowship that any British newcomer seeking social acceptance could surmount only if fortified with the right credentials. Following meticulous perusal, the newcomer would be designated in or out of this sacrosanct community. Without question, being out was discomforting—the shunning encountered from a Ronald Colman or C. Aubrey Smith at a mixed-nationality cocktail party would make an unaccepted Brit feel like he'd crawled out of the woodwork. Conversely, once in, colony life—with its garden parties and sports—was enjoyable; and Maggie and I appreciated our inclusion.

I still find myself wondering what form of genie converted a troupe of "strolling players" into the snooty arbiter of its own countrymen. It could have been snobbery, based on the possession of luxury homes, swimming pools, tennis courts, and so on. Or perhaps the phenomenon was a *male* disorder, born of a nostalgic yearning to emulate the insularity employed by the gentlemen's clubs of London's Mayfair and Belgravia. On the other hand, colony rejection might have been due to certain diehards' believing that "Oxford-accented" Britishers should limit their acquaintanceships to those of similar "good breeding." To let up on such discrimination might be the first misstep to colony infestation by low-class British vaudevillians and the like.

Whether the good side of the colony outweighed the bad is a matter of conjecture. But one fact remains—credentials or not, the approved acceptance into the most exclusive consortium west of the Atlantic lay with one man alone . . . Hollywood's and Britain's great film and stage patriarch, C. Aubrey Smith. His nod represented the welcome mat or the brush-off.

Having known Aubrey well, I'm convinced that he can't have been happy with the assignment. I truly believe that, at heart a simple soul, he was the victim of the old-school-tie, stiff-upper-lip implorations of so many of his world-famous compatriots. But Aubrey went along with the job and, despite its dinner jacket–in–the–jungle mentality, the British film colony flourished. As for Aubrey, through the passing of years I was lucky enough to have him in three of my films, and he was always worth his weight in both performance and grizzle. Offscreen he was unforgettable, crustily imposing, dominantly erect, the perfect personification of graceful gentility, and, perhaps not surprisingly, kind to the point of being adorable.

Aubrey's home was where Coldwater Canyon crests the Santa Monica Mountains, affording breathtaking views of the San Fernando Valley to the north and the sixty-mile-distant Santa Catalina Island to the south. The house was lovely, crowned by a weather vane stoutly portraying three cricket stumps topped by cricket balls, and above these, swinging in the four winds, was a cricket bat. Cricket! I never knew what the initial C of

Aubrey Smith's name stood for, but if it wasn't for cricket, somebody had slipped up at his christening. In his youth he received a top-ledger education at Charterhouse and Cambridge, where he acquired his love for the game.

During his many years as a star of the London theaters, Aubrey Smith was best known as a great amateur cricketer. Throughout the half of the world identified as "the empire upon which the sun never sets," Aubrey was affectionately nicknamed "Round the Corner Smith"—a sobriquet earned by the deadly nature of the curve in his ninety-mile-an-hour hardball bowling. At least a generation of worldwide cricket fans bestowed on him adoration akin to that reserved for sports greats in the United States.

My once-over by Aubrey went as I should have expected. Up there at the top of Coldwater Canyon, the great Aubrey gave me a Scotch and soda—very benignly—then started to explore whether I could fit into the colony society. I shall never forget that dear old grizzled face as he got down to serious business with "where'd you go to school?" A bad start. I was in my late thirties and had already achieved more than a degree of success both as a playwright and as a film writer. It hadn't crossed my mind that scholastic background could mean anything at this stage. I had attended a few months at the St. Mark's College primary school in Chelsea, but St. Marks was hardly up there with Eton or Harrow, or with Aubrey's Charterhouse. I didn't know how to reply—so I postponed the dreaded moment by taking a sip of my Scotch. But it was Aubrey himself who unwittingly saved me from possible social exile. Before I could think up an answer to the school problem he came through with what to him was infinitely more important: "Cricket?"

Cricket—*of course!* The keyword to acceptance by these far-from-home Ishmaels. Cricket had come my way after a fashion. I'd played once for the stage against the press. And feeling like a traitor, I'd played for a team of writers against the stage. I'd been known to bat in an occasional run, but my cricket was not anything to boast about, any more than my golf or my tennis. The only outdoor pursuit I've ever really been good at was riding horses; but since I hadn't ridden up to Aubrey's home, there seemed to be little point in bringing the matter up.

Although I had little faith in my cricketing ability, I said quite truthfully that I loved the game. The old man beamed and suggested that I might like another drink, and from that moment on Maggie and I were in.

I followed up by playing in occasional matches on the colony's cricket field north of Griffith Park. Dear, amusing Aubrey, being too old to join in the fray, would pour tea and serve watercress sandwiches to the wives while the husbands gallantly wielded their bats and balls. It was a pleasant way to spend an afternoon, inducing a sense of companionship that frequently continued off the cricket field.

Life was enjoyable. Tennis. Golf. And the abundant horseback riding I adored. Soon Maggie and I kept two horses at the Riviera Country Club stables, from which trails ran up into the unspoiled and wildly beautiful Santa Monica Mountains. We bought a Luscombe airplane and often flew out of Culver City airport to Palm Springs. We also flew to the 1939 San Francisco Golden Gate Exposition on Treasure Island. When I had business in New York, we returned together: a breathtaking flight.

Among our closest companions, Maggie and I counted the newlyweds Brian Aherne and Joan Fontaine, whom I adored. Sometimes Joan and I rode together in the Santa Monica Mountains. Or we stumbled through colony parties, where she knocked over and shattered a Ming vase—I took the blame to spare her embarrassment.

Once Maggie and I flew our Luscombe to meet them at Las Vegas. Yes, Vegas did have a landing strip—short and dirt and existing for practically the sole use of Nevada mine owners and ranchers. One could have bought up the Strip, like much of Beverly Hills, for a song—I remember Wilshire Boulevard at one hundred dollars a front foot! Brian, Joan, Maggie, and I spent the night in what was certainly the first hotel-casino in what is now the overcrowded gambling capital of the world. Next day we landed at Mines Field (now LAX) and enjoyed drinks with Brian and Joan that evening in their home. And our personal and professional friendship lasted for years.

I was in studio demand. Money was plentiful. Maggie was an elegant and popular hostess. We enjoyed season tickets at the Hollywood Bowl and gloried in the opera season at the Shrine Auditorium—where the greatest stars in the world would appear, Gigli and the rest. The great Stravinsky played our home piano, while my cocker spaniel Henry howled from the next room. And only a hundred miles away, easily reachable by plane or over traffic-free roads, was Palm Springs—lovely—little more than a village in those days, completely uncrowded and gloriously relaxing on weekends at Charlie Farrell's Racquet Club. I would saddle a horse and ride out among dunes studded with cactus flowers, or sip a cool drink at a sidewalk café on a warm desert evening. Guitar-strumming cowboy singers entertained for an hour or more, expecting nothing more than a thank-you, a drink, and a couple of bucks.

I've always had a passion for mountains, shared by Maggie. And a further hedonistic element was the presence, rewardingly visible in those smog-free days, of the nearby San Gabriel and San Bernardino mountain ranges, the peaks of San Gorgonio (Old Greyback) and San Jacinto reaching up to almost twelve thousand feet. Nestled on nearby slopes at the seven- or eight-thousand-foot level are Lakes Arrowhead and Big Bear, resorts where one can boat or swim in the summer or break a leg skiing in the winter. I hiked treacherous Strawberry Peak to absorb the view out over the LA Basin and Pacific Ocean beyond.

Among the colony's crème-de-la-crème expatriates, the mention of certain names would raise hackles of pious horror. Disrespectful Errol Flynn, with his well-known penchant for very early teenage mistresses and other unacceptable bents of character, would never have been invited to Aubrey Smith's cricket-bat-adorned home. Not that Errol gave a damn. Personally, I've always been of two minds about Errol Flynn. An invocation in the Book of Common Prayer asks, "Have mercy upon us miserable sinners." Naturally *us* includes Errol—and me, and pretty well everybody else I've ever known. But knowing Errol was never miserable, I have never been able to decide whether he was truly a sinner.

Foreign-born but educated in England, Errol was proud of his looks and physique, also justly proud of his thespian success, which—in Hollywood in his early days of stardom—he was inclined to let press and fans assume was the fruit of born brilliance, discouraging mention of any previous theatrical or film experience. In his book *My Wicked, Wicked Ways,* Errol did admit to having performed in both England and Australia, but by that time it didn't matter.

Having known him as an adventurous soul, I believe his claims that he spent his early twenties fishing for pearls in the South Pacific and prospecting in the jungles of New Guinea. But fortune didn't come his way south of the equator, nor was the red carpet down for his arrival on the West Coast; in fact, it was months before the newshounds Louella Parsons and Hedda Hopper noticed his existence. But once Hollywood woke up to his presence, the metamorphosis hit with intensity faster than fast. I'm sure Errol would have hit the tops in the long run anyway, but there's no question that his mercurial rise to fame was based on the four-letter word luck.

During the early summer of 1935 Errol was granted a low-paid, dead-end form of employment as a "stock artist" at Warner Bros., a job little better than that of a film extra. I'm sure that soon enough Errol, stuck on a dismal corner of the Warner lot, must have been wishing himself back in the wilds of New Guinea, or even dodging sharks while pearl fishing. But along came the once-in-a-million happening. Luck, yes. But fortunately Errol had the looks and ability to justify it.

A miraculous star by the name of Robert Donat had arisen out of the British Isles. He had made two huge personal successes—the first in *The Count of Monte Cristo* for Edward Small in 1934, then as Richard Hannay in my film *The 39 Steps*. Magic! Robert was the one person on earth Warner Bros. needed for their lead in Rafael Sabatini's *Captain Blood* (1935)—the story of a young Englishman who, facing the noose after being wrongfully accused as a rebel, escapes to sea and becomes a pirate. After much gore and gallantry, everything works out fine—Blood gets the girl and hoists Britain's Union Jack in place of the skull and crossbones. Donat was signed. The cameras were set to roll.

They didn't. With the Hungarian-born director Michael Curtiz about to say, "Action," everything stopped dead. The hideous reason? The captain had taken to the seas again, homeward bound to England, the country from which he had once fled.

It was a stunning, not to say expensive, shock. Jack Warner (the not-too-bright, heavily conceited, and oversexed heir to his brilliant brother Harry Warner's great studio) must have been verging on a heart attack, but he survived and the studio had to face facts. Nobody could blame Robert Donat. His doctor gave Robert urgent orders to get out of the extreme dryness of Southern California or face a demise swifter than any that could have overtaken Captain Blood and his pirate ship.

The medical diagnosis was accurate. I know this because a few months later, Gaumont British, Hitch, and I wanted Donat for *Sabotage* (1936). Donat had agreed to do the film, but when it came to production he was still far too sick—even the damp British climate wasn't compensating for the dryness of Southern California. We played John Loder, a good actor and certainly one of the best-looking men on earth—but not Robert Donat. Sylvia Sidney arrived in England, gave a superb performance, but she hated Hitch and never spoke to him again off the set. Nothing could persuade her that natural causes had cheated her out of playing opposite Donat.

John Loder was a delightful character and a great friend who starred in four of my films. He had been the Scotland Yard inspector aboard *My Paris Plane,* and had infiltrated an international gang in *Warn London.* Later, in Hollywood, he joined the cavalry troop I was commanding in the Santa Monica mountains—which brings me back to Errol.

Our problem at Gaumont British was infinitesimal compared to that of Warner Bros. GB's overheads were negligible, but Warner's were immense. And with the pirate ship standing on the soundstage, and highly paid stars such as Olivia de Havilland and Basil Rathbone just twiddling their thumbs, losses were piling up by the minute. But God is kind—even to such low forms of life as Jack Warner—and so came the savior. His name was Harry Joe Brown. Harry Joe, already recognized as a fine moviemaker, was the studio's appointed producer of *Captain Blood.* Harry was one of the most pleasant people to come my way.

As things were looking grim, he went to Jack Warner. Weeks were passing; there was even the chance of other box-office cast members' being forced to drop out because of contracted assignments. The picture had to be made—right now—or be abandoned and losses cut. Harry Joe had a suggestion. He'd noticed a young man among the stock artists, good to look at, maybe with acting ability. Somebody named Errol Flynn.

I can imagine Jack screaming his head off. "A stock artist! For Christ's sake—get me Colman, Gable, Robert Taylor! A star!"

All the top stars were tied up, announced Harry Joe, but this young man—"Flynn!"

"Christ!"

"At least let me test him."

Nearing a heart attack and the clock ticking, Jack had to give the okay. The rest is history. Errol was tested and was magnificent as Captain Blood. All Hollywood wanted him. But Warner swept him up with a pittance contract, signed and sealed. They quickly started a press buildup of him as the exemplification of what a red-blooded young man should be. Both studio and columnists did a great job, and fans flocked worldwide. Jack Warner and his company were becoming richer by the moment. But the goose, Errol, was laying the golden eggs for peanuts.

When Errol moved on to *Robin Hood,* Myron Selznick, creator of the top Hollywood film agency, moved in, arresting Errol in his dressing room between shots. Michael Curtiz was on the set preparing the next take when Myron signed Errol to an agency contract and said, "Now you'll stay put. Don't go near the set. Read a book till I give the go-ahead."

Errol obeyed. Myron went to Jack Warner and said, "My client is through. Sue if you wish—he hasn't any dough—or return him to your stable of underpaid stock artists. But he won't speak one more line as Robin Hood unless he receives two hundred thousand dollars a picture."

Jack must have screamed, but Myron was adamant. Jack had to give way, so from that moment Errol was financially up there with Clark Gable, Cary Grant, Gary Cooper, and Robert Taylor. The meritorious and charmingly handsome Errol was being properly paid for so sublimely sustaining Warner Bros.' wealth and worldwide clout.

No one could blame Errol for his reticence regarding his pre-Hollywood stage and film experience. A young actor on his way up would have been stupid to wag his tongue about an insignificant thespian past. As it happened, I knew the facts. In January 1934 Maggie and I decided to learn to fly. I met a young lady named Billie Rose at a party of the artist-sculptor Jacob Epstein. We became friends, and Billie persuaded us to drive up to Sywell, six miles outside Northampton—one of a trio of little flying clubs that embraced Brooklands and Lympne.

We drove up and promptly fell in love with the flying club, with its little airfield, and with her husband, the ace World War I fighter pilot and future Kings Cup champion, Tommy Rose. He taught us to fly a Gipsy Moth I biplane.

We met world record–breaking pilots of those pioneer days—a dazzling collection—few of them exactly teetotal, and exciting to meet at one or another of the club bars. There was Jim Mollison, who in 1932 made the first east-to-west solo flight across the Atlantic from Ireland to New Brunswick, and Amy Mollison, who crash-landed with Jim on the U.S. coast the following year. Amy had achieved world fame by being the first person ever to fly solo from England to Australia. Jean Batten—who made the first solo flight of the South Atlantic—was also around. And in addition to Tommy Rose, the bars of the three clubs boasted a roster of record breakers—as famous as Hollywood stars in those now-forgotten days—such as C. W. A. Scott, Sir Charles Kingsford Smith, Campbell Black, and others.

But imposing as were so many of these, Maggie and I got the biggest kick out of making a friend of Beryl Markham, who in 1936 was the first woman to fly solo from England across the Atlantic. Charles Lindbergh, Amelia Earhart, and the first Atlantic conquerors, Royal Air Force Flight Lieutenants John Alcock and Arthur Brown, had all flown west to east—the American continent to Europe—always with the prevailing west wind pushing them on. Beryl Markham flew into the teeth of the wind, its prevalence cutting down her chances of survival by roughly 50 percent. Maggie and I were among the well-wishers who saw her off in her single-engine Vega Gull, heading for New York. The weather in England was good. But her book *West with the Night* says that after a thousand miles or so it became increasingly foul. She made it, however, managing to land her faltering plane in marshy mud in Nova Scotia. The New York greeting ceremony, prepared and graced by Mayor Fiorello La Guardia, had to be postponed, but Beryl Markham had done something no woman had ever done before.

But getting back to Errol: during our weekends in and out of the air at Sywell, Maggie and I with Billie and Tommy Rose would frequently spend Saturday evening at the Northampton Theatre Royal, which was gallantly hosting a repertory company. I say gallantly because by 1934 the going had to be tough, both for a theater struggling to combat the talkie invasion and for the actors who had to learn, rehearse, and perform a different play every week. The company was a good one, however, and I'm sure the audiences enjoyed seeing their local favorite appearing as debonair Charles Surface one week and as a youngish Sherlock Holmes the next. Anyway, among the acting troupe was a finely built hopeful named Flynn. I admired him and his work; and when the company was invited out to a Sunday cocktail party at our flying club, I met the young man in person. I think I knew even then that he was destined for a great future—*someplace.*

It wasn't to be in Northampton, though he was doing his best to build up his popularity—at least among a special section of the residents. I'm sure Errol was adored by his audiences, but it seems adoration wasn't enough. He wanted *worship,* not only of his performance of the parts he was playing but of his . . . well, *his* parts.

At that time Errol was living in digs alongside a road used by high school girls on their way home after lessons. As it transpired, an unusual form of lesson was sometimes available. The digs had a large window facing the street. There, or so I was assured, Errol would reward passing damsels by revealing himself—tall, lithe, and completely in the buff. I have no doubt that many of the young "voyeurs," having been granted a look-see at male beauty, took the memory of Errol home and into their dreams. But I can't help wondering what the Northampton police thought about such bare effrontery.

Apart from any kick Errol got out of displaying himself to passing young ladies in the British Midlands, three years later he was a film idol with probably more than half the world's adolescent females craving to see more of him than just his acting ability. The way things worked out, once he hit stardom, Errol seems to have lost interest in public exposure—surely a great loss to a host of lovely young ladies.

Only a few weeks after Maggie's and my arrival in Hollywood, we found ourselves on William Randolph Hearst's special train, which ran every Friday evening out of Pasadena to his fairy-tale castle at San Simeon. The train, in spite of Hearst's professed opposition to liquor, was well provided with any drink a film star, producer, director, social-ite, even writer could wish for. There were five or six luxury Pullman coaches, and pretty well every Hollywood icon who could take time off was aboard.

But on that particular night of my first trip to San Simeon, among the luminaries, from Charlie Chaplin to Clark Gable, from Janet Gaynor to Bette Davis, was Errol Flynn. Perhaps half an hour out of Pasadena, he spotted me and recognition was instantaneous. There I was—some writer from England who had seen him act at Northampton and who had drunk with him at the Sywell Flying Club. He must have been aware that I was the one guy on the train who could grab considerable press coverage by blurting out facts about his histrionic beginnings. I had no intention of doing any such thing; and I was inclined to like this young genie-out-of-the-bottle superstar. But Errol wasn't to know this; and so, wisely but unnecessarily, obviated any tongue-wagging by rewarding me with his friendship. He switched on the charm, of which he was a past master, and kept it pretty well running all the way to San Luis Obispo, where the train disgorged its multimillion-dollar cargo into a fleet of Rolls Royces and Cadillacs.

Accessing the castle grounds was an experience in itself. Once the car fleet reached the gates of the Hearst ranch, there were warning notices for all to see: Beware! Wild Animals! Don't Leave Cars Until Instructed! This wasn't tomfoolery. The thousands of acres surrounding Hearst's San Simeon masterpiece were a refuge for wild animals from every corner of the earth. Lions. Tigers. Bears. I'm not sure about crocodiles, but I do know that the weekend haven of the Hollywood elite didn't need protective guards. Any poor wretch hoping to rob Hearst of even one of his archaeological treasures would have had to fight his way across a savanna more dangerous than anything in Kenya.

From that remeeting on the train, Errol was always pleasant to run into. We often played tennis at the Palm Springs Racquet Club. He was nice to know as an acquaintance—not a close friend. But he *had* close friends, and a person is frequently judged by the company he or she keeps. Errol's winning smile as Robin Hood is still with me, as are the smiles of his Merry Men. He had a genius for collecting buddies whose offscreen reputations hardly fell into the category Merry. The artist John Decker. The actors John Barrymore and W. C. Fields. And so on. I knew them as houseguests and party guests. There is a very large John Decker painting hanging in my living room—a snowscape to which John added, while very drunk, a small figure urinating in the bushes.

A cloud crossed the sky, as in 1942 word came out that the Godlike Errol might have feet of clay. The sacrilegious rumors were nothing to begin with. Just the usual film columnist whisperings of entanglements with this or that glamorous young dame, or of fistfights with characters such as the writer-director John Huston. No matter; in those days a film star could do no wrong. Or if he or she did stray, the vast power of his or her studio would have it hushed up with the speed of light. As Gertrude Stein might have said, "A star is a star is a star." Even today very few of us ever see a falling one.

But Errol's claim to disfame came like a thunderbolt when headlines hit of his arrest in connection with a hugely publicized charge of the statutory rapes of Peggy Satterlee and the "San Quentin Quail," Betty Hansen. The scandal rocked the industry and ended only when Errol was dragged back from the jail gates by the wizardry of the famous defense attorney Jerry Geisler, swiftly summoned by Warner Bros. at the prospect of their biggest box-office icon going down as a child molester. Thanks to the brilliance of Geisler's rhetoric—undoubtedly aided by large payoffs to the right people—Errol left the court pure as the driven snow. Sex before marriage with teenagers? Robin Hood, content with Maid Marian, would *never* have thought of such a thing. Nor would Errol, according to Jerry Geisler and Warner Bros. So Errol remained the soul of chastity. Warner was content, and Jerry Geisler was considerably richer.

Through Errol, I also met Betty Hansen, and earned a trophy of a stuffed California quail, still on my bookcase. Imagine my consternation to find her age had been misrepresented!

〜 〜 〜

## Interlude: The Spy at Split Rock

There were weekends when Maggie and I would fly together across the deserts and mountains of Southern California, Arizona, and Nevada—Maggie as the captain of our Luscombe, me as "spare pilot" who could take over the controls when expertise was unnecessary. I must admit that whenever landings or weather presented any form of crisis (and two or three of them were pretty hair-raising), I was happy to leave our mutual survival in the hands of "the Captain." But there was one particular sky-ramble that was not so dangerous as sinister.

We were flying from Las Vegas, heading south-southwest to the landing strip at Palm Springs. Our flight was crossing the lonely expanse of the Mojave Desert, fifteen thousand square miles of desolation stretching from bone-dry Death Valley in the north to the Colorado Desert in the southeast. The vast desert was trisected by only two roads: State Highway 42 heading northeast to Vegas, and Highway 32 proceeding east to a subtropical little city named Needles, which, with a summertime *midnight* temperature of 112 degrees, was said to be the most torrid spot in the United States.

There was nothing below us but unending sand, brush, cacti, Spanish bayonet, Joshua trees, and salt flats, the abode of rattlesnakes and Gila monsters. As if to break the arid monotony, barren mountains reached up six thousand feet or more: treeless and desolate, aeries for vultures. We had to climb to around ten thousand feet, keeping fingers crossed lest a recalcitrant engine should place us in hell. Stories are told of motorists leaving their stalled cars in the swelter of the Mojave who die of heat and thirst.

We flew on over rugged peaks and desert nothingness and were glad to be in a plane rather than a car. We were doing a comfortable hundred miles an hour, and the desert receded beneath us, never even a hermit's shack in sight. We avoided a section of desert mapped as the Devil's Playground—weren't interested in playing games with the devil. Nothing . . . until . . .

We had come down to around six thousand feet, flying between a towering upthrust on our left and a slightly lower bastion on our right. Our map had directed that we avoid a restricted ordnance zone where tank warfare could be practiced and artillery shots fired without hurting a thing except jackrabbits, which I like, or coyotes, which I don't.

Quite suddenly Maggie spotted it, pointed it out to me—not the Devil's Playground, but something considerably more intriguing. We were puzzled. We knew that even out here in the mostly uncharted vastness of the Mojave we were looking at something that supposedly shouldn't exist— maybe it was just a trick of the eyes. Or was it? We came down to a few hundred feet, only for our eyes to confirm what they had refused to believe. There was a *landing strip,* nestled among narrow canyons between sharply rising sand-swept buttresses, shadows of which rendered the strip's presence almost indiscernible.

We were fascinated. We had aerial maps, not well topographed in those days, but with light aircraft capable of only short hops, no strip in the vastness of a desert should be overlooked. This one had been overlooked, so far as our map was concerned. Curious, we decided to land—spiraled further, put down on the strip, gazed around. Weird! A dirt strip but no hangar. Tucked to one side and tied down with what looked like rotting rope was an ancient open-cockpit biplane—dirty, looking like something that would never fly again. In front of it was a rusting gas pump. Nothing else. No sign of life.

We didn't know what to do. Had we flown into a time warp? Were we viewing the dream of a ruined past? Sitting there, motionless amid a world of loneliness, we could only mutter conjectures, none of which made sense. We had found something that couldn't be there. Or if ever it had been, why had it been abandoned to the desert winds?

We heard a rustling. It sent a slight shiver down my spine. I'd been through some hard-to-refute ghostly experiences in my life. Could this be another one? The rustling, coming from the right, was developing into the sound of footsteps. Our eyes switched past the ancient biplane to the side of the cliff . . . and there was a man *emerging from a cave in the rock.* He approached, slowly but deliberately, came alongside. The gent was of middle height, middle-aged, rugged, with filthy matted locks brushing cheeks that looked like they hadn't met up with a razor in months. But it was his eyes that compelled attention—hypnotically piercing. He spoke, and his accent wasn't American or Latino. It could have been German, Russian, Polish, but it was understandable to the point of being riveting. I remember the short exchange of dialogue, starting with his flatly demanding words, "What d'you want?"

Maggie and I were taken aback, as much by the question as by its brusqueness. What *did* we want? Nothing really, except to know how we had put down on an airstrip that didn't exist. Maggie, her mind always quicker than mine, answered the question. "Gas. We'd like some gas." The cave dweller nodded, proceeded to that rusting pump, and got on with the job of gassing us up. But only for seconds. He stopped. He had pumped in rather less than two gallons, but his eyes were demanding now as he said, "You didn't need gas and you knew it. *Why're you here?*"

I answered, stumblingly because I didn't know the real answer. "We're heading for Palm Springs. Lotta desert to cross. We thought it safer to gas up . . . I mean, like we saw your strip from the air and—"

He broke in. "You'd 'ave more'n enough gas to get you to El Centro or even Yuma City. You didn't come in for gas."

At a loss I muttered weakly, "Happy to hear we're okay. How much do we owe you?" He ignored the question, asked again, "Why're you here?" His hand had crept down to his right-hand pocket . . . it suddenly crossed my mind that he might be reaching for a gun. The hand stopped short of the pocket as Maggie, always calm, said, quite truthfully, "We were flying across pretty wild desert . . . not much known about it. We spotted your strip and dropped in out of curiosity."

"Curiosity killed the cat!" The words spit like a bullet.

None of this made sense. But there was no point in pursuing the matter. The gentleman's right hand was still lingering around that pants pocket. Nothing to do but get out of there and let our friend go back to his cave, and the quiet that we had seemingly disturbed.

It wasn't as easy as all that. I brought greenbacks from my pocket, said, "Well . . . thanks . . . so long and . . . how much?" But he showed no interest. Seemingly all he wanted was to see our Luscombe get the hell out of his canyon.

"Why don't you go?" he said.

The tone was more than harsh, as though we'd been guilty of invasion of privacy. So there was nothing for it but to respect the gent's wish. Maggie taxied the Luscombe, turned it, came back into line for the takeoff. But I still wanted to pay for the gas we'd bought. No way. The guy shook his head and I remember noticing that his matted locks shook in time to the head shake.

But for the first time his tone seemed to be reasonable as he warned, "Watch out. There's a downdraft as you head out of the canyon. Bank too close you could end up at the foot of Split Rock. Stay to the right. Safer . . ."

This was probably good advice, for which any amateur aviator should be grateful. I said, "Thanks for the tip. You're a great guy."

The answer came back fast. "Forget it! I'm not interested in picking up pieces of wrecked aircraft around these parts."

There seemed little more to say . . . except I sometimes kid myself that I'm a friendly soul. So I said, "Good to have known you. Any time you're around LA give me a call at . . ."

He cut in again: "I never come to LA. Get out of here! Watch that downdraft at Split Rock."

That was it. We got out, banked right as instructed, but even as we passed the gentleman below, I could swear I heard him say, "Don't come back!"

I'm sure we didn't want to, although we'd got away with a couple of gallons of gas for free.

We landed at Palm Springs and spent the night in a bungalow at Charlie Farrell's Racquet Club. The adventure was behind us, but we devoted quite a while to poring over our air maps of the Mojave. A dead end. That hidden strip remained hidden, and in no place could we find indication of a hazard called Split Rock. So much for curiosity, unsatisfied—well, at that time. But an answer of sorts *was* to be forthcoming.

It was perhaps two years later, after Japan had joined hands with Hitler for the seemingly mutual conquest of the American continent, that I read in the *Los Angeles Times* of a raid on a hard-to-spot landing strip in the Mojave, of the seizure of a suspected foreign agent who lived beside the strip in a cave laden with electronic communications equipment. I know nothing about radio or radar or the mysteries of short wave, but it appeared that the gentleman who had given us two gallons of gas with the request to "Get out of here!" was somehow in electronic communication with both Japan and Germany. The cave was a center from which intelligence could be transmitted across vast areas. It's a long time ago, but I remember reading something to the effect that the strip was destined to be the key locale for the hour-to-hour exchange of information when the forthcoming invasion of the States—Japan from the west, Hitler's Germany from the east—came to its fruition.

Glancing way back, I feel that that foreign agent wasn't as bright as he should have been. I know that if one has something to conceal, rudeness is prohibited. "A soft answer turneth away wrath" (Proverbs 15:1). And it's true! I've met more than my share of secret agents in my life—ladies and gentlemen working both for and against us. The secret of success lies in openness. A friendly attitude can cover a host of unrevealed machinations. But with the attitude of that unwashed cave dweller and his determination to get rid of us, he might as well have been wearing *spy* on his hat.[23]

# 10

# War in His Pocket

What began as a 1937 contract with Universal Pictures had passed through two comfortable years during which neither Maggie nor I could find any cause for complaint. Many good colony friends. Comfortable and financially gratifying employment. Things looked good.

Except—it seems that Old Man Satan—perpetually apprehensive that peaceful enjoyment might instill in mankind a belief in faith, hope and charity—decided to inject a fly into the ointment. There are events that can't be forgotten—and shouldn't be: the doings that started around 1933 and that, following the "domino theory," led the world steadily toward John Donne's tolling bell.

I know that few Hollywood British colony members were foreseeing disaster. The Great War had cost so much in blood—eight million dead—that the world had said, "Never again." But, sad to relate, in the 1930s a feeling of uneasiness crept up on the colony as discomforting news came from home.

It was generally known that an Austrian named Adolf Hitler—a far-from-successful commercial artist who by rabid, rabble-rousing speeches delivered in a Munich beer garden had thrust his way up to the chancellorship of the German Reich—was becoming a nuisance. Nobody out here, American or British, took Hitler seriously—this in spite of the fact that he had written a book called *Mein Kampf* in which he stated his missions. Nobody bothered to read the book. The world should have. Most particularly it should have been studied by Britain and France, who by an early show of power could have stopped Hitler in his tracks.

Neither nation moved a muscle—not even when refugees seeking safety, sanity, and anti-Hitlerism came flocking into Paris, London, Hollywood, and Beverly Hills. Many were just against the upstart chancellor and his missions. Some were in fact fleeing for their lives because the first of *der Führer*'s vowed missions was visibly taking shape. Its nature? Nothing less than the complete cleansing of German blood, entailing the eradication of the evils that had led to Germany's defeat in the Great War. Only by blood purification, insisted Hitler, could the German population regain its rightful heritage as the world-dominant master race.

So with the advent of Hitler came a national exodus of artistically creative German talent. Suddenly, famous names—many of them worshiped—were becoming conspicuous by their absence or death, and not all of them Jewish, by any means. Nazi enthusiasts must have felt that something was missing—on the radio they could not listen to the music of Felix Mendelssohn, Leon Jessel, Kurt Weill, Erich Korngold, or any other composer whom Hitler designated Semitic. Only the most politically harmless plays or comedies were performed in the theaters, and the illustrious Max Reinhardt with his great theater spectacles had gone with the initial emergence of Hitlerism. The German film industry, second only to Hollywood as a provider of world entertainment, had collapsed. Erich Pommer, the brilliant Jewish head of Universum Film AG—who had come up with *Metropolis* and *The Blue Angel* and many of the greatest movies ever made—had left Germany while the going was still possible.

Heil Hitler! Abschied Deutsch film industry!

Others—film producers, writers, directors—went too. Big names. Bertolt Brecht. Heinrich Mann. The young but fast-rising Billy Wilder. *Ehrenarier* (honorary Aryan) Reinhold Schünzel, a fine director who had also been a top Berlin theater comedian. The always-creative writing and directing brothers Curt and Robert Siodmak. Erik Charell, not a Jew but strongly anti-Nazi and the director and mind behind *The Congress Dances*—which remains for me the most attractive musical film ever produced. But perhaps the greatest loss to the German film industry, swept away to Hollywood on the flood of anti-Hitler talent, was Fritz Lang, director of *Metropolis, Dr. Abuse, The Nibelungs,* and *M*—the movie that put Peter Lorre on the filmic map.

Meeting with many of the "get-out-of-Germany" contingent over here, I became firm friends with both Pommer and Lang. On the first day of our acquaintanceship, Fritz told me of his recent departure from Berlin. Pommer had already headed for the United States, and Universum Film AG was rudderless. Fritz was summoned to the Chancellery, to a personal meeting with *der Führer,* who promptly ordered him to take over the film industry. Fritz, knowing perfectly well what saying "no" to Hitler would mean, wasn't hesitating. That night he took the train for Paris. After a couple of days in Paris, he headed for Le Havre and the next ocean liner to the States.

For many years until his death, Fritz was a dear neighbor. We worked together in 1954 on a spy story titled *Journey to Nowhere,* but when I traveled to Europe in 1955 to write and direct *The Count of Monte Cristo* television series, Fritz could not replace me, so our *Journey* went nowhere. As to Pommer, our friendship wasn't restricted to California. I met with him amid the ruins of a devastated Berlin just after the war.

So the German and Austrian film bigwigs came to Hollywood, which assimilated them as over the years it had assimilated Ernst Lubitsch, Charles Vidor, Michael Curtiz, Gottfried Reinhardt—and scores of others, including members of the British film colony, who never thought of themselves as aliens anyway. Since England had settled the colonial Eastern Seaboard, they felt they had a right to be here. Actually, looking back, I don't believe the majority of our colony members gave a damn about these foreign arrivals. This was perhaps understandable—they didn't play cricket.

So the late 1930s slipped by. Anything happening in Germany—thousands of miles removed from Southern California—was uninteresting to the majority here, as there were *truly* newsworthy items around, such as the fact that a famous gangster-hoodlum had been stabbed to death in an equally famous film star's Beverly Hills bedroom—both unclad. Awkward. How would Megafilm Company with twenty or so millions tied up in the film star's next two movies talk the star-loving public out of this one? Telephones and dining tables were buzzing at this real news!

As to the British colony, our initial apprehension was slipping away. In the LA newspapers, references to Hitler ("Who's he?") or the Third Reich ("What's that?") would be on a back page, if mentioned at all.

But the Munich Pact of September 1938 came as something of a jolt to our colony members. To many it was reassuring. There would be *peace in our time* and nothing to worry about, because Chamberlain and Daladier knew what they were up to. But there were members unprepared to sink back into a state of trustful torpor. Some were interested to know how our countrymen at home were feeling about the way things were going. A lucky chance to get the answers appeared—perfect timing. Dear old Aubrey Smith, who had been away in England for some months, returned to Beverly Hills. The film colony seized the golden opportunity.

Some eighty of us, headed by Ronald Colman, arranged a welcome-home dinner party for our patriarch, taking over Chasen's restaurant for the evening. Aubrey was happy, in good shape, and all of us were expectantly and optimistically awaiting his account of the recent happenings. The many-tabled dinner concluded and the great moment came. Aubrey rose, harrumphed, then started, gruffly but definitely. "Of course, as I'm sure you all know, the situation couldn't have been more disastrous, boding I fear great ill for the future."

There were murmurs of surprise. So in Aubrey's opinion the recent turn of affairs had been disastrous, and worse was to come. This was an unexpected attitude, not what we'd hoped for. But the murmurs quickly hushed as we awaited clarification of the ominous words. It came. Aubrey, dominating the room as only he could, harrumphed again and continued: "I said disastrous, and believe me, I'm not overstating the case. As I'm sure you'll all have read, the first test match against Australia at Manchester's Old Trafford was calamitous. The Aussies annihilated us. Run after run, with our bowlers helpless to stop the avalanche. The second match at Lords was equally discouraging and . . ."

Cricket! The five test matches between the visiting Australian team and England. All five games lost! Disaster! Dear Aubrey made no mention whatever of the Munich Pact or of Hitler's or Chamberlain's behavior. But he did make some consoling remarks about certain up-and-coming young British cricketers who could make a difference in the next round of test matches.

Sad to relate, the next round *didn't* come along, and wouldn't for many years. Undoubtedly, many of those likely young cricketers—Britain's hopefuls—never lived to wield another bat or bowl another ball. Nor, I guess, did most of the Australian players, gallant young men who, when it came to the crunch, proved eager to bleed and die for the mother country, England. War! Years of it, as other forms of "test matches" were fought on the sands of North Africa, over the skies of Britain, and in the Normandy landings. Aubrey never lived to see Britain defeat Australia; but up there, where of course he is, I know he must have been proud that the cricketers of both sides merged into one team and fought and prevailed together.

I'll say right now that these pages were never intended to be a chronicle of war—rather, an attempt to record the way nearly a hundred years of the bloodiest century of all time applied to me, and for a number of years to Maggie. In this regard our confrontation with the news of the start of

World War II stands out starkly. Almost comically. It came to us, not with a bang or a whimper, but with the sudden cessation of a dance band, leaving us and scores of other fox-trotting couples reeling absurdly on a dance floor.

In 1939 the Sunset Strip had several fine nightclubs and a dozen first-class restaurants—French, Italian, Russian, Hungarian, you name it. My warmest memory is that one "dressed" for an evening on the Strip, the ladies begowned, men in tuxedos or even white tie and tails. Sadly, the once-shining jewel has long since lost its glitter. To appear on the Strip in a tuxedo these days could invite a mugging.

At the top of the Strip's ornateness was the Trocadero, the "Troc." The club was owned by Billy Wilkerson, publisher of the all-powerful *Hollywood Reporter*. Consequently, stars, actors, producers, directors, and so on were compelled "to be seen" at Wilkerson's nitery or face a stinking *Hollywood Reporter* write-up when it came to the next movie. Equally, *not* to advertise in Wilkerson's daily could entail a bad review. To exacerbate this form of blackmail, almost nightly the two top film columnists, Louella Parsons and Hedda Hopper, who hated each other, occupied VIP Trocadero tables, tapping any gossip as it waltzed past—seizing any scrap of film dirt juicy enough for publication. In a way, Louella and Hedda were as powerful as the *Reporter* itself; and it was imperative that any individual who craved a Hollywood career should kiss the asses of these two harridans whose pens could create or destroy. Fortunately, the rules for how to get along in Hollywood didn't apply to writers, who were a low form of movie life unrecognized by the fans.

Louella was the kinder of the two. She'd print anything outrageous enough, but she'd admit to being in the wrong when she was. For example, not long after I married my second wife, Betty, I was in Mexico City writing and codirecting *The Prince of the Church* (1952) for Manuel Reachi's Promesa Film Company. Some "dear friend" informed Louella that I had left Betty while divorce proceedings were contemplated. Louella printed the story in her *Los Angeles Examiner* column. Betty read it and called me in Mexico. I called Louella, who apologized and promptly sprung into print denying the false rumor. But Hedda—confident that no entertainment figure would dare sue her for fear of dire reprisals—would stick by any statement she had made, however damaging. She knew the bigger the hurt, the bigger the public interest, and the bigger her importance. Hedda was a bitch, but Louella possessed a human streak.

September 1, 1939: Maggie and I were nightclubbing at the Trocadero. Nobody could complain of what one got for one's money. Always a first-class dance orchestra, top-drawer entertainers such as Lena Horne, Edith Piaf, and Billy Eckstine. We were enjoying each other's company. Our ballroom dancing wasn't up there with Astaire and Rogers, but we got along without treading on each other's toes. We had nothing to grouse about. Maggie was beautiful and popular, and our tenor of living was as good as anybody could ask.

It must have been around midnight when the dance band came to an abrupt stop, leaving couples swaying out there on the dance floor. A voice came over the speaker system, informing us that Adolf Hitler's panzer divisions had invaded Poland and that Warsaw was under bombardment from the German Luftwaffe and the advancing tank corps.

I knew little about Poland. In 1934 a play of mine, *Big Business*, which had first faced an audience at the Beaux Arts Theatre in Monte Carlo in 1932, was produced in Warsaw after translation into Polish by Bernard Shaw's translator, Florian Sobieniowski. I was informed that the play was a hit; Sobieniowski sent me stills of the stage production and glowing reviews in Polish, which I could not read. But the payoff was that *there never was a payoff*—not even one Polish zloty. I hope Mr. Sobieniowski did well out of it, maybe retired and was lucky enough to get out of Warsaw before September 1939.

For Maggie and me the immediate business was—what next? We didn't have to wait long for a partial answer. Home from the Troc around two o'clock in the morning, the telephone rang before we could sleep. It was the fine playwright-actor-director Elliott Nugent calling to ask if we were aware that our country was at war. Britain had issued an ultimatum to Germany to withdraw the invading troops immediately or the United Kingdom and France would stand by its treaty with embattled Poland. Of course, everybody knew Hitler would ignore the demand, so Britain declared war within hours.

Colony members were in a bind. Most of us, happily ensconced in Beverly Hills, Bel Air, Brentwood, Malibu, and so on were legal residents of a country that we had practically adopted as home. But few of us had become American citizens. Warmly welcome in the States as we were, somehow taking the Pledge of Allegiance to a nation not our own could have been conscience-wrenching. With the outbreak of war in Europe, we were aliens in a neutral country—and to complicate matters, a country in which a hardening frame of mind was becoming noticeable. Some war over there? None of our business! Locally, a highly popular revue, *Meet the People*—starring Nanette Fabray—was enjoying a lengthy run at a Hollywood theater; and the box office was distributing copies of a song touting, "The Yanks aren't coming, this time let *God* save the King."

So what were the British to do? Go back and fight for a country that a large percentage of colony members hadn't visited for years, perhaps decades? Actually, some of the males had fought in World War I. Some had lost limbs, such as Herbert Marshall, who got along on a false leg after 1917. But going back to England wasn't as simple as might have been expected. Into my forties, I found myself wondering if my ability with a machine gun could still be of use. I discussed the matter with Eric Cleugh, our Los Angeles British consul general.

Eric said adamantly, "For God's sake, Charles, be your age. D'you think they'd want you stumbling around under a Lewis gun? Grow up!"

Complicating planning was the concerted opinion of my countrymen that the war couldn't last beyond Christmas 1939. After all, what chance would the Germans have with General Maurice Gamelin's French army manning the impregnable Maginot Line? On Germany's eastern flank was the vastness of Communist Russia, representing a third of the world's landmass and, with the exception of China, the greatest array of manpower on earth. Buoyed by self-assurance, our British colony continued to believe Hitler had made a supreme but expected error.

The colony was wrong. Two weeks after Hitler's attack, Russian armies were swarming across Poland's eastern frontier. Nazi and communist warriors embraced at Brest-Litovsk in celebration of eternal brotherhood. Stalin had backslid on any understanding his nation had with the Western Allies and had switched to the side of the hated Adolf Hitler—splitting Poland between them. All Europe heard the Warsaw radio station defiantly broadcasting a Chopin polonaise until the very moment of death or last-ditch surrender.

On the day the news came through that Russia had entered into the Poland caper, I was walking through the MGM Thalberg Building and ran into the fine American writer Laurence Stallings. I liked Stallings, and later in the war he was to become actively pro-British. But now he was chuckling, "Charles, heard the latest? What chance will England and France have with Stalin in Hitler's corner? Better tell your pals back home to give up before they've nothing left to give."

I wasn't resentful. I could understand Stalling's attitude. In neutral America the fact that Europe had split into opposing factions made for interesting news, but this was nothing to disturb a good citizen's sleep—in the long run those guys would sort out their differences. Of course, there were hotheads, people like Franklin D. Roosevelt who showed concern. Otherwise, the United States was content to be a spectator.

Changes taking place on the far side of the Atlantic? Hell! Changes were taking place in Southern California, and not necessarily for the worse. In 1939–41 existence in Hollywood and Beverly Hills remained better than agreeable. Life, laughter, and what passed for love stalked the Sunset Strip. Unexpectedly, Billy Wilkerson's Trocadero bowed out, but coincidentally Charlie Morrison's Mocambo was moving in; and diagonally across Sunset Boulevard, Ciro's was filling any gap. At the same time, to add to the industry's satisfaction, "Prince" Michael Romanoff, the self-proclaimed heir to the Communist-seized Russian throne, opened Romanoff's Restaurant, a cozy retreat for the film elite on Rodeo Drive in Beverly Hills.

Like Chasen's, established three years earlier, Romanoff's quickly achieved clublike recognition with cliquey exclusivity. This meant any voyeuristic out-of-towner coming to Romanoff's in the hope of glimpsing film celebrities would politely meet with "Sorry, all our tables are booked." And Romanoff's and Chasen's were alike in another way. After dining at Chasen's, habitués would relax, play backgammon or gin rummy, or even table tennis on one of the tables in the attractive rear garden. At Romanoff's one would dine, relax, and play—principally chess, of which Mike Romanoff was a devotee.

So *my* life in Beverly Hills continued smoothly. The studios, which had never been more active, were keeping me plentifully employed; and my superb agent, H. N. Swanson, always had writing assignments waiting for my availability. The Hollywood British colony, with its horses and polo, dogs, black-tie dinners, and mint julep garden parties, proceeded on its unjolted way—perhaps like an ostrich burying its head in the Southern California sand.

But none of these happy-go-lucky attitudes could eliminate the continuing apprehension felt by colony members. Some said we should have stayed at home and let our votes have some bearing on Chamberlain's peace-in-our-time illusion. Too late. We were resident aliens, and voteless in Britain. With our home country in deadly peril, many of our members, stiff upper lips and cricket notwithstanding, were shaken out of their torpor, questioning how the hell we could help when crossing the Atlantic to England was forbidden by Britain itself—unless one could come up with acceptable proof that one's presence over there would truly contribute to the war effort.

Very few of us had an ironclad reason for being granted passage on one of the few ships crossing. David Niven held a reserve commission with a crack British army regiment. I believe Richard Greene was an army reservist. So they could go—and did. But what possible reason was there for the British government to grant limited ocean passage to a onetime eighteen-year-old corporal?

The more I pondered the problem, the wider and more uncrossable seemed the Atlantic. Suddenly my groping mind hit on an idea—which was simply the realization that in over a dozen years, I had hardly eaten a meal that hadn't been paid for by my two middle fingers pounding at a typewriter. So how about writing? I considered the matter, hesitated. Crazy! A pen couldn't kill Nazis.

Or could it? I learned that the English playwright Ian Hay, appointed Director of Public Relations at the British War Office, was now Major General John Hay Beith. I knew Ian Hay. We had been friends at the time that he supplied some excellent dialogue for my screenplay-adaptation of *The 39 Steps*. And as public relations was akin to propaganda, I believed I saw my chance: propaganda! Maybe my pen, though in no sense a sword, could still represent some form of weapon. So in late summer 1939 I wrote to Ian—sorry, Major General John Hay Beith, and sent him a propaganda idea titled "Hitler Is Dead."

During that "Twilight War," a forever and a day of waiting and wondering, my home bar became something of a semiregular watering hole, where colony friends could indulge in deep discussions on the possible escalation of the European crisis. Discussions inevitably proved an unsatisfying waste of breath but a reasonable excuse for the downing of a Scotch or two—or three—or four. The most consistently regular house guest was my longtime pal Sir Cedric Hardwicke, and other watering hole companions included dear George Melville Cooper, the delightfully amusing Alan Mowbray, and my favorite monster, the gentle and highly intelligent Boris Karloff, certainly one of the kindest and most generous individuals I have been proud to meet.

All of us had been in World War I as young men. Cedric had been a second lieutenant commanding a platoon. Melville Cooper was a young second lieutenant captured by the Germans during their mighty March 1918 offensive. Boris, our senior, may well have had a captaincy. Alan Mowbray and I had both been corporals, Alan at twenty-one, and I at eighteen. But all of us—corporal to captain—had known our war amid the mud, filth, and carnage of the trenches, hardly the best school in which to acquire the arts of field marshalship.

We considered ourselves to be hardened veterans, strategists who would study maps of Europe over my bar counter, theorize, fight battles both bloody and political until—usually over the third Scotch—we would come up with ideas as to how to bring Hitler to his knees and avoid bloodshed altogether. Most of the ideas were wild and woolly. Alan Mowbray suggested Britain should bring the entire Grand Fleet out of Scapa Flow and have it sweep the North Sea clean of German herring-fishing boats, thus depriving the Nazis of bloaters and kippers. After consideration, this thought was abandoned—bloaters and kippers also being a staple dish of the British Isles. No matter; discussions proceeded—disagreements, heated arguments—the whole getting nowhere and ending in a form of stalemate over a final Scotch and our decision to leave the future to minds in closer contact with the conflict.

General Beith replied, "We have gone into your *Death of Hitler* scheme. It is most ingenious, but I am afraid it is old stuff. The idea that Hitler is dead and represented by an understudy has been rather overworked here of late. In any case I understand that the policy of the Ministry of Information and BBC is to issue no statements which are not absolutely true. This being so, I am afraid I shall not be able to interest them very much!"

Disappointing. But with my mind now fixed on the idea of writing propaganda in England, I wrote to him again. I didn't need money. All I wanted was authority to cross the Atlantic to write anything that could be helpful in the way of anti-Nazi propaganda.

Not so understandable was his reply to my second letter, which delivered a major setback—worse even than Eric Cleugh's damper on my Lewis gunnery thought. Beith thanked me for my offer but said that for the time being he couldn't see any way in which I could be of immediate help to the war effort, at least not in Britain. He did, however, come through with what, emanating from a major general, was more of a command than a suggestion. He prophesied that the war would spread across the globe; and recognizing this, I should get on with my career and go on writing in . . .

Hollywood! In other words, instead of being permitted to come home and share Churchill's "blood, toil, tears, and sweat," I was told to stay out here, continue to write movies, and luxuriate.

Although pleasantly phrased, the letter's opening paragraphs seemed irrational, slightly contemptuous, or shrugging off my offer of service as negligible. But with further perusal, I saw the reasoning. Beith pointed out that I was an established Hollywood screenwriter turning out two or three major feature movies a year, which were vehicles for some of the greatest film celebrities on earth. This was true. Pictures of mine would star the Americans John Wayne, Gary Cooper, Ray Milland (who became a naturalized citizen in the 1940s), Paulette Goddard, and—on the pop side—such huge box-office moneymakers as Nelson Eddy. So Beith's command became clear to me. I was to get on with what I was doing, come up with as many star-attracting movie vehicles as possible, but make every effort to inject some form of anti-Nazi message into every picture I wrote. What better way was there to influence world audiences than to have them seeing their idols take up arms against or lose sympathy for Nazi Germany? Today this would be called brainwashing. At that time it was propaganda—on the grand scale—and I quickly had to admit that Beith's letter made sense. Also, since "Orders Is Orders," it was a means of helping my country that I gladly grabbed at.

Actually, Ian's suggestion affirmed what I was already doing, and, looking back, I don't think I did a bad job. My doomed *Cause for Alarm* featured a Nazi agent spreading terror in Italy. And my short novel *War in His Pocket* was being published in *Bluebook* magazine. Putting anti-Nazi propaganda into the sumptuous Nelson Eddy musical *Balalaika,* however, called for subterfuge. Eddy didn't notice the insidious injection, but the German director Reinhold Schünzel, who had fled his country when Hitler got going, highly approved.

But I wasn't the only member of the self-exiled Bennett family. Maggie *knew* that she possessed something that could surely help her country. By the spring of 1940 she had intentionally accumulated thousands of solo miles as a Luscombe aircraft pilot—just what the Air Transport Auxiliary badly needed. She wrote to the ATA, stating her very considerable experience and asking Britain to accept her services. With cross-Atlantic mail being in a state of chaos, she knew it would take time to receive her answer and orders. And this entailed waiting—a tiresome business—but so is war a tiresome business.

Maggie would eventually leave for England in the early months of 1942. She traveled by rail across the United States and then flew by Yankee Clipper to neutral Lisbon, then on to London. Arriving home, she was immediately pressed into ferrying fighter aircraft for the RAF Air Transport Auxiliary.

∽ ∽ ∽

## Interlude: Hitler Is Dead

The following was submitted to the British Ministry of Information.

### Strictly Private and Confidential

Till now this has been a war of nerves in which the [propaganda] effect on civilians and behind-the-line communities has been considered of greater importance than actual troop action. Propaganda is playing a greater part than ever before in warfare. Already we have been unloading pamphlets rather than bombs over Western Germany. I believe the following suggestion could be vitally useful in this direction.

The theme of the suggestion lies in three words—*Hitler Is Dead!* I understand that our propaganda angle in Germany has been and is that we are fighting not the German people, but the Nazi regime—in other words, we are fighting Hitler himself. Undoubtedly it is Hitler who is holding Germany together just now. If Hitler were removed, it is more than probable that we would see the crack-up of the entire Nazi system.

I conclude that if our agents *could* assassinate Herr Hitler, they *would*. The fact that no one has succeeded in killing the man so far suggests that he is much too well guarded to make such an eventuality possible. In consequence we must kill him by some other means—kill him by propaganda.

Thus—the start of the campaign must be insidious. The BBC receives and broadcasts an unconfirmed report from Poland that Herr Hitler was killed during a visit to the German reserve lines during, say, the first weeks of September. The BBC, of course, refuses to place any credence on this report and *says* so over the air. In fact, in the eyes of the BBC, this first report would seem to be just "wishful thinking" on the part of some obscure Polish authority.

But—other reports come through—persistently. It is rumored that the funeral of a certain German captain, killed in the corridor fighting, was attended by personages of no less importance than Goering himself. A further report hints that enquiries have been instigated by British agents in East Prussia—a curious fact has come to light—a fact which is passed on by short-wave radio to Germany. It seems that the said dead captain was a mythical personage. Admittedly, he has been buried, but—curiously—no proof of his ever having actually existed can be found—his name is missing from German army lists. The inference is becoming clear. Herr Hitler *was* killed in Poland. He received a military funeral under a false name.

Other rumors come in. A German prisoner in Poland reports that he actually *saw* Hitler die—that the Führer died very gallantly. Reports come in—and are duly rebroadcast—of a night of alarm and disturbance at German Army Headquarters in the Field. In fact, gradually even the conservative BBC is beginning to believe that the original reports *may* have had some basis of truth.

Then—suddenly—England has admitted the truth of the situation. Hitler *is* dead—the Hitler who is now chancellor of Germany is a *double!*

Now to let Germany know.

Our agents in Germany will already be at work, insidiously spreading the gradually strengthening report by underground means. Short-wave radio will have been transmitting the reports to Germany all along. Admitting that most Germans do not listen to English short-wave broadcasts—some *do.* The story will already be passing from mouth to mouth, though probably the very danger of admitting that the story even *exists* will so far have prevented the German authorities from issuing any form of denial. To *deny* that Hitler is dead is only to spread the rumour—a rumour which will be safer if not even officially discussed.

But—our aeroplanes get to work. Pamphlets. Millions of them. The first of these bear just three staring words in great black print—*Hitler Is Dead!*

These pamphlets are followed up by others. Germany is definitely told—from the air and *over* the air—that the Hitler who is ruling them is a fake. Germany is bombarded with photographs—two, side by side—one of the original Hitler and one of his present double. The pamphlets point out in simple language that the shape of a man's ears cannot be disguised. The double we are shown is Herr Hitler's living image—but the ears are slightly different. By this time the German police will undoubtedly be attempting to destroy and seize all pamphlets—but many of the photographs, the statements, will be in the hands of soldiers, civilians, peasants. The word-of-mouth report will be growling like a rolling snowball. Millions of Germans will refuse to believe the staggering rumor—but they will discuss it just the same, and presently the whole of the Reich will be aware of it.

The German government will be forced to take action. Contemptuous denials will be issued. But the very real merit of this particular propaganda lies in the fact that *the more stoutly the report is denied, the greater amount of publicity it will be getting and the more credence it will be receiving!* Soon many alarmed Germans will be asking the vital questions: Is this thing true? *Can* this thing be true? In point of fact, German officialdom itself will be backing up the growing suspicion. The German people have been ordered not to listen to short-wave broadcasts from enemy countries. Why? The answer to this question will seem to lie in the fact that the government is still making a desperate effort to conceal the hideous truth from its peoples.

Our short-wave and aeroplane propaganda will be continuing. Now we will be out in the open, definitely telling the German people that they are fighting for a Führer *who no longer exists.* In other words, we will be striking at a fundamental of German character—the German love of being led. Naturally, we will be telling the German people that they are mad to shed their blood on behalf of a man who is actually nothing better than a *film crowd worker.* The man Germany loved and followed so blindly is dead. Are the German people so crazy that they will follow a ghost?

With the report gaining in momentum, Hitler may at last be forced to deny the story himself—over the air. *But we will have prepared for this.* Insidiously, our pamphlets, our radio broadcasts, will have been suggesting that *the* Hitler voice which speaks on the air is no longer Hitler's. The German people can be told that the voice they will be hearing—*have* been hearing for weeks now—is that of Herr Ernst Thingummyjig—late star actor of the Berlin State Theatre—first-class character actor and acknowledged master mimic.

This propaganda angle must be intensified—the double appearing in public—the actor mimicking the dead Hitler's voice on the ether. Intensify the *fake* angle.

And then suggest that all is not well at Berlin. Tell Germany that the German Cabinet is breaking under the strain of following a leader who

Lilian Langrishe Bennett (ca. 1885).

*All materials are from the Charles Bennett Estate Collection.*

Lilian Bennett acted in melodramas produced by the Miss Lilian Bennett Repertoire Company.

CHILDREN OF THE NIGHT.
BY ARTHUR W. SKELTON.

Charles Bennett, child actor, ca. 1913–15.

At tea aboard S.Y. *Mariposa,* in *The Marriage Market.* Bennett is at far right (ca. 1914).

Bennett, on the left, in the silent film *John Halifax, Gentleman* (1915).

Publicity shots of Charles Bennett, juvenile actor (ca. 1916).

Bennett during World War I. He is at right in the group shot (ca. 1918).

Bennett as an avenging Romeo with the Alexander Marsh Shakespearean Company (ca. 1923).

Bennett when he was an actor at Bristol Little Theatre in 1924.

Charles Bennett, playwright and actor (ca. 1925).

Charles Bennett, playwright and actor (ca. 1928).

# SHAKESPEARE MEMORIAL THEATRE FUND.

### STRATFORD-UPON-AVON.

**Patron - HIS MAJESTY THE KING**

HENRY AINLEY.
THE DUCHESS OF ATHOLL, M.P.
THE EARL OF BALFOUR, P.C., F.R.S., O.M.
MISS LILIAN BAYLIS.
LESLIE BLOOM, Esq.
THE VISCOUNT BURNHAM, C.H., LL.D.
and THE VISCOUNTESS BURNHAM.
THE VISCOUNTESS COWDRAY.

HIS EXCELLENCY THE FRENCH AMBASSADOR
and MADAME DE FLEURIAU.
SIR JOHNSTON and LADY FORBES-ROBERTSON.
SIR ALFRED FRIPP, K.C.V.O., C.B.
SIR ISRAEL GOLLANCZ, Lit.D.
THE HIGH COMMISSIONER FOR CANADA
and MRS. LARKIN.
THE LORD LEIGH, J.P.
THE AGENT-GENERAL FOR QUEBEC and MRS. LEMIEUX

VIOLET LORAINE.
ALEC. L. REA, J.P.
GORDON SELFRIDGE, Esq.
MARIE TEMPEST.
HIS WORSHIP THE MAYOR OF STRATFORD
and MRS. E. R. THOMPSON.
MRS. MATHER THOMSON.
DAME MAY WHITTY.
MISS WINIFRIDE WRENCH.

## TWO PERFORMANCES OF

# OTHELLO

## AT THE APOLLO THEATRE

### SUNDAY EVENING, APRIL 3rd, at 8 p.m., and
### MONDAY MATINEE, APRIL 4th, at 2.30 p.m.

UNDER THE AUSPICES OF THE LYCEUM CLUB STAGE SOCIETY
President - Mrs. ALEC L. REA

### ALL - STAR CAST including

| | |
|---|---|
| Charles Bennett | Robert Loraine |
| Gertrude Elliott | Alan Napier |
| John Gielgud | Ion Swinley |
| Esmond Knight | |
| Elissa Landi | Ernest Thesiger |
| Hamson Lawson | Herbert Waring |
| Olga Lindo | Ben Webster |

## Play Produced by A. E. FILMER

Stalls 15/-, Dress Circle 12/6 & 10/6, Upper Circle 5/-, Pit (reserved) 5/-, Gallery 2/6

All communications to : Mrs. CLIFTON BOYNE, 140, Long Acre, W.C.2.    Telephone : Regent 1761

DAVID ALLEN & SONS, Ltd., London and Belfast

Playbill for *Othello* (1928). Bennett appeared in an "All-Star Cast" of the play under royal patronage, April 1928.

The playwright and screen-story writer Charles Bennett, ca. 1930. (Photo by Claude Harris)

BRITISH INTERNATIONAL PICTURES LTD., ELSTREE

*present*

The First British
Full Length " All-Talkie " Super-Film

## " BLACKMAIL "

*From the Play by*
CHARLES BENNETT.

REGAL, MARBLE ARCH, LONDON
Friday, June 21st, 1929.

British International
Picures' publicity booklet
for the film *Blackmail*, 1929.

## " BLACKMAIL "

*From the Play by* CHARLES BENNETT.

### THE CAST

| | |
|---|---|
| ALICE WHITE | ANNY ONDRA |
| MRS. WHITE | SARA ALLGOOD |
| MR. WHITE | CHARLES PATON |
| FRANK WEBBER | JOHN LONGDEN |
| TRACY | DONALD CALTHROP |
| THE ARTIST | CYRIL RITCHARD |
| THE LANDLADY | HANNAH JONES |
| CHIEF INSPECTOR | HARVEY BRABAN |

DIRECTED AND ADAPTED BY

## ALFRED HITCHCOCK

*To be preceded by*
*A British International "Talkie" Short,*
*" In an Old World Garden."*

Poster for *The Last Hour* (1930).

Poster for *The Secret of the Loch* (1934).

Bennett with Alfred Hitchcock (ca. 1936).

Charles Bennett and Maggie "Faith" Bennett in 1937. (Photo by Walter Bird)

Bennett with Cecil B. DeMille, ca. 1941. (Photo courtesy of the Academy of Motion Picture Arts and Sciences)

Charles Bennett in Hollywood (ca. 1942).

Bennett with his polo pony, Mex, ca. 1944.

The First Mounted Patrol of the California State Militia, ca. 1943.

Betty Jo Riley (1940).

Betty and John Bennett (1948).

Charles Bennett, at home with his family, ca.1952.

Bennett directing *Madness of the Heart* in 1948. (Photos by Norman Gryspeerdt)

Bennett directing
Margaret Lockwood and
Paul DuPuis in *Madness
of the Heart*, 1948. (Photo
by Norman Gryspeerdt)

Bennett meets
with his
literary agent,
H. N. Swanson,
ca. 1951.
(Photo by Lou
Jacobs Jr.)

John Bennett at California
Military Academy, with his
mother, Betty Bennett (1962).

John Bennett, honor cadet,
California Military Academy,
1962.

*(Above)* Photo inscribed to Charles Bennett: "To my first and beloved writer. Love Hitch" (ca. 1977). *(Below)* Bennett was rediscovered on videotape (ca. 1990).

Bennett during the *Blackmail* rewrite (ca. 1991).

Bennett, with Angela Lansbury, displaying the Writers Guild of America, West, Laurel Award for Lifetime Achievement in 1995. (Photo by Bonnie Clarke)

John Bennett contemplating Charles's death (1995).

doesn't exist anymore, except in the people's imagination. Hint, and then definitely state, that the morale of the army is suffering as the *truth* seeps through to the battlefronts. Never give pause to the barrage of *dead Hitler* propaganda—the pamphlets, the radio. Redouble and intensify the statement—*Hitler Is Dead—Why are you fighting for a leader who is dead?*

It is possible that this propaganda angle may even have its effect on Hitler himself. It *must* of necessity be galling for a man of Hitler's egoism to be moving through a world in which many millions of people will be believing him to be just a two-cent actor. Hitler is almost a madman anyway. Properly handled, our propaganda campaign might send him completely out of his mind.

And now—if you have read this far—please reread and assimilate. As I said before, the great merit of this whole setup lies in the fact that the more stoutly the story is denied, the more persistent it must necessarily become.

# 11

# A Secret Agent

May 10, 1940: without ultimatums or declarations of war, Hitler's divisions swiftly seized Denmark and Norway. And within days came the vast tank assault on France. The Maginot Line collapsed. Belgium collapsed. The French army collapsed. Northern France was swiftly overrun. And the already mauled British Expeditionary Force, unprepared for tank warfare, retreated to the Channel coast at Dunkirk.

The United States took notice, up to a point, but still as a spectator. It seemed that only pro-British President Roosevelt and his direct associates were seeing the writing on the wall. Though Roosevelt's warnings went unheeded, not so the swift march of events. Soon large sections of America's press, professedly disinterested, were finding the news too spectacular to consign to the back pages. The pro-Hitler *Chicago Tribune,* ecstatic at the way things were shaping up, was triumphantly telling America that Britain's imminent defeat was demonstrating the rightness of America's neutrality. The stupid little United Kingdom should long since have seen reason and subscribed to the Führer's "Christ-like design" for a thousand years of peace.

Also heralding Britain's doom, famous American voices were being raised. The public hero Charles Lindbergh, who months earlier had been Hitler's guest and the recipient of Nazi awards, was telling America that the continuance of strict neutrality was imperative in the name of the world's future. In London, Ambassador Joseph Kennedy—amassing a vast fortune by practically cornering the Scotch whiskey market—was advising Churchill to seek peace with Hitler before being faced with unconditional surrender.

So where did members of the British colony stand? Some were experiencing a backlash from what was going on in Europe. Increasingly, there was awareness of anti-British feeling proliferating in circles that had previously been friendly. This hostility was creeping up insidiously; and though facing the fact wasn't pleasant, pinpointing its cause wasn't difficult.

Many Americans had been quite rightly disturbed by the rise of fascism, first Mussolini in Italy, then Franco in Spain. With the spread of anti-fascism in the States, there came a wave of sympathy toward anti-fascist Soviet Russia, and out of that emerged a form of procommunism. I'm not saying this attitude was shared by the majority of Americans—far from it. But the wave spread noticeably through Hollywood film circles, where communism was becoming the fashionable dream of the left-wing intelligentsia. Great Britain was at war with Germany, and indirectly with Germany's convenient ally Russia; and any enemy of Stalin and the Soviets was anathema to the left-wingers.

In many Hollywood film circles, anti-British feeling verged on unconcealed ugliness. Too often, both vocally and in print, left-wingers were referring to Churchill as a filthy old fascist—declaring that the sooner Stalin and Hitler shut Churchill's big mouth, the better for everybody, including those fucking English fools who were allowing the old son of a bitch to lead them by the nose.

I had to be cautious. In those first two years of Hitler's triumphs, my main obstacle was the great studios' fear that any film hinting at anti-Nazi or pro-British sympathy would infuriate the twelve million–plus members of the German-American Bund—to the heavy detriment of box-office potential in states such as Wisconsin and Illinois. So the studios remained rigidly neutral, while at the same time reaping billions of bucks by disgorging sop that avoided mention of the war across the Atlantic.

But with my services now in demand, I was able somewhat to pick assignments. This made it possible to write parts that would ensnare box-office names who might not realize they were indulging in anti-Nazi poison in the guise of popular entertainment. This tactic worked to my gratification, as my movies received a big showing in world markets. Among them were two films in which I actually broke the Hollywood taboo against anti-Nazi subjects. The first was *Foreign Correspondent* (1940), produced by Walter Wanger and directed by Alfred Hitchcock, and the other was a war film, *Joan of Paris* (1942).

Walter Wanger had acquired *Personal History*, written by the foreign correspondent Vincent Sheean, and he had some six or seven writers trying to get a film out of it. No way. Sheean's memoir was a fine piece, reporting the progress toward war as seen by an American journalist stationed in

Berlin; but there was no story, no element on which to hang a screenplay. Nonetheless, Wanger, sure that a film would be forthcoming, borrowed Hitchcock from David Selznick and jumped way ahead of the cameras. The string of writers got no place; and there was Hitch, sitting impatiently in an office at United Artists, frustrated at having been hired to direct a nonexistent script.

Hitch was further irritated when he learned that David Selznick had loaned him to Wanger at $7,500 a week, while under his Selznick contract, he—the loanee—was pulling down only a weekly $2,500. He was actually receiving a weekly stipend of $2,250, since Myron Selznick, Hitch's agent, got 10 percent of the $2,500. David, Myron's brother, profited a clear $5,000 a week. There was nothing Hitch could do about it: a contract is a contract.

Wanger must have been chafing at paying out $7,500 a week while his hired property twiddled his thumbs. Something had to break, and it was Hitch who persuaded Wanger to call me in. I hadn't worked with Hitch since *Young and Innocent,* three years earlier in England. But since I'd written six pictures for him, two of them my originals, Hitch knew I could tell a story.

Spies and murder, pursuit and suspense, had been 60 percent of my creative meat, and both Wanger and Hitch were happy with the story. *Foreign Correspondent* was essentially anti-Nazi propaganda; but to avoid Hitler's wrath, Wanger never allowed the heavies to be identified as German. America was not in the war; therefore, there were no Nazi armbands, no "Heil Hitlers." The dialogue spoken by the enemy heavies could not be in German, so all their dialogue was spoken in reverse. A line like "Kill him" became "Mih llik." Hitchcock might have defied Wanger, but Hitch's fear overrode the film's propaganda importance. Don't offend, don't take a chance. Yet Wanger's wariness made no difference—audiences knew that the unidentified heavies were Nazis.

*Foreign Correspondent* was a smash hit everywhere—except, I conclude, in Germany and the Nazi-occupied countries where it would not have been shown. Joseph Goebbels, Hitler's brilliantly dangerous propaganda chief, called the movie "a masterpiece of propaganda, a first-class production which no doubt will make a certain impression upon the broad masses of the people in enemy countries"—enemy countries of course being Britain and its colonies. When we heard of Goebbels's commentary, both Hitch and I were flattered.[24]

Critics' reviews were tremendous; and I was more than gratified because, coming at the height of U.S. neutrality, the film's success was proof that my storytelling could pull its weight for the Allies. *Foreign Correspondent* was nominated in 1940 for six Academy Awards, including Best Picture, which Hitchcock won for *Rebecca*. I gleaned further satisfaction that it earned me an award nomination in the newly designated category of Best Original Screenplay (though that was won by Preston Sturges for *The Great McGinty*). Robert Benchley not only played in the movie but contributed some inimitable dialogue such as only he could write.

After *Foreign Correspondent,* Swanson involved me in writing something at Columbia called *They Dare Not Love* (1941). Although not one of my favorite efforts, the film had the personal appeal of being a useful propaganda story line about lovers torn apart by the Nazis. But the whole thing at Columbia Studios was utterly ridiculous, an experience few writers would want to go through. On your first day there, you were invited to lunch with the studio head, Harry Cohn, in the executive dining room. When you came in, there were all the top people of Columbia sitting around. Harry Cohn said, "How wonderful to see you, Charles. Welcome!" You sat down. At this point he pressed a button, and the chair under you collapsed—and you fell on your ass. Everybody laughed, laughed, laughed. This was evidently the greatest joke in the world, that Harry Cohn could collapse a chair under his latest writer. So I never went into the executive dining room again. Harry Cohn was the most revolting character in the world, with a foul tongue all of the time.

My screenplay was from a spy tale by James Edward Grant—hide and seek in the United States with Gestapo agents until George Brent, playing a German prince, returns to Austria to free some of his countrymen. It was a bloody good story. Filming was started by the brilliant film director James Whale, but Cohn tossed him out after the first week.

When I finished *Dare,* my agent sold me to Cecil B. DeMille to reconstruct *Reap the Wild Wind* (1942). DeMille had the writers Alan Le May and Jesse Lasky Jr. working on the film. But they got into trouble with the construction, the architecture, and didn't know where the story was going. DeMille fired them both, and I did a miraculous job of reconstructing the story. C. B. was crazy about my job, and we became close friends. He asked me to write the script, but I said I couldn't write the American sailor dialogue, so he rehired Alan Le May. I told the story and Alan wrote the tough dialogue. It was a perfect collaboration.

One night I went to a magnificent party at the mansion of the producer Stephen Ames—a multi-multi-multimillionaire—in the Holmby Hills. At the bar was Harry Cohn.

"Charles, how wonderful to see you," he said. "Tomorrow we go into production on your movie."

I said, "Oh, lovely! Good luck."

"Oh, we won't need it. We love you dearly."

I was Cohn's closest friend in the world. So the following day, I said to Alan Le May, "My new picture is starting filming today at Columbia; let's go on the set."

We came up to the Columbia gate, and the security guard at the door, who knew me perfectly well, said, "Yes, Mr. Bennett, what do you want?"

"I want to go on my set," I said. "My picture is shooting for the first time today."

He said, "Oh, wait a minute. I have to ask Mr. Cohn's permission for anyone to go on the set."

I said, "Oh, that'll be all right. Mr. Cohn is my friend. We talked at a party just last night." So he got on the phone to Cohn.

And I could hear Cohn on the phone, "Do you think I'd let that stupid s.o.b. of an Englishman on the set? Tell him to go away!"

What the hell can you do with people like that? One night I was his closest friend. The next day I was a stupid s.o.b. of an Englishman.

In contrast, DeMille was a very kind, gentle man—despite all that crap of his being a bully. He may have been tough on the set now and then, but who isn't? I remember the first time I met the costume designer Edith Head in DeMille's office. I was fascinated to see the vast respect with which the great C. B. treated her—DeMille was always respectful to what he recognized as true talent. He was no bully. He was the kindest, gentlest person I knew; and I loved him dearly.

DeMille used to invite me to his immense ranch, Paradise, in the local mountains. The first time I was up, there were hundreds of deer grazing on his front lawn! He protected them every year during hunting season. And each morning, on his way out to a stone-walled swimming pool, DeMille would stop and say, "Good Morning! How are you today?"—to a spider!

So there I was at work on *Reap the Wild Wind,* and it hadn't got a climax, and DeMille was getting nervous. "What are we doing with the end of the picture?" DeMille turned to me in a conference, as if I should know! As it happened, I did. I had thought up an ending that morning in the bathtub. John Wayne and Ray Milland, both bitter rivals for the hand of Paulette Goddard, are exploring a shipwreck in diving helmets. Just as they set about to fight each other, they are interrupted by a giant squid. I acted out the whole scene for DeMille, playing all the parts, including the giant squid. Dead silence in the room—everybody watching DeMille for his opinion. DeMille sat there, completely transfixed. He sighed, "Yes, Charles, in Technicolor!" The scene was shot and was probably much of the reason the film was so successful.

Jesse Lasky Jr. wrote of my ability to entertain DeMille in *Whatever Happened to Hollywood?* "Charles would swagger and glower in an impersonation of the heavy to be played by Raymond Massey. Then Charles would mince out a delicious imitation of Paulette Goddard's Florida belle. He'd ape Ray Milland's effete aristocrat, or the heavy-shouldered, jaw-jutting challenge of John Wayne's First Mate. But too often his office performances were better than the scenes themselves. The written word missed the swaggerings, struttings, eye rollings of our spellbinding Charles. DeMille would complain that we hadn't got it on paper, quite ignoring the fact that would have been next to impossible."

Thank you, Jesse, for the fine review! I had honed my acting skills over many years.

I have asked myself whether I inserted propaganda into *Reap*. The overall sense of the film favored Yankee individualism, but there was nothing specific. Yet I believe this was more than compensated for by my involvement with DeMille in pro-Allied undercover activities, which I will discuss shortly.

Alan Le May—although American as apple pie—was as pro-British as Roosevelt himself. Every morning before getting down to the job, he and I would listen to the latest radio reports, hoping for the best, but dreading the worst. He was a great man, as was DeMille. Not infrequently DeMille would sit with Alan and me, sharing our hopes. Perhaps the most painful affliction attached to growing old isn't the passing of the years so much as the passing of friends.

I've known many Hollywood producers who would have resented loss of such "valuable working time"—saying in effect, "I'm paying these bums to write a movie for me, not to listen to the radio." Jack Warner required his writers to work nine-to-five office hours. I didn't take notice of this; but other writers spent their afternoons playing gin rummy. Cecil B. DeMille, bless his heart, wasn't like that.

Looking back, I think that my favorite wartime film—no, the favorite of *all* of my pictures—was *Joan of Paris* (1942), which I cowrote for RKO after Ellis St. Joseph. I loved it because it was more human, more in touch with my hatred of Nazi Germany, my love of my country, and my feeling for France. It was a sad, beautiful story of a girl who dies in the cause against the Nazis. To me, the tragedy of it is that it wasn't played by proper stars—it should have been played by Cary Grant and people like that. Instead, RKO cast two completely unknown Europeans, Paul Henreid and Michèle Morgan. As a result, audiences stayed away, it didn't make money, and my heart was broken.

I was proud of *Joan of Paris*. It was potently anti-Nazi! And I felt that John Hay Beith would be gratified that he'd asked me to "put the message across" from Hollywood. Also, I was more than proud of RKO Films, which, with the young producer David Hempstead, had dared make an openly anti-Nazi movie before Pearl Harbor awakened Hollywood's moguls to the big dough in being nice to Britain and nasty to the Axis. The reviews of *Joan of Paris,* released in theaters just one month after the attack on Pearl Harbor, were as good as or better than any I had ever received, and it was acclaimed as one of the best pictures of the year.

It also had a lighter side, plentifully supported by the performance of an overweight young actor, Laird Cregar, who was superb as the Nazi governor of occupied Paris—a gentleman who would eat grapes, always gracefully, as he condemned noncollaborating Parisians to death. Cregar's departure from inevitable top stardom was a tragedy. At the age of twenty-five, and intending to become a juvenile leading star rather than a character actor, Laird went on a diet to drop from 280 to 150 pounds. He dropped—sure enough—as dead as the heroine of *Joan of Paris* before a Nazi firing squad at film's end. Laird Cregar's death was a great loss, particularly to 20th Century Fox, which was determined to develop him into a box-office bonanza.

I took first writing credit on a highly collaborative, overtly pro-British propaganda film called *Forever and a Day* (1943). *Halliwell's Film Guide* claims *Forever* was notable for having the longest-ever list (twenty-one) of credited cowriters, including C. S. Forester, Christopher Isherwood, John Van Druten, and James Hilton. I doubt whether the picture's box-office returns were great, but its collection of British film colony members among a score or more of top stars, from Charles Laughton to Merle Oberon to

Ray Milland and C. Aubrey Smith, was impressive and possibly useful for building public opinion in favor of Britain.

But writing propaganda was not enough. I wanted to be more actively involved, but what more could I do? Jesse Lasky Jr. made the point that I could ride a horse. "Charles Bennett would appear, dustily booted from a polo match. He flew planes, rode like a Cossack and could on occasion steal scenes from the boss [DeMille] who had always been second to none in 'office performance.'" I had never seen a Cossack ride; neither, I imagine, had Jesse. Anyway, how could equestrian ability help in days when such cavalry feats as *The Charge of the Light Brigade* were out of fashion?

December 7, 1941: invasion appeared to be only a matter of hours. We waited. Our coastal cities were blacked out from San Diego up to Seattle, and an attack was expected night after day after night. Expecting the worst, everybody was wondering what was holding the Japs back.

I was at work for David Hempstead at RKO, putting the final touches to a good screenplay, *Challenge to the Night,* not produced. Our greatest challenge was the immediate danger visible to anyone riding in the Santa Monica Mountains overlooking the vast expanse of the Pacific. Out there stretched millions of square miles of ocean, teeming with enemy ships and submarines. And what was our defense? From my interest in aviation, I knew too well how important and undefended was our vitally important Southern California area. It was important because the core of the aircraft industry—Hughes, Lockheed, Douglas—was here. If Japan had seized those plants while the door was wide open, the U.S. ability to produce an air defense or offense would have been sliced by maybe 80 percent.

A resident alien, I jumped at an opportunity to become the acting commander of Company D, 1st Battalion, 39th Regiment, of the California State Guard. We started immediately in December 1941, receiving our License to Bear Arms on December 21, 1942. In 1943, when a California state court held that resident aliens could not serve with the actual State Guard, Company D was split into two sections—Company D remained with the California State Guard, but our alien group became the First Mounted Patrol of the California State Militia, attached to Company D. I remained commander of the First Mounted Patrol until my departure to England in the spring of 1944, turning over its command to a horseman and future president, Ronald Reagan.

Both Company D and the First Mounted Patrol were cavalry, carrying out antisabotage duty around the military aircraft centers such as Douglas Aircraft, and security patrols into the brush-covered Santa Monica Mountains looking for evidence of enemy infiltration. In hindsight it seems ridiculous that our little cavalry troop should stand watch over such facilities. My son John remarked of the patrol: "An immigrant militia toasting martini-filled helmets was polo's defense of the free." It's true.

One time, when commanding the cavalry troop, I came at a full gallop across the extended polo field at Riviera Country Club—twice the length of a normal polo field because a quarter mile or so was kept for practice purposes. Suddenly Mex, the wonderful polo pony that I'd acquired from the car designer Dutch Darrin, became alarmed by something. He turned—and he could turn on a dime, one of the things that made him great in polo circles—and I came off. Why in hell I wasn't killed, neck broken or something, I shall never know. The speed must have been something over twenty, maybe twenty-five, miles an hour. But I survived. It could be that somehow I instinctively went back to my early twenties, when I was playing Romeo in all the smallest little mining towns in England. I had learned how to fall, after kissing Juliet for the last time and crashing down three or four steps to my death. Off the polo fields and into the hills, Mex had nerves of steel and could easily pick his way along razor-back ridges where no trails existed.

I have learned recently of a National Park Service plaque which states that a wartime spy lived up Rustic Canyon in the Santa Monica Mountains. Swastikas were found painted on the interior walls of a generator shed, and there was evidence of radio equipment. I knew that property well. It was located upstream of the Will Rogers ranch, and it belonged to a senior Douglas test engineer, Norman Stevens, who was troubleshooting bombers before the Battle of Midway. He had installed the generators to power his house and irrigate his orchard—there was no other source of electricity—where he intended to lie low with his family if the Japanese invaded. Our troop frequently scouted down through the dense thickets of sumac adjacent to his property—and I recall meeting the engineer. But our patrols were on public land, so I cannot speak to the unlikely truth of what the Park Service found on his private property.

I suppose it possible that a foreign agent could spy on this important engineer while working as his farmhand. I also suppose that painted swastikas might be construed as evidence of spying—though a spy who would so advertise is a fool. Certainly the possession of radio equipment is no crime, particularly if assembled by a brilliant, reclusive engineer. But I have a more likely explanation. The engineer was a prominent theosophist, a cult that finds special significance in that very ancient swastika symbol. So maybe his handyman, perhaps an occultist, painted swastikas with his employer's approval. Of course this does not rule out spying, or any mystical art. But one thing is for certain: the conjecture of a psychic saboteur targeting Douglas Aircraft provides an intriguing story I should have written, but did not.

Along this line, film historians have asked whether I was responsible for Hitchcock's story *Saboteur* (1942). I gave many ideas to Hitch, and the story does resemble my travelogue *Love Goes West,* though headed in the other direction, from Los Angeles to New York City. It is possible that we discussed over cocktails my cavalry troop and developed the idea of a saboteur at Douglas followed up by a chase thriller. But whether the idea for *Saboteur* was his or mine, Hitch took it to David Selznick. Eventually, Peter Viertel wrote the film as his first picture; but he couldn't stitch Hitch's ideas together to highlight the melodrama. After it debuted in April 1942, the *New York Times* drama critic called *Saboteur* a relentless wild-goose chase in imitation of *The 39 Steps.* It is said that imitation is the sincerest form of flattery.

Anyway, the Japanese didn't invade. Instead, Japan's military machine was let loose on the Dutch East Indies, Malaya, New Guinea, chalking up vast gains week after week until the great U.S. victory in the naval battle of the Coral Sea dislocated the Japanese timetable. We all know what happened next. It took just short of four more years until the horror of the atom bomb brought Japan to its knees.

Very soon after the war I rode again through the Santa Monica Mountains. This time the Los Angeles County Fire Department asked me to help map the trails. I did so, while DeMille paid my studio salary.

With DeMille's help, I did become involved in a third war activity, in addition to writing propaganda and commanding a cavalry troop. For years, plays and films about detectives and spies had been my bread and butter. Between 1940 and 1944 I served as a spy, doing very considerable undercover work for British intelligence, the FBI, and U.S. Naval Intelligence. Very few people in the world knew that Cecil B. DeMille was mixed up in the Secret Service, and for a long time in this town the top meetings took place in his private office. I would get a call from DeMille's secretary, saying—in a nasal voice—"Mr. Bennett, Mr. DeMille would like you to come across to his office." I would say to Alan Le May, "Excuse me, but Mr. DeMille wants to see me." I would go across the hall, and there would be Richard B. Hood of the FBI, the head of naval intelligence, people like that. And I would be asked to do certain jobs, most of which I never entirely understood.

Sometimes I just passed along information that came to me. In January 1943 I reported rumors concerning a young American soldier photographing Fort MacArthur's gun emplacements and inadvertently passing on his knowledge of troop movements. I was assisted at this by my mistress at the time, Peggy Morrow Field. In March 1943 I kept track of a Dr. Guenther Stern with multiple aliases, who encouraged me to promote his story idea about Mexico; and in June I forwarded my correspondence with Dr. Stern to Lieutenant Robert Calloway of U.S. Naval Intelligence. On another assignment, I interviewed the actor Miles Mander, composer Jimmy Campbell, and film writer W. F. Lipscomb about a film associate, Jeffrey Bernard, recently arrived from England, and assembled a dossier regarding the possibility of his being a German secret agent. Lipscomb described Bernard as an untrustworthy, "rough and tough customer" and a member of the C. M. Woolf gang.

On one occasion the head of the British Secret Service asked me to sail down the coast looking for possible submarine bases—an odd request, and I didn't do it. There was another instance when I had to enter a German agent's living room to see whether a certain picture was hanging on the wall; this scenario seemed like a scene I might have written.

There was one assignment of especially perilous character. I was asked to befriend a wildly pro-Hitler German Jewess (yes, I said it right!) suspected of being a Nazi agent and cousin to Joseph Goebbels. Dorita was very attractive and had a razor-sharp mind, and—as I came to know and adore her—I felt a certain shame at what I was doing. But through Dorita I got to know the *head* of the German Secret Service in California. He attempted to influence my writing at Columbia Studios, presumably knowing I was a spy. Of course, I knew this to be dangerous work—one slip, and no more Charles Bennett. But I liked doing it, and the danger was fun!

Maybe Dorita was what the Secret Service suggested, an Axis spy who had scouted attack sites against the Suez Canal, and who was carried by sedan chair across the Andes of South America to search out locations for a secret base. But despite what was said, I cannot be entirely certain about Dorita's role. Maybe our suspicions were without any real basis. It wasn't my job to know. My job was to stick around and be Judas Iscariot. I was taking directions from much higher echelons than I could ever be in touch with, so I did my job—believing my little bit would eventually lead to the destruction and obliteration of Hitler and all he stood for. Maybe Dorita was the complete innocent, maneuvered by others—I hope to God she was, because in a way I loved her and she became a lifelong friend.

Then there was the question of Errol Flynn and his scoundrelous friend Freddie McEvoy. In his biography of Errol, Charles Higham accused Errol of being an Axis spy. But during my days with British intelligence, it was Freddie who was enemy number one, and he came close to murdering me. According to Higham, McEvoy and Flynn smuggled Nazi agents across the border from Mexico. I can well believe this of McEvoy. But for Errol, much as I liked his flair, I knew he possessed only one interest, which was how much Errol got out of it—no matter who paid.

Strangely enough, a lot of my espionage was against our own ally, Communist Russia. I was asked to do things that were anti-Soviet. I remember all sorts of idiotic things—I won't go into detail—but only because it was known, even then, that Stalin's Russia would be our eventual enemy.

Another slant on my secret activities concerns the insertion of false but useful accounts of me in the Hollywood trade papers. For three months beginning in March 1939, there was mention in both the *Citizen News* and *Los Angeles Examiner* that I had published in England a serialized biographic novel titled *Mountain Monarch* about King Zog of Albania. In December 1940 the *Los Angeles Daily News,* the *Herald Express*—and was it *Variety?*—all claimed I was writing the biography of General Juan Almazán, strongman of Mexico, with plans to travel there to set up a film. Perhaps this rumor was floated with the intention to send me to Mexico on an intelligence assignment, or perhaps to attract German attention for other reasons. In 1942 both *Variety* and the *Los Angeles Examiner* had me editing the *New World Encyclopedia,* which gave me reason to travel. But the most preposterous insertion appeared in 1943 when *Variety* mentioned my writing a *Glossary of Military Terms for Writers*—for the life of me I can't imagine the value of that ruse.

Good news arrived in the autumn of 1942, conveyed by Sidney Bernstein of the British Ministry of Information Films Division during his visit to the States. He said the Ministry of Information (MOI) had approved my traveling home to Britain to write propaganda there. I knew Sidney—later Lord Bernstein and chairman and creator of Grenada TV—during my Hitchcock days, and I was happy to learn I would be working initially with so gifted an old friend. He explained that I could travel to England to work with the MOI Films Division as a consultant on British-American film propaganda. Happily, I wrote to him that I would proceed back to England under my own steam, as it were, as soon as I was clear of present assignments at Paramount Pictures. I expected to be finished by February 1943, though it actually took a year longer.

No matter—by then I was at work on first-class assignments and pro-Allied propaganda. Still collaborating with DeMille and Le May, I wrote the anti-Japanese Gary Cooper film *The Story of Dr. Wassell* (1944), which received full Navy and Washington cooperation. I was the constructionist, and Alan wrote an immense amount of its tough American dialogue, at which he was awfully bloody good.

James Hilton has been credited for the story. This is wrong. Hilton never took or was entitled to any credit on this movie. Alan and I wrote the screenplay from Dr. Wassell's own statements, and later—for publicity—DeMille had Hilton put out a novel about Wassell. DeMille was unhappy about the novel because Hilton had told nothing but the strict truth, whereas Alan and I had fictionalized the situation to increase its box-office appeal.

In 1943 I wrote another screenplay for DeMille at Paramount—*Rurales* (1943, not produced)—a large-scale picture about the Mexican Revolution. It was designed to knit the bonds between the United States and Latin American countries, and it received cooperation from Washington. Because of the propaganda importance of these pictures, it was quite impossible for me to walk out on either of them. I considered this as important as if I were in uniform.

Looking back, I suspect—what with DeMille's in-studio involvement in intelligence gathering and international propaganda—that the Paramount Studio mogul Adolph Zukor was also neck-deep in dealings with the State Department, British and naval intelligence, and the FBI. Such a concentration of influence in one mogul would make a fascinating historical study.

Eventually, I finished at Paramount and traveled by rail to New York. The trip gave me time to think about how life and fiction sometimes overlap. Not long before, I had been tossing around story ideas, planning a national magazine story, *Shore Patrol,* based on our 1st Mounted Patrol, also a book titled *Ferry Pilot,* based on the experiences of my wife Maggie. But by May 1944, as I boarded a munitions freighter, the *Sam Rich,* with two other passengers—a supercilious British government accountant and the head of Denham film lab—nothing seemed so immediately interesting as my monthlong dangerous convoy crossing, and the prospect that I would soon be home.

~ ~ ~

## Interlude: A Suave Villain

The worst of Errol Flynn's "Merry Men," and perhaps his very closest friend, wasn't fit to live at all. Memory can be short; but of all the characters who have come my way, the Australian-born Frederick McEvoy Esq. is surely among the least easily forgotten, his wayward presence on this planet being in my view up there with those of Caligula, Jack the Ripper, and the permanently jailed Charles Manson. "Freddie" was a suave villain—a character type I have exploited throughout my film and literary career. Innumerable columns have been written about him—even a book. I don't know whether the scribes derived their knowledge from hearsay, research, or personal contact. For myself, I'm writing from a none-too-prized acquaintanceship, coupled with what I believe might have been my total nonexistence after March 1942.

Freddie's profession was simple. Using St. Moritz in Switzerland and Cannes on the Côte d'Azur as his base of operations, he built a stunning career out of marrying wealthy heiresses and then accepting a million or so in return for a quiet divorce. Among his major marital acquisitions was the heiress to Standard Oil billions, Beatrice "B" Cartwright, who—though crippled, in a wheelchair, and thirty-two years his senior—paid him off royally for her freedom. Over dinner one night in Nice, "B's" brother, William Rogers Benjamin, who was then financing my Glenn Ford movie, *The Green Glove* (1952), in the south of France—an original screenplay adapted from my unpublished novel *The White Road*—told me he had a file eighteen inches thick detailing the infamies of his ex-brother-in-law.

Tall, slim, with the perfect build of an athlete—even more handsome in his macho way than his friend Errol Flynn—Freddie was a Cresta Run bobsled champion, a bronze medalist for Great Britain in the four-man bobsled at the 1936 Winter Olympics, and one of the finest skiers on earth. He was also one of the greatest scoundrels unhung—utterly ruthless and psychopathically uncaring about everybody and everything beyond his own comfort.

We were casually acquainted, occasionally in Cannes but more often at the ultraluxurious Palace Hotel in St. Moritz. The magnificent monarch of the ski and bobsled runs would always be around, certainly one of the best-looking and most treacherous gigolos in the world.

I remember a murderous occasion along a St. Moritz ski run. I had tumbled in among the trees, when down sped Freddie; he stopped nearby (he did not see me). He waved another skier to pass him. The trouble was, he waved his friend off the run onto a dangerous patch, which, at the speed of travel, should have caused his intended victim grave personal injury. Happily, the gent survived the fall and was, no doubt, adequately reassured by Freddie's suave and unconscionable apology. But after watching this intended malice, I shuddered my way down the slope to meet Hitch over a stiff drink at the Palace bar.

But in 1939 unkindly fate tossed a monkey wrench into the serenity of McEvoy's works, inconveniencing his trouble-free existence. Nazis swarmed into France, sources of caviar and Champagne dried up, rich heiresses fled their homelands, and Freddie was forced to make a decision regarding his own immediate future. Being a born leader, he might have sought service in the British army. Fearless on the most dangerous ski slopes and the St. Moritz Cresta Run, he could have been an inspiration to desperate men fighting on a stricken field. No way—risking his superbly valuable skin for his country wasn't Freddie's idea of fun or how to get the best out of life.

Instead, the gallant thirty-three-year-old married Beatrice. It was reported that she gave Freddie an allowance, and one day each week to make love to other women—and then he prudently fled to the strictly neutral United States. A wise move. Not only would he be safe from any meddlesome British authorities who might have hit on the fact that a certain F. McEvoy was highly eligible for the draft, but the wealthiest ladies and healthiest pickings were now found anywhere from Palm Beach to Beverly Hills. So as the war shut down Atlantic travel, God's gift to affluent females exited Europe for the United States—and as it happened, none too soon.

Although I'm sure Freddie didn't know it, at the time of his departure for America the British War Department was putting out feelers, seeking him for questioning on a matter that justified his being shot for treason. It was suspected, perhaps unjustifiably, that McEvoy had been negotiating the sale of his talents to the highest bidder, Nazi Germany.

According to Errol Flynn's biographer Charles Higham, in his *Errol Flynn: The Untold Story* (1980), Freddie arrived in the United States accompanied by Beatrice. With her generous support, he flourished rewardingly, no doubt telling himself that this spot of bother between Hitler and Churchill couldn't last indefinitely, and he would presently return to St. Moritz and Cannes to pick up where he had left off. Freddie took up residency in Miami, from which, Higham claims, he traveled to the Caribbean to arrange for Axis U-boat refueling bases along the Atlantic coast of Mexico and Central America. Certainly Freddie was capable of such treachery; but I do not speak from experience in these matters.

As was his birthright, citizen of the world Frederick McEvoy had it happily made in neutral America—except for a sudden, out-of-left-field disaster! Pearl Harbor. Overnight the United States was Britain's ally. No longer could Freddie regard the United States as a safe haven; and those wretched Brits could even request his extradition. Hell—a personage as great as Freddie couldn't be expected to bury himself in some squalid hideout. So, trusting his never-failing sagacity, he divorced Beatrice and moved from Miami to Mexico City to occupy his time on Nazi assignments, running gold, guns, and drugs from Mexico to California. From Mexico he often reentered Hollywood to stir up pro-German, anti-British feeling in the film industry.

A miscalculation: in March 1942 across the border he came—and met me!

The setting for our reunion was the wide terrace of the top-social Los Angeles West Side Tennis Club. As usual, the assemblage was a Hollywood columnist's dream. And among the film idols was Errol Flynn. Freddie's back was to me.

Errol called me across, saying, "Freddie, you two have been around the same spots quite a bit—could be you know Charles Bennett?"

Freddie turned, and for a moment (no more) I glimpsed the perturbation in his eyes. Not because he had momentarily dismissed the likelihood of other frequenters of St. Moritz in Southern California, but because—and of this I'm sure—he was aware of my connection with intelligence services.

Being Freddie, he recovered fast, pleasantly suave as ever. We downed our drinks and the group broke up; but unless I'm overrating my importance, this wasn't the end of it. A few days later Freddie was out of the country, playing for safety.

No problem—he took a meal ticket with him. Relying on his macho presence and the charm that never failed to captivate so many and so much, Freddie indulged in a whirlwind courtship of the attractive, eighteen-year-old Irene Wrightsman, daughter of the Standard Oil tycoon and multimillionaire Charles Wrightsman. He confirmed the deal by insisting on an immediate Gretna Green–style marriage (that is, an elopement) followed by a romantic flight across the Mexican border. It has been said that Errol Flynn, disguised as the chauffeur, drove the car that whisked the lovers into Mexico and matrimony.

A master stroke: Freddie was back in a permanently neutral country, safe from nosy U.S. and British intelligence agents—and along the way he had acquired a bride who was the key to money, money, money. Pretty, too. Even bedable. A pleasant change from some of the harridans on whom, for a price tag of a million or so, he had been compelled to bestow a portion of his masculinity. I understood that a child was born of their love match, another calculated piece of McEvoy self-assurance. Freddie must have been patting himself on the back.

But with bells celebrating Freddie and Irene's Mexican nuptials, I have jumped ahead of myself—and need to backpedal to what I suspect was an apropos event. Freddie's meeting me at the West Side was an obvious shock, conceivably alerting British intelligence to his presence in town. So I was to receive a shock myself just twenty-four hours later, and still two days before the couple left for Mexico. A coincidence? I'll never know.

After a day at home working for DeMille on *The Story of Dr. Wassell,* I helped myself to a drink and went out into my Coldwater Canyon garden for a rest. My home was just one of four that formed a tiny, unexplained oasis amid orange groves that stretched to the south for a mile or more, almost to the semi-isolated Beverly Hills Hotel and its Polo Lounge, beloved by the film industry. It was a lovely evening, the sun setting blood-red over Santa Monica.

Blood-red indeed. A bullet—shot from the chaparral-studded hill on the opposite side of the canyon—whistled past my left ear, burying itself in property later owned by the costume designer Edith Head. I have no proof that Frederick McEvoy had anything to do with it; there were deer around our canyon in those days, and an illegal hunter might have missed his mark. But I do know that Freddie was still in California and would have been happy to know that I'd been rubbed out. If Freddie was behind the shooting I'm sure his hired triggerman received a merciless McEvoy tongue-lashing. Deserved. I'd done better sniping in Flanders fields.

I am sure Errol was not involved. He had faults, but homicidal proclivity wasn't one of them. In fact, I'm inclined to believe that titling his book *My Wicked, Wicked Ways* sprang from a narcissist's bravado rather than a cloven hoof.

But I didn't like this situation one little bit—who'd know when and where the next bullet would come? And I experienced genuine relief when informed that the honeymoon couple had arrived in Mexico.

According to all fairy-tale romances, Freddie, Irene, and offspring should have lived happily ever after. No such thing. There was a worm in the woodwork—namely, Papa Charles Wrightsman.

I knew Wrightsman, a congenial soul to drink with at one or another of the three Hollywood nightclubs. But when it came to acquiring and keeping millions, it seems that Freddie had met his match or better. It is related that, faced with his daughter's continuing marriage to this unspeakable character, Wrightsman went after the bridegroom with the most devastating weapon at his disposal. He cut off Irene's allowance, saying, in effect, "You have a husband. Let him keep you—I won't'!"

Sad! Suddenly, the luxury-loving McEvoy was asked to scrape up a living to support a penniless wife and child. But Freddie wasn't beaten. Gallantly facing misfortune, Freddie continued his highly paid, nefarious U-boat schemes—which I presume were directed against the Panama Canal. Higham reports that FBI Director J. Edgar Hoover had a personal interest in Errol Flynn's Hollywood sex scandals, and he kept an exceptionally tight surveillance of Freddie during Errol's 1943 and 1944 visits to Mexico.

The only sense I can make of Errol's coming and going is that he had become useful to U.S. intelligence. After publishing his biography of Errol, Charles Higham confided to me that he was now convinced that Errol was a double agent, listed as working for British intelligence. If Flynn had been enlisted—possibly under threat of exposing his Hollywood shenanigans— then his Acapulco visits were exceptional fishing expeditions.

With the cessation of World War II, the scoundrel was back in Europe roosting comfortably in liberated Paris, grabbing a fortune by black-marketing the coinage of still-reeling nations. Within months Freddie headed back to his old hunting grounds, St. Moritz and Cannes, resuming his profession of super-social stud, to the delight of many wealthy ladies flocking back to their prewar haunts.

Things, contacts, meetings often dovetail. Pertinent to this is that some time in 1947, the war over, I became acquainted with the exceedingly wealthy Woolworth heiress Barbara Hutton—meeting her first at a wedding party that she and her husband, Cary Grant, gave for the Earl of Drogheda's daughter, Lady Patricia Latham. I liked Barbara and, although I never became a close friend, I was always happy to run into her. But the point is that on every occasion our paths crossed after her break from Grant, there at her side, like a permanent shadow, was Frederick McEvoy. They didn't marry; but I'm sure Freddie never lost a penny in consequence, and possibly collected more by playing hard to get. Barbara was both an easy touch and a prominent subscriber to Freddie's high-priced necessities.

Anyway, Freddie flourished. Charles Higham reports that McEvoy continued to smuggle guns, gold, and drugs—shifting his base to the Mediterranean in 1950 when rebels in North Africa wanted gun shipments from Nice and Marseilles. The last time we met, in Cannes in 1951, his finances seemed to be catching up with those of Onassis. His private yacht, *Black Joke,* employing a crew of eleven and sleeping twenty guests, was among the most beautiful on the Mediterranean. Enjoying a nightly black-tie appearance at the casino, Freddie kept the penthouse atop the Carlton Hotel. Ex-King Farouk of Egypt, the most famous habitué of the world's top luxury stomping grounds, couldn't have lived it up more exuberantly.

In 1951 Cannes, Nice, and Monte Carlo had once again taken on the cloak of benign grace, whose presence rendered mutual politeness as mandatory as the donning of evening clothes after 6 P.M. Hence, if one happened to contact one's attempted assassin, custom requires the greeting be courteous. So a veneer of charm and civility was very much existent at my final meeting with Freddie in the casino at Cannes. Although I'm sure his dislike for me was as great as ever, his smile was winning as he said: "Charles, I don't think you've ever been aboard my yacht. Too bad. I'll arrange a little dinner party. I'm sure you'll enjoy it."

I probably would have, but it wasn't to be. Not that I feared being slipped a Mickey—unlikely with other guests present. But my return to

Hollywood was imminent. A pity! It's known that Freddie's schooner parties were fun, with kilted bagpipers parading the deck. Perhaps they should have piped the Scottish lament "The Flowers of the Forest," because only a few short months later Freddie died under circumstances that he would never have dreamed possible.

Charles Higham relates the details of Freddie's death. At the end of October 1951, Freddie sailed from Nice to Morocco to smuggle a cargo of drugs. The crew mutinied and Freddie was stabbed; but with the help of a partner in crime, he survived a superficial wound and fought off the crew. At that moment a freak storm blew in, causing the yacht to heel over violently, in danger of capsizing. The engine room exploded, and the ship drifted dangerously before the gale. Freddie abandoned ship with his third wife—a lovely Paris model, Claude Stephanie—and swam for shore through the heavy surf. He made it to the Moroccan shore, but she was several yards behind, going under, exhausted.

Higham concludes his account with: "Now Freddie took the one decent action of his life. He dove back to rescue his wife. But he, too, was exhausted. . . . A moment later, locked in Claude's arms, he was carried away into the sea." Even Errol Flynn relates in his autobiography that this was the one unselfish act of Freddie's life.

A romantic vision! But not the version I was told when I inquired shortly after the fact. Freddie died attempting a rescue not of his beloved wife, but of her extravagantly expensive jewels sinking in the churning Mediterranean. McEvoy drowned for greed! A perfect demise, so happily foretold by Clarence's dream in *Richard III*:

> CLARENCE: Lord, Lord! Methought, what pain it was to drown! . . .
> Inestimable stones, unvalued jewels,
> All scattered in the bottom of the sea:
> Some lay in dead men's skulls; and in those holes
> Where eyes did once inhabit, there were crept,
> As 'twere in scorn of eyes, reflecting gems,
> Which woo'd the slimy bottom of the deep,
> And mock'd the dead bones that lay scattered by.
> (act 1, scene 4)

The suave villain is a favorite character written into many of my plays and films. Most notable were Prince Nichola in *The Last Hour* and Stephen

Fisher, the Herbert Marshall character in *Foreign Correspondent.* In the late 1950s I pleased myself writing a comedic play about a Freddie McEvoy character on the French Riviera. *The Unspeakables* (1959, not produced) tells the story of the "international white trash," gamblers and gigolos who lived by seducing heiresses and smuggling. They sold charm and grace for title and social position, living by such ethics as: never steal from anybody who can't afford it; never embarrass anybody except your equals; be kind to animals, and civil to your wife.

*The Unspeakables* represents the pinnacle of my social and political cynicism. But as entertaining as the play was for me to write, it did not sell. About five years later, a Riviera-based, gigolo-themed comedy, *Bedtime Story* (1964), was released, starring Marlon Brando, David Niven, and Shirley Jones—and more recently I've heard of *Dirty Rotten Scoundrels* (1988). But neither of these resembles my play.

# 12

# Unto the Breach

June 1944, 10:30 A.M., King's Cross Railway Station: arriving from Edinburgh, and greeted with as warm a welcome as any expatriate could *not* wish for!

Carrying two suitcases, I strode proudly out under the terminus's impressive front portals just as a buzz bomb hit and exploded across the station's entire front square, annihilating the Regent Theatre and much around it. I had personal feelings about the Regent, having played there in *Blackmail* late in 1928. This was where Nigel Playfair presented an unforgettable production of *The Immortal Hour,* and where once I had seen John Gielgud play Romeo opposite the Juliet of Gwen Ffrangcon-Davies.

The spectacle was appalling. Crowds were running this way and that, anywhere to escape the splintering aftermath of the bomb's blast. Everything was in turmoil: fire trucks screaming up, ambulances arriving, leaving the dead but gathering up the wounded.

I was quickly informed that because bombs were coming in every ten minutes or so, sometimes in barrage or volley form, London's bus transportation was, if not entirely chaotic, decidedly chancy. The good old "Tube" underground system, reaching into almost every corner of the metropolitan area, was running; but I wasn't in favor of lugging my suitcases from train to train at station change points. Luck was with me. The almost impossible happened. A cab came by, feeling its way through the litter. I grabbed it. "The Savage Club, please."

Watching warily for any newly presented V-bomb hazards, the driver was affable, almost my closest friend when he learned I had just got in from the States. He was just as eager to know what things were like over there as I was eager to acquire firsthand information of what I'd come home to.

"From America, eh?" he observed. "Must be great to be over there."

"Sure, of course, but I wanted to be over *here.*" I replied, aware that I'd been complaining of the quiet nonchalance back in Beverly Hills.

The driver appeared puzzled, but only momentarily, dismissing any bafflement with, "Well, everyone to 'is own fancy. For me, I'm partial to a bit o' peace 'n quiet."

After passing too many shattered ruins through Bloomsbury and Mayfair, my pal deposited me at the Savage Club mansion on Carlton House Terrace, which by the luck of the game was still unhurt. The cabbie and I parted affectionately. And so it was among those first hours in London that I became aware of the fantastic sense of camaraderie that exists in a city under bombardment. It was as if everybody were everybody's friend. Coming home from everybody for himself, this mutually helpful attitude was a warm revelation.

The Savage Club entrance was empty, not a soul around—and right now the tick-tick-ticking of a flying bomb was coming across the sky. You could see them approaching, crossing, each possessing a shining red light that looked even more ominous by night. Always the bombs ticked as they came over—reassuring us that while the bomb ticked it wasn't about to hurt anybody. I hesitated, deposited my suitcases to one side, then went on up the wide stairway. I hadn't forgotten the location of the bar—and sure enough, it was where I'd known it to be back in 1937, when I'd consumed a farewell drink before heading for the States. It was a very large room, and its bar counter was full. Perhaps twenty-five or thirty members were drinking—except they weren't, not a single one. All of them—most with glasses poised in their hands—were dead still, eyes alerted ceiling-ward as they listened to the tick-tick-ticking.

The bomb's engine cut out. The ticking ceased. Dead silence, everybody awaiting the explosion. A silence during which the bomb, heading north, could now change direction, possibly execute a complete turn, and then come plunging down on the area it had passed over. The blast came—perhaps a quarter of a mile away but almost deafening. The entire room shook, then settled down. The dreaded moment was over. Instantaneously, my brother Savages babbled back to life, imbibing, laughing, finishing interrupted sentences. It struck me that this wasn't so much a babble of relief as of customary acceptance. The bomb had hit; the danger had passed. A cluster of brother Savages, who at that moment might well have been dead, were still living—and making the most of it. "Cheers, Jim! What'll you have? Care for another? Same again, Ronnie?"

Then a way-back actor friend of mine named Edward "Teddy" Chapman spotted me hovering in the doorway. He gasped, "Charles Bennett! Charles, you bloody fool! You were safe in America. What the hell are you doing here?" A nice greeting, followed generally by a warm welcome. Old buddies—new ones, too—were swiftly plying me with drinks. Scotch whiskey was unavailable, but gin and bitters were plentiful. We talked of my twelve-ship convoy crossing aboard the *Sam Rich* munitions transport, and of my firing a Lewis gun at two Norwegian-based Nazi fighter-bombers above the North Sea. Presently, with a bunch of welcomers around me, I was sitting down to a reasonable lunch. My cabbie had been right; food could be found if you had funds and knew where to look.

A bedroom was available, and I stayed overnight at the club. I can't say I slept well—with nightfall those flying bombs hadn't called it a day. In his book about World War II, Winston Churchill tells us that on June 15, 1944, more than two hundred missiles came over within twenty-four hours, and over three thousand in the following five weeks.

My mind was on Maggie. We had been apart for years, and my anticipation was high. Never had the clown sung so truly . . .

> CLOWN: O mistress mine! Where are you roaming?
> O! stay and hear; your true love's coming,
> That can sing both high and low.
> Trip no further, pretty sweeting;
> Journeys end in lovers' meeting,
> Every wise man's son doth know.
> What is love? 'tis not hereafter;
> Present mirth hath present laughter;
> What's to come is still unsure.
> (*Twelfth Night*, act 2, scene 3)

Before going to bed that night I had managed to get Maggie on the phone. It wasn't easy, but patience did the trick. At that time she was stationed at an ATA field at Hamble in Hampshire, some 130 miles from London. She responded enthusiastically, said she was so happy to hear my voice, happy that I'd arrived safely, and said she would apply for a few days' immediate leave. She hoped to call me tomorrow.

She did just that and told me she would be arriving at Waterloo Station around five o'clock in the afternoon. I grabbed a suite at the Savoy Hotel that had a living room, bedroom, and wide windows overlooking the Thames. Later that afternoon I was heading for Waterloo Station—walking. As I hiked across Westminster Bridge, a bomb came over, ceased to tick, circled and plunged into the river about two hundred yards upstream. The splash was immense, although the explosion was somewhat squelched by the water.

A Cockney gentleman pushing a barrow alongside me nodded toward the aborted blast and remarked, "That fucked 'im up a bit."

Maggie's train arrived at Waterloo only about thirty minutes late. I shall never forget how dear and neat and wonderful she looked in her pilot's uniform. She was a beautiful woman, had a perfect figure, on which the ATA officer's uniform fit superbly. We had been married for fourteen years, but I was practically falling in love with her all over again. That night we repaired to the Savoy around two in the morning, where we spent nearly an hour at the living room window watching the sometime clusters of red-glowing V-bombs coming across South London and the Thames. I think we were glad to be together again. I know I was.

Maggie had been granted seven days' leave in London, and the next day she had things to do and people to see. I too had things to do, my first thought being to report to Jack Beddington at MOI headquarters. Upon my arrival, Jack lost no time in assigning me work on a piece relating to the famous El Alamein desert victory in North Africa, under the auspices of Sidney Bernstein. Jack Beddington turned out to be an entirely agreeable man, and I quickly felt that I had made a new friend.

My wardrobe trunk arrived at the London docks aboard the *Sam Rich*. For years war-torn Britain had been under the strictest ration laws with regard to clothing—perhaps only one new suit allowed per person in maybe two years. But I was about to become the best-dressed man in London. The trunk contained five almost new suits and a six-month-old tuxedo. Sad to relate, I was happy, though I should have felt guiltily ashamed. But much sadder to relate, a V-bomb hit the *Sam Rich* a day or two later. It seemed utterly tragic that a ship that had gallantly survived so many dangers at sea should have made it home to die at the dock.

Jack Beddington assigned the English playwright and Oscar-winning screenwriter William "Bill" Lipscomb to go with me into the East End dockland and garner propaganda material about the doodlebug (V1) havoc. Like me, Bill had been Hollywood-acquired, scripting *Clive of India*

(1935) and *A Tale of Two Cities* (1935) for Darryl Zanuck, and *The Garden of Allah* (1936) for David Selznick. Bill was happy to learn details of his old friends in the colony, but our assignment was pretty gruesome. Delving through a ruined block of dockworkers' homes, rescue workers came upon the decapitated head of a child. Bill and I were glad to put that afternoon behind us.

On my fifth night at the Savoy Hotel, Maggie went off to dinner with a fellow ATA officer pilot, Herbert Newmark, one of the nicest and most civilized persons who'd ever come my way. I arrived back at the Savoy around midnight. Maggie hadn't yet shown up, so I went to bed. I was still awake, listening to the tick-tick-ticking and reassuringly distant explosions of V-bombs, when the door from the living room opened and there were Herbie and Maggie, side by side *holding hands.* I was taken aback. I shouldn't have been. Word of my Hollywood capers had surely crossed the Atlantic—most particularly, details of my long and expensive frolic with a Hollywood mistress, Peggy Morrow Field ("Peitsy"). But Maggie had offered no remonstrance, no accusation; and there was none now.

Her opening words summed up everything: "Charles, I want a divorce. I'm going to marry Herbie."

Shock? Maybe, but this climax to so many years of rose gardens mingled with stinging nettles was not unexpected. There was little I could do except behave in a reasonably civilized fashion. I knew that Maggie *had* been truly happy to see me again and our deep affection for each other remained a fact of life until Maggie's death put *finis* to a romance that had never quite died. I slipped on a robe and used the house phone to order Champagne—a lot of it. Maggie, Herbie, and I sat up together in the living room for at least three hours, wishing each other luck and love . . . and that was that. "Laugh, Punchinello!"

In the morning Maggie went back to her job flying Spitfires and Tornados at Hamble. But before kissing me a now sisterly au revoir, she gave me the key to her one-room apartment in the vicinity of Gloucester Place, inviting me to use it until I could find some place to deposit myself.

Strangely, the happenings of those twenty-four hours weren't over. The next afternoon I dropped into the Savage Club to pick up my mail and was confronted with a second shock—this time, not unpleasant. There was a letter from Peitsy that came as directly to the point as had the Maggie-Herbie announcement of hours earlier. Peitsy said that, as deep and everlasting was her affection for me, she had fallen in love—"please, Charles, don't be too upset"—with the actor Louis Hayward, and she was going to marry him. Stating it baldly, I admit to having been vastly relieved. Her letter made no mention of the $10,000 settlement I had already made on her when leaving Beverly Hills. Possibly she was employing it as a dowry, not that Louis needed her money.

I liked Louis Hayward—a pleasant, somewhat minor film star. Bizarrely, it was only at Louis's death in 1985 that I sustained another shock. I became aware that I had kept a lady pinnacled as an upper-crust member of Los Angeles society. The *Los Angeles Times* obituary column listed his ex-wives, naturally blazoning Ida Lupino, but topping even Ida was Peitsy—the *socialite* Margaret "Peggy" Morrow Field.

This word is approached with deep respect by Los Angeles columnists, since it signifies birth, background, and, above all, old Los Angeles money. Indeed, even top film stars can't be mentioned in the same breath. Perhaps I should have been proud that a product of Chelsea's perpetually impoverished artists' colony had actually provided for a top-notch *socialite*. I might have derived a kick out of patting myself on the back and counting my "achievements." Not so. My mind didn't work that way. I am still inclined to view good or bad fortune simply as the way things happen.

The following morning I pulled out of the Savoy and worked my way to Maggie's pied-à-terre. I sidled past what was left of the front door and stumbled through interior ruins, ascended crumbling stairs, and found Maggie's room in the surprisingly livable rear of the onetime mansion. Settled in for the night, my perspective was requiring readjustment. To quote Cole Porter, here I was, "all alone in this big city," and I wasn't happy about it. I knew that the MOI would keep me busy, but these other elements had come faster than had seemed probable. Maggie, whom I had never ceased to love, had gone with the wind—in which she would be devoting so much of her future. And Peitsy, who had become little more than an expensive nuisance, was finding new fields to conquer.

I was bedding down in the room of my soon-to-be ex-wife, and, modern attitudes notwithstanding, there are limits. I was aware that I had to find sleeping quarters of my own. But where? In 1940 whole areas of London had been blitzed almost beyond recognition. Hundreds of hotels, apartment houses, and homes had been wiped out. Newly bombed-out citizens were everywhere. So where was an intruder from the comforts of Beverly Hills to find a resting place?

During our stay at the Savoy Hotel, I had not visited my beloved haunt, the Savoy Grill Room—an error corrected that evening. The Grill hadn't changed during my seven-year absence. I was told it had twice lost its windows, but it certainly hadn't lost its luster or its bevy of famous patrons. The always graceful maître d'hôtel Manetta expressed pleasure at my return to London and ushered me to my favorite old table—his memory equal to his charm. I hadn't been seated five minutes when John Gielgud stopped by to say hello. I'd first met John in 1927, when we'd appeared together in *Othello* at the Apollo Theatre. But we'd become better acquainted eight years later when he'd starred in my Hitchcock film *The Secret Agent.*

John wasn't the only old friend to greet me. Henry "Harry" Kendall and Gladys Cooper waved from across the room; and welcoming me home warmly was Hitch's *Lodger,* Ivor Novello, whom I had met in 1935 when Maggie starred in his play *Party.* I wonder how many people today remember that in 1915 this very young Royal Naval Air Service fighter pilot wrote one of the very greatest songs of the Great War, "Keep the Home Fires Burning," an air that shatters me on the rare occasions that I hear it. Nostalgia? Either that or memories of 1918 and the teenagers who never came home to a fire kept burning for them.

Ivor explained that he, and others of the supper crowd, would not be leaving the Savoy when the Grill shut shop because many were sleeping guests of the hotel itself. Not above, as Maggie and I had been, but way below. After grub, many patrons—theater people like Alfred and Lynn Lunt, then at the Aldwych in *There Shall Be No Night,* descended into the hotel's cavernous cellars to sleep through the night's bombings and reemerge on the morrow.

I have sometimes wondered if I was born under a lucky star. I was ordering dinner when twenty-four-year-old James "Jimmy" Woolf sauntered in. Jimmy was the younger son of C. M. Woolf, the chairman, managing director, and proprietor of General Film Distributors (GFD), who had nearly scuttled my *Man Who Knew Too Much* and *39 Steps.*

I had first met Jimmy in June 1937, soon after Maggie's and my arrival in Hollywood. After staying at the Château Elysée, we were comfortably ensconced in a Mexican-style bungalow court called La Ronda, just around the corner from the now sadly deceased Garden of Allah and that cradle of starlets, Schwab's Drug Store. Jimmy Woolf, residing across the cactus-adorned patio, was a likable, somewhat oversophisticated youth of seventeen, the possessor of an unshakably languid manner and a lazy but not unattractive drawl. We were soon on visiting terms, bungalow-to-bungalow, and our early acquaintanceship developed into a lifelong friendship—his life, not mine. As I have too many other old friends, I've outlasted Jimmy by more years than I care to count. But 1937 . . .

The all-powerful C. M. Woolf owned 50 percent of Hollywood's Universal Pictures, almost as a plaything, and he sent Jimmy to Universal to study Hollywood's know-how. Jimmy was in immense demand at every top film industry party from Hollywood to Bel Air. Strangely, it seemed that Jimmy could not have cared less. The average teenager would have been thrilled at shaking paws with such living legends as Louis B. Mayer and Groucho Marx. Not so Jimmy. The seventeen-year-old would come up with any excuse, however lame, to avoid the social whirl.

Jimmy was one of the most observant people who has ever come my way. I'd swear the youth had an almost uncanny ability to read minds, which gave him an unfair advantage when it came to the rest of us. This gift paid off fifteen years later when he and brother, John, created Romulus Films and Remus Films. It was Jimmy's perception regarding an audience's likes and dislikes that pointed his way to such box-office bonanzas as *Moulin Rouge, Room at the Top,* and *The African Queen.*

I haven't forgotten one Sunday morning in June 1937. Eyes glowing, Jimmy came across to our bungalow, a copy of the *Los Angeles Examiner* in hand. In those early days Hearst's always devoutly pious Sunday edition of the *Examiner* devoted its entire front page to classified ads. I don't think either Hearst or his editor was particularly interested in their nature so long as the money rolled in. Jimmy had spotted a mid-page item and was intrigued. It read:

Lonely Tonight? Don't Be. The Best in the West.
Just Call—[Telephone Number] and a Lovely Lady
Will Be Your Companion within Minutes.

Jimmy couldn't wait. He called from my phone and drawled, "Hello! Good morning! I'm interested in your best in the west advert. I'd like to ask, would some nice young lady care to have dinner with me this evening?"

The reply—a woman—was enthusiastic. "Of course! Name and address, please."

But Jimmy had other things to ask, foremost being, "How much?"

The answer was ten dollars an hour.

Jimmy's drawl was more markedly lazy than ever. "Nice . . . except one last question. If I take the young lady to bed, is that inclusive?"

Apparently Jimmy sensed shock over the line. Of course he was talking to a madam, but when it comes to prostitution, rules of etiquette are observed.

The reply came back abruptly. "That, sir, must be between you and the lady. None of my business."

Jimmy accepted the downright lie, drawled, "Thank you for your courtesy," and hung up, without leaving name or address.

Dear Jimmy. I'm glad I was fortunate enough to have known him. He died of a heart attack, perhaps twenty-five years ago (1966) at the Beverly Hills Hotel. He'd gone to bed and was reading *The Valley of the Dolls*. Maybe the thought of grabbing its film rights and coming up with another hit movie excited him to the extent of his taking off for another valley, happier I hope, than that of the dolls.

But back to 1944 and the Savoy Grill: languidly casual as ever, he glanced around, spotted me, and strolled over. It had been seven years since our days at La Ronda, but he'd changed little and I was happy to hear that drawl again. We had supper together, for which Jimmy paid. Jimmy asked where I was staying. A good question—I told him that as of tomorrow or the next day, depending on how long my conscience would allow me to take advantage of Maggie's generosity, I would be resembling a stray dog looking for a home but unlikely to find one.

Jimmy nodded understandingly and drawled, lazily but speculatively, "Charles, are you afraid of these bombs?" I gave the matter a moment's thought, decided I wasn't, and said as much. Jimmy looked gratified. "Good. My aunt's scared stiff of 'em. She's getting out of town tomorrow— going down to Somerset. You can have her flat."

Luck! I couldn't believe my ears. In a devastated city where apartments were nonexistent, I was being offered one on a silver platter—or at least on a supper dish. I asked incredulously, "You sure of this, Jimmy?"

"Why wouldn't I be—my own aunt? The flat's in Dorset House at the top of Baker Street. I've a flat there on the fifth floor. My aunt's on the ninth; only two stories below the roof and that's the trouble. If a bomb hits Dorset House, the ninth floor will be history. But, Charles, do you want it?"

Did I want it? Ninth floor. Why would I care? Ever since the trenches of World War I, I'd been a believer in the Cockney soldier's phrase "If a bullet 'as yer nyme on it, chum, dodge or not, it'll find yer." The same philosophy applied to buzz bombs—just substitute doodlebug for bullet.

I repeat: I believed I bore a charmed life. It never occurred to me to seek refuge when sirens were wailing. I found the descending bombs more interesting than alarming. So I moved into Dorset House. The small but comfortable flat was all I needed—and as to being so high up, maybe I was feeling that should a bomb hit, I would be nearer to heaven than hell. Thanks to Jimmy Woolf, I'd found a home and was content.

Jimmy's fifth-floor apartment had a private bar. Writing up on the ninth, it was nice to descend for a refresher when a break from the job seemed desirable. As to Jimmy's job, it took some time to figure out what he was actually up to. On some days he would be wearing a Royal Air Force uniform, but he didn't seem to be attached to any wing or unit. I presently fathomed that his stint was to round up performers for Royal Air Force concerts, a job for which C. M. Woolf's son was peculiarly suitable. His aptitude for dropping into the Savoy Grill for supper, or the Milroy Club for an after-hours drink, put him where the stars would most likely be twinkling. Jimmy, with his winning drawl, could probably line up a Beatrice Lillie or a Douglas Byng over a couple of brandies. Thus, he was providing tip-top entertainment for young RAF pilots who, living night to night through the flak of Germany, could surely use a laugh or a song or two during periods of respite.

An endearing side of his nature was his delight at passing along happiness to others. Almost immediately after my taking his aunt's flat, he decided that my stay in England would be more comfortable with a nice young lady friend—not a live-in companion, but somebody warm, responsive, and available should an attack of loneliness overwhelm me.

Curiously, looking back over a long lifetime, I can't remember ever feeling truly lonely. When I'm on my own, I am happy to write. Call it an obsession or hobby—at least it prevents me from craving companionship. This may be a blessing or an anomaly; and maybe because of it, I've missed a lot. But much as I enjoy other people's society, I've always been content to get back to the solitude of my desk.

Never mind. Jimmy Woolf's thoughts were kindly ones, and within days of my move into Dorset House he brought a delectable young maiden to my apartment for an introductory drink. After bestowing beneficent rites on us, he withdrew gracefully, leaving us to enjoy each other's company. Anne—that's as far as I'll go with her name—was intelligent, amusing, and sweetly reciprocal. According to Jimmy, she wasn't a bad young actress, and I pray that she achieved a successful future. In any case, she moved into my leisure life for about five weeks, never refusing a supper date at the Savoy Grill, and always happy to come back to Dorset House for an affectionate nightcap. Our relationship broke up because, aware that I would shortly be heading for a quiet divorce, the dear girl suggested it might be nice if we could share a wedded future.

I remember her saying, "I'm sure Maggie won't mind"—which was a generous attitude toward a shortly-to-be-dispensed-with wife.

Not being exactly on the lookout for a bride-to-be, I was afraid dear Anne's vision of our future together signaled "Nuff!"—"*Finis!*" Our parting was affectionate and amicable.

Jimmy would come up with other pleasant diversions. He loved poker and made a point of throwing a weekly poker game in his flat. The players, mostly theater people, were usually old friends. Rex Harrison had an irritating habit of winning. And among the regulars were the wonderful actress-comedienne Isabel Jeans, Roland Culver, Heather Thatcher, and— on Sunday evenings, when the Ambassadors Theatre was closed—Henry (Harry) Kendall, the star actor-comedian of those lovely wartime revues *Sweet and Low, Sweeter and Lower,* and, ultimately, *Sweetest and Lowest.* The games were congenial, as we ignored the explosions of doodlebugs. But the stakes were higher than normal—in a city where any old moment could mean curtains, money seemed to have lost its importance. Also, none of us was exactly on the breadline. For me, the poker games served as a relaxation from a sometimes lengthy term at the typewriter.

Anyway, what with an apartment and a purloined typewriter, I was sitting pretty; and the assignments that Jack Beddington came up with kept me happy. Forget Hollywood! Let Errol Flynn continue to save the world by chasing the Japanese off a make-believe Burma Road, or bombing an equally make-believe Tokyo. Things were *really* happening in Europe— such as British and American troops fighting Nazis in northern France while London continued to smile off the grapes of wrath.

Deservedly or no, I was smiling too. My life was proceeding smoothly, often enjoyably. When not out of town on a Ministry job, I'd spend the day writing and, in the evenings, often as not, I'd hie me to the Savoy Grill and, if in warm company, on to the dusk-to-dawn bottle-party club, the Milroy. This was the only all-night spot in London, and its rules were entirely its own. It was run by Johnny Mills (not Sir John, the actor) in partnership with the popular dance bandleader Harry Roy. Roy's band would play from around ten in the evening till daybreak while night owls would eat, drink, and be merry.

By British liquor law, the enterprise was illegal—except for a neat piece of circumvention. In return for very nearly a king's ransom, members would purchase a bottle or so of liquor, which became the personal property of the purchaser. No known law stipulated that folk couldn't partake of their own liquor at any place or at any hour of the day or night. The result: "Skål!" Drink, love, and laugh! And if a bottle or two were left unfinished in the small hours—or around dawn, when even the most hardened revelers would call it a night—the bottle or bottles would be labeled with the member's name and stowed away until the next visit. The shenanigans worked. The club ran as though on oiled castors. The waiters were solicitous. The food was excellent. Scotch whiskey and champagne flowed like the Niagara River rapids. Nero fiddled while Rome burned; and if there was death outside in darkest London, within the warmth and brilliance of the Milroy there was food, drink, and dancing.

I spent many enjoyable hours there and never felt blameworthy. The majority of Milroy patrons were folks for whom the war represented a pretty full-time job—well-known war ministers and military and naval types footing it neatly to "Lili Marlene," and American uniforms mingling gratifyingly with those of Britain and Free France. As London went through an all-time low in its bloodstained history, the Milroy came up with well-deserved but hard-to-find amusement, granting hours of blessed relief to those desperately in need. Sad to relate, a fat wallet was key to its comforts; but solace for some and tough going for others will always be a way of the world. Looking back over fifty years, I feel that the Milroy served a useful purpose—a shining light in requisite darkness.

When visiting London these days, a not-infrequent occurrence even in my dotage, I am happy to find myself still an honorary member of its successor club, Les Ambassadeurs. Into my nineties, I have acquired a bad habit of outliving people I've known and liked. But there's little I can do about it, and I'm bound to catch up with departed friends like Johnny Mills and Harry Roy. But never mind. I'm now writing about 1944, the continuing war, and my work for the British Ministry of Information.

৸ ৸ ৸

## Interlude: The Problem of the Purloined Portable

Soon after my arrival in Britain, I was faced with a dilemma. I should have known that typewriters would be on the unavailability list. I should also have realized that instruments at the MOI offices, heavy with official use, would be equally unavailable. I hadn't had the forethought to bring a portable from California; so here I was, in need of a typewriter infinitely more than a mistress—and this time Jimmy Woolf couldn't be a provider.

But once again Lady Luck was at my shoulder. Drinking with a brother Savage, I was grousing about the problem of being a writer minus a major tool of his trade. My companion was sympathetic but unhelpful, and the conversation drifted off to other subjects. But it was interrupted by the voice of everybody's-friend-bartender, John. He was replacing a behind-the-bar telephone as he said, "Couldn't help overhearing what you was saying, Mr. Bennett. I took it upon myself to check with a pal o' mine; just hung up. You want a typewriter. You can have one tomorrow."

My ears pricked up. There could be no trouble, he explained. Simply go to a basement drinking-club in Regent Street at precisely four o'clock tomorrow afternoon. The door would be locked. Tap sharply on it twice, then three times more slowly. He gave me the street number and told me exactly how to proceed. I was to go to the bar counter and order a dry martini—very dry. Apparently "very dry" were the key words, because a uniformed sailor would join me at the bar and pass me a package that would contain a Remington portable typewriter. In return, I was to pass the sailor twenty-five pounds in cash, no questions asked.

I knew this was skullduggery. I would be receiving stolen goods, property of the Royal Navy. And though this should have filled me with shame, I grabbed at it—not in the sense of *pillage* but in the category of *fortunately appropriated.* The sailor would march off with ill-gotten gains and dear John would undoubtedly receive a percentage of the overt transaction. But the Remington was a vital necessity, and I was telling myself that it would be serving our country—via the MOI rather than the Royal Navy. So, next day, I ordered a dry martini—"very dry."

A sailor emerged out of the woodwork and planted a brown-paper package on the counter. The dialogue was crisp: "Mr. Bennett. Sir?"

"Right."

The naval gentleman tapped the package. "You're wanting this 'ere. Twenty-five quid."

The cash was passed. The sailor departed. I bought another martini, not so dry this time, shared a drink with the bartender, then headed back to Dorset House and found the Remington to be all I'd hoped for.

I went home to my Dorset House flat at the top of Baker Street. But Sherlock Holmes was *not* around to point an aquiline finger and say, "Elementary, my dear Watson. *He* did it!"

# 13

# A Foreign Correspondent

During my first month in England, I stayed a short weekend with my old friend Sholto Douglas, commander in chief of Coastal Command. I had known Sholto since 1932. He and his dear wife, Joan, had the apartment above Maggie and me at 4 West Halkin Street, and the four of us became immediate friends—a friendship that was to last for around four decades. Upon learning that I was back in London, he took the first available opportunity to invite me to his residence adjoining Coastal Command Headquarters. Both Sholto and Joan were wonderful hosts. And they were still keeping in touch with Maggie; Sholto was very proud of her flying prowess with the Air Transport Auxiliary.

The most exciting point was when Sholto took me down into Coastal Command's vast underground operations room. To say that I was overwhelmed by the efficiency of this undertaking, not to speak of the spectacle, would be an understatement. On one side of this vast chamber were boxlike cubicles in which sat important air force officers and their assistants. Facing them was a perhaps 150-foot-wide wall map of the command's extent. It was a huge section of the world displayed like a mural, not only the shores of the British Isles, but almost the entire North Atlantic, stretching south to the Caribbean and north beyond the shores of Newfoundland. Swarming over the great map on ladders were young members of the Women's Royal Air Force (WRAF), planting flags or markers to indicate the latest known positions of Atlantic convoys, Nazi wolf packs, and the like, for Coastal Command to strategize.

As Sholto and I emerged from the deeply descending elevator and came into this vast room, he stopped beside a box where an air commodore appeared to be in charge of the evening's observations.

Sholto asked, "Everything in order?"

The answer was crisp: "Moving along, sir. No complaints."

Sholto glanced across to where three WRAFs were planting markers off the southern tip of Greenland. He asked entirely casually, "Cape Farewell?"

"No change since my last report, sir. There are two down below, but our frigates have 'em marked and are working at it. They won't get away."

"Keep me informed," said Sholto.

As we ascended into a peaceful evening where sheep were actually grazing in the fields, I was conscious of a shiver down my spine. "They won't get away," the air commodore had said; and I was conjuring up the thought of ordinary, decent young German sailors, obeying the wretched Hitler's dictates and, possibly at that very moment, being blown into deep-sea oblivion by dropped depth charges.

I didn't like it, but Sholto was completely unperturbed. Destroy a hundred or so Germans? All in a day's or a night's work. Meanwhile, "Cocktail hour, Charles. Dry martini?"

Over dinner I told Sholto and Joan about my convoy crossing. Sholto took it all for granted, his attitude being, "Lucky you got through."

He added, "There was little I could have done to help you. The bulk of my aircraft were staging for the Normandy beach landings."

I was glad I hadn't known this when Nazi planes were approaching the *Sam Rich* over the North Sea. Coastal Command's job was to provide convoys with air protection; but the herding home of just twelve ships down the coast of Scotland meant nothing compared to the success of the invasion of Nazi-held Europe.

But what fascinated me was Sholto's interest in my recent Lewis gun experiences. Sholto in his early twenties had been one of the most highly decorated fighter pilots in the RAF—Military Cross, Distinguished Flying Cross, Croix de Guerre. Yet even on previous occasions he had expressed pride in the fact that I had been decorated in World War I. At a cocktail party I remember him presenting me to friends with the remark "Young Charles was awarded the Military Medal for Bravery in 1918—aged just eighteen." All of which means that Sholto was a generous man.

Anyway, I do want to put on record how grateful I am for the memory of the now dead Sholto, who granted me at least a fleeting glimpse of real war on its grandest scale. Thanks to Sholto, I was lucky enough, for a weekend, to be in touch with the true machinery of conflict at its most deadly. How many of us on this earth have been that fortunate?

Upon my return to London, I was again on the sidelines. Yet the sidelines could also be a vital part of the machinery of war. And Jack Beddington showed no inclination to have me spend my return to England whooping it up at the Savoy Grill or the Milroy. There were jobs to be done, although the rationale behind some of them seemed a little obscure. But the MOI figured that I possessed a certain ability to put words together, and words are important when writing propaganda.

I was sent down to Cornwall for a day or two on behalf of the MOI. Looking toward St. Michael's Mount, I saw the vastest aircraft carrier imaginable beating by. Its size almost dwarfed the island, but it was a reassuring sight, particularly as, when I returned to London a day or two later, buzz bombs were coming over every few minutes or less.

I went to Devon with an MOI introduction to Viscount and Viscountess Astor—both enigmas when it came to British high society, as both were born in the United States. Lord Astor (Waldorf Astor) was the son of William Waldorf Astor, one of the world's wealthiest Americans, who became a naturalized British citizen in 1899, and then became 1st Viscount Astor in 1917. His son (the 2nd Viscount) was educated at Eton and New College, Oxford, then made his own mark in England by breeding racehorses, as proprietor of the great London newspaper the *Observer,* and then as a member of Parliament for the Sutton (dockland) Division of Plymouth. I found him a gracefully charming individual.

Inheriting his father's title and thus moving up into the House of Lords, Waldorf Astor had to relinquish his parliamentary representation of Plymouth, but Nancy Astor was promptly voted MP in his place. A Virginian debutante, Lady Astor was surely one of the most interesting characters of this century. Nancy was adored in Plymouth, in fact adored in Britain generally, and not without reason. Apart from becoming the very first woman elected as a member of Britain's Parliament, she spent a great deal of her busy career working for and succeeding in establishing innumerable women's rights.

I fell for her genuine charm and personality. From the first handshake, I found her exciting, forceful, a live wire; and she seemed to receive me with genuine pleasure. After a congenial lunch at the Astors' attractive and fortunately unbombed home, Nancy escorted me, entirely on foot, around the ruins of the fine old city. I had known Plymouth when the little Bennett family, unpleasantly broke, had spent much of 1910 there, but in 1944 I was viewing a very different town. Blood-curdling. The destruction was horrible. Whole streets were gone, among them the one in which we had semi-existed.

Nancy Astor wasn't content with displaying ruins. She reintroduced me to lovely Plymouth Hoe, the great parkland area overlooking the famous harbor from which Sir Francis Drake had sailed with his small but gallant fleet to defeat the vast Spanish Armada in 1588. Nancy—I can't help calling her Nancy because that's who she was to me—even insisted on taking me down to the ancient wharf from which the Pilgrim Fathers had sailed for the New World on September 6, 1620. Perhaps she was rightfully proud of her Plymouth constituency's association with the land of her birth.

She even suggested that when things settled down a bit—the war and its inconveniences—I might care to visit her at Cliveden, the Astors' famous estate, where everybody from Winston Churchill to Joachim von Ribbentrop had been frequent weekenders. The Astors can be forgiven for hosting von Ribbentrop. At that time he was the German ambassador to Great Britain; and nobody—Nancy Astor least of all—could have foreseen that within a bare three years this monster would be the architect of the Hitler-Stalin pact that made World War II possible.

Sadly, I never got around to accepting what I knew was a genuine invitation. Too late now. I should have grabbed it when I was back in London in 1947–48. I didn't; and since I'm not a multimillionaire, my chance of staying at Cliveden has now faded into the might-have-been. Anyway, Nancy Astor was unforgettable.

A day after leaving Plymouth, I was joined on another foray by Bill Lipscomb. Jack Beddington decided we should get a glimpse of a Welsh coal mine in wartime. Somewhere amid the rugged peaks and slagheaps of Glamorganshire, we came on the mineshaft and were received royally. We boarded a huge elevator, which in no time plunged us down more than a mile into a world as bewildering as it was unexpected.

Back in 1923 our repertory company actors were invited to visit local industries, such as the Shelton Iron Works at Etruria, Staffordshire, but nobody invited any of us to descend into the pit. So my visit to that mine in South Wales was a new experience. I suppose I'd conjured up visions of grimy tunnels, narrow and low to the point of enforced stooping and crouching, a warren inhabited by coal dust–besmirched mine workers. But what Bill and I saw below the mountains was a revelation.

We were confronted with a spectacle as welcoming as the foyer of

London's Dorchester Hotel. The tunnels were as airy, spacious, and brightly lit as any London tube station; the area facing the elevators compared well with the below-street Piccadilly Circus. It had been breathlessly hot a mile above, but Bill and I had descended into a climate such as one longs for on a humid summer's day. Our greeters were bright-faced, nattily attired officials, any one of whom might have taken a shower only minutes back. The welcome was hospitable; I remember thinking that if the gates of hell should be as inviting as this, I'd have no cause for complaint—at least initially.

Our initial bedazzlement wasn't to last. Coal mines are coal mines, and the real job was scooping out the product that could keep a country rolling, particularly in wartime. There were railroad tracks and coal-carrying freight trains running this way and that. So Bill and I, arrayed in overalls to protect us from the coal dust, boarded one of the trains and started on our way. Innumerable side tracks ran off in various directions, leading perhaps toward scary labyrinths such as those Jules Verne wrote about in his *Journey to the Center of the Earth*.

As our wide, well-lit tunnel narrowed, the electric lighting and airiness continued—but not my sense of comfort. Presently the train reached the point at which tracks and trains could proceed no farther, seemingly the raison d'être for the mine's existence. The tunnel was becoming a burrow gouged out of rock, and soon Bill and I were almost crawling our way forward. After what seemed to be infinite minutes of ferreting, we emerged into the area before the actual coal face.

We were in a long, rock-roofed gallery no more than six feet from floor to ceiling, and there were the miners, chipping away at the coal face. Nobody looked at Bill or me as we crawled in. The gentlemen, mainly in their fifties, were too busy at their job. Chip, chip, chip: transferring the fruits of their efforts to shovels thrust through shafts toward trains waiting to convey the cargo to that brilliant world at the foot of the elevators.

There was an arresting angle to our exploratory journey, nothing to do with the grizzly-looking miners who had spent at least a third of their lives down there. Working alongside the old-timers was a completely new generation of coal-face chippers, boys—well almost. Eighteen- or nineteen-year-olds deep in the bowels of the earth. I had read the book and seen the film *How Green Was My Valley*. I think I knew that being a coal miner was an inherited profession, passed from father to son. But these bright-looking coal-face chippers didn't look like the descendants of generations. Most of them looked more like youthful products of my childhood in Chelsea. I wondered—but not for long.

Back amid the luminosity fronting the elevators, a smartly dressed young assistant manager explained the phenomenon. They were teenagers certainly, assiduously doing the same job as men three times their age, but only because they had objected to becoming a part of an army whose job it was to kill. So rather than shooting a rifle, these conscientious objectors chose to spend many hours, day or night, extracting coal from a rock face instead of extracting life from a German or an idolizer of Mussolini. It never crossed my mind that these young men were cowards, and I never harbored resentment. In fact, my mind may have been tinged with admiration. Obviously, they were brave enough to stand up for their convictions. But personally, although I possessed no nostalgic love for the life I'd survived in the trenches of World War I, I knew that, had I been eighteen again, I would have preferred daylight and danger over conscientious self-condemnation to the pits.

Shortly after our return to London from southern Wales, Bill and I left again on an MOI assignment to badly battered Dover. The Normandy landings had taken place, but with the outcome of our invasion still in the balance, almost the entire north coast of France remained in Nazi hands. Dover—only twenty-one miles across the English Channel from the Pas de Calais—had been since 1940 under direct artillery bombardment. It represented the epitome of England's defense against Continental encroachment—the actual front line against the Nazi enemy.

With a sea frontage of barely half a mile, the town nestles into a quilt-like down that is narrowly protected on either side by those steep white cliffs. We were led through the town, past defenses strong enough to have repelled any immediate enemy landing. But the most exciting revelation was burrowed into the deep bowels of the white cliffs themselves—and I'm not writing about gun emplacements, which were rightly taboo even to the MOI. What excited Bill and me were the emergency hospital facilities hidden deep in the cliffs: wards, emergency operating rooms, everything needful in the event of a truly devastating attack.

At last, standing at England's front line, I felt I had achieved what I had hoped for since 1939. As I gazed toward France from the loom of Shakespeare's Cliff, I recalled Gloucester's sentiment from *King Lear*:

GLOUCESTER: There is a cliff, whose high and bending head
    Looks fearfully in the confined deep:
    Bring me but to the very brim of it,
    And I'll repair the misery thou dost bear
    With something rich about me: from that place
    I shall no leading need.
(act 4, scene 1)

Bill and I were expected to know what the great American public would listen to, with respect to propaganda. But in my heart I had the feeling that few folk in Beverly Hills and environs were a bloody bit interested in what was going on down a British coal mine, or what Nazi bombers had done to Coventry Cathedral.

Chasen's, Romanoff's, the Mocambo, and Ciro's were still flourishing. Japan hadn't invaded the West Coast, and the war had drifted across the Pacific to unheard-of places such as Sumatra and the Malay States. Any tidbits passed along by William Lipscomb or Charles Bennett would be swiftly forgotten over a cocktail at La Rue. Beverly Hills, however, wasn't the keystone of what was left of the "Free World," and the MOI, with its reports stretching across the globe, was not to be ignored.

So Bill and I could still hope to perform jobs that might carry some importance. During the ensuing ten months, I wrote at least eight films, and all but one was aimed at the Continent. My first was to be narrated in Italian, designed to convince those defeated peoples what gangsters they were allied with. Then I wrote a script for the Greeks demonstrating how England kept its promise to aid them against Italian and German aggressors. I wrote two films aimed at France, and one at Holland, along with a couple of documentary films about British mines and shipping on the Tyne. My final assignment for MOI was a film lecturing the British people on the importance of voting. It was released just before the elections, and I was unprepared for the labor landslide that followed.

Neither was I prepared for the opportunities thrown my way. When the English film industry cottoned on that I was back in London, assignments, offers, and the like started coming in fast. I adamantly turned my head the other way. I wasn't looking for money; but I was planning for after the war, and being only forty-five years of age, I certainly felt I had not yet reached my peak.

Adamantly turned my head? Well, that's not strictly true. There were a couple of exceptions. The American producer Edward Small sent me fifteen thousand dollars to write a first screenplay of *Lorna Doone*. And I received permission from the Ministry to write *The Trial of Madeleine Smith* for Laurence Olivier and Vivien Leigh. Two Cities Films, a leading production unit of the Rank Organisation, paid me about four thousand pounds for the script. These payments were very welcome because I was working for nothing but expenses at the Ministry.

My screenplay was about a seventeen-year-old Madeleine Smith, charged with murder and acquitted in 1857. I was contracted to direct the picture, which made me very happy, because I loved my screenplay. Laurence Olivier was to produce, and his wife, Vivien Leigh, would play the young Scottish suspect.

Over a sparse, war-rationed lunch at the Garrick Club, Larry talked to me of his admiration and gratitude to Filippo Del Giudice, head of Two Cities Films. He said Del Giudice had given him carte blanche to make films and deliver messages so necessary during those desperate war years. Take *Henry V*—Larry was the star, director, and producer. Del Giudice was head of the production company, the studio, the money.

I had first met Laurence Olivier in 1927 at London's recently formed Arts Theatre Club. I'd describe the Larry of those days as shy, diffident, retiring, and not easy to know. But neither was he easy to forget. So when I met him again, he was by this time a famous actor, director, and personality. In a way, the reunion was a shock. The shy young man of 1927 had become an entirely self-possessed individual with a mind that, unlike those of most producers of my working acquaintance, could leap ahead of a writer's thought with gratifying swiftness. I soon found that talking with the matured Larry was an intellectual and creative delight. Yet behind Larry's not infrequent flashes of brilliance, I still sensed that same retiring diffidence. That barrier that had once seemed to be shyness might now be construed as aloofness. But it wasn't aloofness. Under Larry's exterior, one finds a man who takes a quiet delight in friendship and in increasing the enjoyment of other people. This became clear to me over the next few weeks.

During the Blitz the question of morale was all-important, and the job of artists was to entertain and help buoy the national spirit. When I went to Glasgow on MOI business, coincidentally Larry was there, playing through a repertoire at the King's Theatre. Since Glasgow was Madeleine Smith's city, we took advantage of the lucky coincidence. Larry performed in the evenings, but in the daytime we put in many usefully exploratory hours. Joined by the novelist Compton "Monty" Mackenzie, we delved into the secrets of the still-standing Smith residence, where through a small sidewalk-level window Madeleine allegedly passed cups of hot cocoa—well laced with arsenic—to her young lover, Pierre Emile l'Angelier. We explored the woods of Rowaleyn above Gare Loch, where Madeleine first made love with the young Frenchman. We traveled to Edinburgh and visited the scene of the trial. And we examined Madeleine's yellowed-with-age—and sizzling—letters to her lover. Finally, with all the thoroughness of Sherlock Holmes, Larry unearthed evidence, never known or produced at trial, that most certainly would have sent the young lady to the gallows. Luckily for Madeleine, our discoveries came nearly a century too late. She was acquitted because of insufficient evidence.

And we took time to be tourists. Larry learned that I had never seen Stirling Castle, so he rented a car and off we went. Larry, like a professional guide, showed me around the great fortress, parading the magnificent battlements with all the pride of the king of the castle and obviously reveling in my appreciation.

In using the word reveling, I should add that Larry's emotions, though genuine, always seem to be underplayed. Fortunately, he carried this trait into his art, be it film or theater. Theatrical history relates that in 1742, David Garrick astounded a Drury Lane Theatre audience by speaking Shylock's lines naturally, as though he were actually thinking them. This was a violent change from the ranting delivery then acceptable. The audience was mystified, but before the evening was over it was enthralled by a new acting technique—underplaying.

In our century Sir Gerald du Maurier, who could throw away a line and yet have its force hit the back of the gallery, was recognized as the master of this art form. Sir Gerald is no longer with us, but Larry is; and his underplaying, when necessary, is the tops. Nothing could be gentler, more quietly wistful than his "Upon the King" soliloquy (act 4, scene 1) in the film version of Shakespeare's *Henry V* (1944). I was lucky enough to be present at the film's premiere at London's Carlton Theatre. His performance was so compelling that when a V2 bomb fell less than a quarter mile away, seemingly tilting the theater upside down, Larry's quiet delivery had the shaken audience hushed and listening again for his whispered words even before the shock of the bomb had subsided.

The same Larry who could hypnotize an audience with a whisper could also stir it to frenzy. In the same film young King Henry exhorts his troops before the walls of Harfleur:

> HENRY: Once more unto the breach, dear friends, once more;
>     Or close the wall up with our English dead. . . .
>     On, on, you noblest English.
> (act 3, scene 1)

Larry's delivery carried his audience way beyond Harfleur, reminding the wartime world that Hitler's "Fortress Europe"—his envelopment of a defeated Continent—could still be breached, given the guts to attempt it. Larry's ringing tones, Shakespeare's words, were sounding when the wall was breached on the beaches of Normandy.

And there was something else I loved about Glasgow. A friend of mine—the fine actor Roland Culver—said if I happened to hit Scotland, I should look up a pal of his who owned a Scotch whiskey distillery. I took Roland at his word, with the result that on my return south I was the unheard-of possessor of two cases of Red Hackle Scotch whiskey—and this at a time when just one bottle was worth its weight in platinum. I was immediately the most popular character in London theater and film circles—for so long as my cases of Scotch lasted.

# 14

# Unconquered

On January 31, 1945, I opened a discussion at London's PEN literary society with a question that has plagued me in one form or another since Al Woods first asked me to rewrite act 3 of my play *Blackmail,* which culminated in the Tallulah Bankhead press fiasco. "But why do they have to alter the book?" I asked. "It seems an awful tragedy that a fine story should have to pass through the hands of another writer—possibly not so competent as the original author." Little did I realize that these remarks would foreshadow difficulties in my postwar career.

With the European war concluded in May, I sailed for Beverly Hills as one of fourteen civilians and 17,000 GIs aboard the *Queen Mary,* carrying two bottles of Scotch in hand. Possessing liquid gold, I was again the center of attraction. And flush with European victory and my own importance as a propagandist, I returned on a Hollywood crusade. I was fed up with studio bureaucracies, moguls, and their formula method. Then, as now, a studio would approve the making of a film if it could be shown to be a variation on some earlier film; and once approved, legions of writers would work on the story. That system was a machine that crucified creativity and demoralized the writer.

I published my concern in an article titled "Rank Enthusiasm" in the November 1945 issue of the *Screen Writer,* published by the Screen Writers Guild and edited by the communist Dalton Trumbo. My article challenged this system by pointing out, none too subtly, that American films were not popular in Britain because the British public was enthusiastic only for British pictures, and such enthusiasm permeated the industry from the ground up. Enthusiasm would begin with the writer, and then pass contagiously to the producer and the director. Studios like the Rank Organisation were eager to exploit that enthusiasm as a commercial asset, encouraging the individual creator—or individual team of creators—by giving a green light without front-office interference. Emphasis was on quality, not commercialism.

I gave as an example Filippo Del Giudice, "a man who honestly believes that the only people who should be allowed to produce pictures are the artists who can themselves create them." And I concluded my article with this slap at Hollywood: "There are far too many formula writers, producers and directors in this world. . . . The British film industry flourished once before . . . but the industry died when it started to emulate the Hollywood product, and to import the Hollywood *know-how.*"

My warning to the studio system proved timely as, within a very few short years, low-budget filmmaking undercut the studios. The collapsing studio system turned to costly epics, out of reach of independent filmmakers. And the nearly fateful coup de grâce occurred as audiences tuned in on the ascendance of television.

But in the meantime, imagine how unpopular I became with Hollywood studio moguls! Charles Bennett—persona non grata! Greek tragedy has a name for my defiance—hubris. No matter. I had in my possession a contract to return to England to work for Two Cities on *The Trial of Madeleine Smith,* followed by yet another film, *Miracle of Peille.* I believed I was in a safe position to snub my nose at Hollywood.

I also had an ally in Cecil DeMille, who respected real talent. My first assignment back from Europe was on *Unconquered* (1947), starring Gary Cooper and Paulette Goddard, with Boris Karloff as an Indian chief! It seems a strange coincidence that I would be writing a film whose title so aptly characterized my attitude, but that's the way it was. At $5 million, *Unconquered* was DeMille's most expensive spectacle to date, a sort of *Perils of Pauline* with Indians and pre-Revolutionary gunrunners. The *Hollywood Reporter* described it as "primitive in its passions; exciting in its action; colorful and spectacular in its pageantry."

When the film was finished, it was claimed that the screenplay was derived from a novel by Neil H. Swanson. My screenplay wasn't written from any novel—the novel was written from my screenplay! This is what had happened with my story *The Clairvoyant*—and *The Story of Dr. Wassell:* people thought it gave the picture more importance to say it was written from a novel, so that's the way it was represented.

DeMille was on the firing line in a left-turning Hollywood. In March 1945 he reacted to his loss of air time with the American Federation of Radio Artists by declaring, "There has been built up in this country an unelected government superseding in power and authority the elected government. And a dissenting voice raised against this unelected but all-encompassing power is condemned to obliteration." Interestingly, Ring Lardner Jr. wrote an article titled "The Sign of the Boss," published in the same Trumbo-edited copy of the *Screen Writer* that launched my crusade. Lardner criticized DeMille's defense of "every workingman's right to independence from any united stand of his co-workers, or, in broader terms, the superior authority of the individual over the organized group." DeMille, in Lardner's assessment, stood for anarchism.

It has been said that DeMille enlisted me in undercover right-wing political activities.[25] That's not strictly true. My undercover activities had been for the Allied war effort. Once World War II was concluded, my right-wing activities upheld the screenwriter's art and autonomy against faceless studio collectivism. There is nothing so important in this world as talent, and it cannot be compromised. But in the exploding context of meetings held by Joseph McCarthy and the House Un-American Activities Committee, my crusade for individualism against the studio system closed ranks with DeMille's fight against Hollywood communists. All this would come to a head in 1950, when I supported DeMille's anticommunism at the Directors Guild; I was later barred from MGM as a result.

Unfortunately, while at Paramount on *Unconquered,* a discomfiting letter arrived explaining there had been a delay on *The Trial of Madeleine Smith.* I wrote to Larry, who replied in January 1946 that he had shelved the idea. He explained that Vivien Leigh was ill and could not work on any picture for another eighteen months at least, after which she would certainly owe several pictures elsewhere. This was troubling news, considering my crusade.

My flight instructor, Tommy Rose, had often taught as his second prime rule (the first never to land under stalling speed) to avoid flying blind through overcast. But being born stupid, I broke the second rule in June 1946. Only once!

In those days I frequently got up very early, logging an hour or so of solo flying to San Juan Capistrano or Glen Ivy Hot Springs for breakfast, before going to Paramount to work on *Unconquered.* With perhaps only twenty solo flying hours to my credit, I took off at around seven o'clock that morning from the dangerously short landing strip at Culver City.

The morning was gloomy, overcast down to around two thousand feet, but there was still plenty of room for wandering around over Los Angeles County. I came up to the overcast, and then, in a fit of complete gibbering idiocy, I decided that if I flew up through the clouds, I'd find rewarding sunshine above. Within moments I was in the most ghastly trouble: I couldn't see a thing. Heavy clouds billowed, and wreathing mist enveloped me. I didn't know whether my plane was on an even keel, on one side, or even downside up.

Looking back over what will all too soon be a hundred years, I can honestly state that I have been truly frightened only twice in my life and this was one of those occasions. I wrestled the joystick, jerked it this way and that—up, down, completely unaware whether I was climbing or going down.

Pure luck! I was going down. Quite suddenly I emerged sandwiched between that deadly overcast and closely huddled homes below. But my plane was on its side, the left wing heading directly and much too fast for a crash landing on the homes of many perhaps still-sleeping citizens. I jerked desperately at the joystick. To my relief, the craft responded and leveled off, but only around three hundred feet above scores of clustered little suburban homes. I pulled back and ascended fast, to find at four hundred feet or so that the overcast had lowered and appeared to be closing in.

Crisis! I was in one piece, so was my aircraft—so were maybe a score or more of those citizens down below. But I was lost! Those homes meant nothing to me at all. I knew I had to land. But where was I? Over Inglewood? Downey? Santa Monica? I banked around, horribly aware that those characters below could all too soon be on their way to a mortuary with me. And then—the good Lord bless Louis B. Mayer—I spotted the monolithic hugeness of one of the MGM studio soundstages.

It gave me my bearings and I seized on them, coming in to make a nervously bouncing landing on that Culver City strip. I remember sitting out there on the runway, still shuddering, for a good twenty minutes or so before I had recovered sufficiently to taxi the craft back to what passed for its hangar.

DeMille liked to lunch with his writers, though our conversation seldom had any bearing on any film in preparation. The famous C.B. had a genuine interest in civil and private aviation, as back in the 1920s he had owned an airport; and he knew about my early-morning, two-hundred-mile or so breakfast trips. So at lunch that day he came up with his almost habitual question, "Where'd you fly this morning, Charles?" Without thinking I came back with what I still believe to have been the truth, "Almost into eternity." Soon after, in September 1946, I sold my plane and gave up flying.

Completing work for DeMille, I went across to Universal International to work on *Ivy* (1947) for the director Sam Wood. *Ivy* was a good script. Joan Fontaine starred as the femme fatale, one of my favorite character types—the beautiful and intelligent murderess, the siren who lures men to their deaths. Sam wanted alterations, and I had to fight him, but eventually I got my screenplay through. While working with Joan and Sam, I realized something about many directors I have worked with. Sam knew where to put the camera, but he was dependent on everyone around him, and in particular on his art directors. Too many directors say, "But I'm not sure about here . . . what do you think?"

One night I was on the set and Joan came to me and said, "Charles, this scene? I desperately want to know what to do with it. I've talked to Sam and he seems to be completely inarticulate. He can't explain to me what he wants."

So I told her what the scene was about, how to play it, and she went back and played it. But the fact is, it wasn't Sam Wood's direction that made her good. It is my opinion that only about a score of directors were really creative people. Hitchcock was a genius director; his ideas were tremendous. DeMille was creative in his way, because he knew what he wanted. But mainly the writer is the person who does it, always praying it isn't changed at the last moment without his knowledge.

I will never forget the horrible ending to *Ivy*. My son, watching it on the telly, said, "Oh, that's a sudden end." I said, "That's not the way I wrote it." The ending, as far as I was concerned, had Sir Cedric Hardwicke, the detective, giving some sort of reasoning for what had happened. But no, not a bit of it. Boom! Desperately sudden.

After *Ivy*, in September 1946 I again traveled overseas for several months. Finding encouragement as Rank asked me to do some preliminary work on *The Trial of Madeleine Smith*, I rented my house to the gangster Bugsy Siegel, and then headed to England and Scotland, and on to the Continent.

Bugsy was a murderous son of a bitch, but he was also the nicest, most genuinely charming man—adored by Beverly Hills society. I had dinner with him at his expense for three hours at a Russian restaurant on the

Sunset Strip. You'd never believe he was one of the biggest killers of all time. He was the perfect tenant, and he actually improved the house by installing a huge mirror in the living room—to guard against any gunman approaching from the garden. But three weeks after his lease expired, the Mafia gunned him down at the house of his mistress, Virginia Hill. Except for the fact that I'd returned from Europe and wanted my home back, Bugsy would undoubtedly have been shot dead from my driveway.

My European trip was extraordinary in two respects. First, I joined Maggie and Herbie on their honeymoon, skiing with them in Switzerland. But most interesting was my invitation to Germany by the marshal of the Royal Air Force, Sholto Douglas, then the commander of the British Zone of Occupied Germany. Our conversation turned to the recently completed Nuremberg trials, and Sholto told me something I will never forget. He said the toughest action of his entire life had come when, as one of the quartet of Allied commanders, it had been his turn to affix his signature to Hermann Göring's death warrant. His respect for Göring as an adversary went back to their dogfights in World War I and had even survived the fury of the *Reichsmarschall*'s night Blitz.

Robert Wright—Sholto's biographer and assistant—told me that on one occasion at Nuremberg he passed within two or three feet of Göring. They exchanged a glance, and Robert said he'd never in his life seen such vicious hate in anybody's eyes—hate so great that it made him shudder—but partly at the thought of what Göring might have done to a defeated Britain, including the hanging of Winston Churchill. The luck of the game.

Now as the guest of Sholto Douglas, and just months after the war's end, I visited the Russian-sector ruins of a devastated Berlin, having a memorable dinner with the German friend I'd met in Hollywood, U.S. Army Colonel Erich Pommer. Erich and I, with two adorable young German lady survivors—one of whom was later to become a Hollywood film star—enjoyed a foursome dinner in a shattered restaurant.

An interesting aspect of the evening was the future star's account of how she and her parents had survived the *Feuersturm* of Hamburg, her hometown. A fleet of a thousand or more Allied bombers would come over, night after night; but rather than unloading bombs at random, their job was the planned annihilation of the city, chunk by chunk, target after target, one night after the next.

Citizens caught on to the pattern and took advantage of it, the solution being to lie low amid the rubble for the next night—almost sure that the

Allied air fleets would be busy elsewhere. The survivors would then move on, to the *latest* annihilated district, to lie low for another twenty-four hours before moving on again. Of course, sanity dictated never spending a night in an as yet unbombed area. It was a weirdly desperate method of clinging to existence, but it worked.

I visited Hamburg two weeks later and observed the devastation of the great German port city. It was midwinter, and snow lay heavy on the ground—but not enough to cloak the hideous carnage. Nor did a chilly wind eliminate the fetid smell of death, which still lingered now and then on the air. Remembering what I had seen in Plymouth, this sight established in my mind that the Nazis got what they had asked for.

Sholto put a plane and pilot at my disposal to fly wherever I wanted—though cautioning me to stay out of trouble because there was not much he could do to assist. Much to the horror of my pilot, I told him I wanted to visit the ruins of Hitler's bunker near the Reich Chancellery building.

Upon entering those restricted premises, I met a forbiddingly armed Russian guard whom I bribed with a pack of cigarettes. He waved me through unaccompanied into Hitler's rooms. More than a little nervous, I snooped through the corridors, wondering if I would come out alive—my heavy winter coat had considerable value on the black market. I walked past the spot where the Führer committed suicide and entered into his and Eva Braun's sleeping quarters. Wanting a memento, I reached under her bed and snatched a gas-mask canister, which I secreted under my coat. I also took a finned incendiary bomb—both items I treasure among my keepsakes.

Back at the plane, my pilot was very much alarmed by my absence—a full hour beyond the time we were to depart—and he was only too happy to get the hell out of there!

# 15

# No Escape

In 1945, within a few months of my return to Hollywood from London, I had met twenty-two-year-old Betty Riley, a secretary in the office of my Beverly Hills tax accountant. Betty was bright as a whip and fluent in English literature and poetry. She was a hit in Hollywood—looked like Ingrid Bergman and had the best figure in town. Hitchcock wanted to give her a screen test, but Betty declined. He could have made a success of her; he could show any actress exactly the way a scene should be played—this little fat man telling a beauty how to act. Jack Warner chased Betty; I told him to leave her alone, so I never again entertained any thought of working at Warner Bros. Studio. No matter! I still intended to take my career stratospheric as a writer-director on *Madeleine* and *Miracle*. As it happened, I did work again at Warner Bros.—and wished I hadn't. But more of that later.

In February 1947, just back from Britain and Germany, my life took a monumental turn. I proposed marriage to Betty and married her within the week. We returned from our desert honeymoon on March 11. A few days later, a telegram arrived from Sir John Davis, the number-two man at Rank, saying my *Madeleine Smith* script was dead. Instead, he said, they would switch me to direct another movie.

March 15, 1947—the murderous ides of March!

CAESAR: Who is it in the press that calls on me?
   I hear a tongue, shriller than all the music,
    Cry "Caesar!" Speak, Caesar is turn'd to hear.
SOOTHSAYER: Beware the ides of March.
CAESAR: What man is that?
BRUTUS: A soothsayer bids you beware the ides of March.
(*Julius Caesar*, act 1, scene 2)

After that date, things did not go as I had hoped. Whereas in the 1920s Parisian critics had raved at my Julius Caesar, soon Hollywood film industry buzzards picked at this Caesar's corpse. There were unwanted contractual commitments, lousy directors and writers deconstructing my stories, lost opportunities and worthless agents, ideas too advanced for their time, suicide, revenge, and theft. I was banned from a major studio as the film industry collapsed and television rose ascendant. Marital problems and illness afflicted me at home.

> Antony: The noble Brutus
>    Hath told you Caesar was ambitious:
>    If it were so, it was a grievous fault,
>    And grievously hath Caesar answered it.
> (*Julius Caesar*, act 3, scene 2)

There was nothing I could do about *Madeleine*'s cancellation. Other people's love lives had messed everything up. Before Larry Olivier could get it into production, his marriage to Vivien was running on the rocks. Presently it broke up, but, without Vivien, there wasn't any Madeleine—not from Larry's viewpoint. To complicate matters, a bit later David Lean suddenly decided he wanted to make the subject with his wife Ann Todd in the lead. Larry released the project and David wanted his own script. He made his picture *Madeleine* (1950)—a lousy script and a box-office disaster. I still love my script, though it only gathers dust in my study.

In place of *Madeleine*, Rank substituted *Madness of the Heart* (1949), which was a horrible story. So much for enthusiasm. Betty accompanied me to England with our newborn. On the flight over, our plane was struck by lightning—a disconcerting omen. From the moment of our arrival, Betty couldn't stand war-ravaged England; and she was ill and wouldn't travel farther. I had to leave London to direct *Madness* on the French Riviera. It's not good to leave your wife and child behind, but I had to direct the film. My star was Margaret Lockwood, a very good actress. And I had a fifty-five-day shooting schedule. Everything was right about it, except the story.

And my humming! I've been humming since childhood, a habit picked up from my mother, who never stopped humming and is probably still at it—way up above. Humming isn't a sin, although it's sometimes an affliction. The worst instance occurred at the Denham Film Studios near London when I was directing *Madness*. I rehearsed the scene; everything was okay. "Quiet! Lights! Sound! Roll 'em! Action!" Utter silence reigned, and Maggie Lockwood and my leading man, Paul Dupuis, started in on the scene. Everything proceeded just the way I wanted it.

Suddenly, from the sound booth came the shout: "Cut!"

I was furious. The performances couldn't have been better. I yelled, "What the hell's wrong?"

The reply came from the sound booth. "Somebody's humming."

Who? Accusing eyes flicked around. No response. Then the truth hit me. While monitoring Maggie and Paul's handling of the dialogue, I had been contributing a low musical accompaniment. Later my sound man told me that he had recognized the tune as a onetime popular ditty called "Dipsy Doodle."

People have asked me over the years, "Why, at the peak of your career, did you not return to England, to resume writing and directing in the theater?" The answer was simple, though I could not speak of it at the time. Betty would not move to England. She became very ill and suffered delirium and extreme pain. I could not leave her and our child. My hasty decision to marry unwittingly ripped out a page that I could never replace. With it went all possibility of renewing my theater career in England.

> Antony: It will inflame you, it will make you mad.
> (*Julius Caesar*, act 3, scene 2)

So I continued writing film and TV from Hollywood. In 1950 I co-scripted *Bangkok* (not produced) with Robert G. North; this screenplay was written for the CIA and was probably intended as a cover. A serious project for DeMille was the complete story treatment of *The Search for the Holy Grail*. It was an epic tale of King Arthur and his Knights of the Round Table, interweaving adventures from Thomas Malory's *Morte d'Arthur* and my occasional sourcebook *The Children's Encyclopaedia* (Arthur Mee, London). DeMille was very enthusiastic about the story, but unfortunately he was sidetracked by such other landmark ideas as *The Queen of Queens*, about the Virgin Mary. Apart from the musical *Camelot,* I cannot recall that any serious version of my epic has yet been filmed. Perhaps if I live long enough, I will pull that sword from the stone.

> Antony: O judgment! Thou art fled to brutish beasts,
>      And men have lost their reason.
> (*Julius Caesar*, act 3, scene 2)

I mentioned that while at MOI, I wrote a screenplay of *Lorna Doone* (1951) for Eddie Small. I think my *Lorna* script was one of the best I have ever written, but since Hollywood as a general rule hates to leave well enough alone, it was eventually annihilated by other writers, and I took my name off it. Around this time Eddie—whom I adored almost as much as I adored DeMille—wanted to make the *Prince of Foxes* with me in Italy. He failed to get the rights, but he told me in all seriousness that he wasn't a bit concerned because he had heard of another subject that we could do in Rome. It was something by some English writer named Shakespeare—dead—so it was in the public domain. "It was," Eddie told me, "about some guy named Julius Caesar," and he assured me that it wouldn't be expensive because "I'm told the sets are still standing." The sets of course were the ruins of the Roman Forum.

Well, Rome it would be, but *Julius Caesar* it wasn't. Instead, I wrote *Black Magic* (1949), *Cagliostro* as it was then called, adapted from the novel *Joseph Balsamo* by Alexandre Dumas. The script was a good one; Gregory Ratoff was hired as director, and Orson Welles played the lead. Between the two of them shooting in Rome, they had a ball ruining the script. Eddie Small was afraid to fly, and since proceeding to Italy by train and boat would have taken too much time, Ratoff and Welles had everything their own way—going completely crazy, rewriting the script as they felt inclined. Ratoff even wrote in a part for himself. The result was utter disaster, such a hideous mess that the picture, when the negative arrived back in Hollywood, couldn't be cut. I spent a week working nights, writing and directing scenes here and there, just to help the eventual picture make sense. The result was that I was against the movie at the time.

But I do think that Orson did a tremendous job as Cagliostro. Curiously enough, I didn't write it for him. José Ferrer was supposed to play the part, but José demanded a three-picture contract, which Eddie Small refused. Cagliostro was a charlatan but, I really believe, a true hypnotist. The movie involved Marie Antoinette and the famous matter of "the Queen's necklace." Akim Tamiroff played Cagliostro's gypsy assistant; and Charles Goldner provided a final payoff as Dr. Mesmer, of mesmerism fame, out-hypnotizing Cagliostro. It was a very interesting picture.

In the 1950s it seemed television might supplant film as the entertainment of choice, and since fewer films were produced, I earned my living by writing and directing for television. I have enjoyed writing novels, plays, and movies, but the only reason I ever wrote anything for TV was for the *money.* I believe I've written more than two hundred TV shows—though I do not have any accurate tally—but I loathe TV. Television is a revolting, horrible sausage factory. Too little money for too much effort. I wish it had never been invented. I have enjoyed directing some of it, but TV writing is a tenth-rate form of writing.

As further cause for my disgust, television destroyed our British film colony. After old Aubrey Smith died in 1948, the colony fizzled into little more than a memory in the early 1950s, when the world's newest plaything tumbled it with a swiftness comparable only to the collapse of the Berlin Wall. As TV almost finished off the (till then) unassailable feature film industry, fewer and fewer top-flight movies were made, and the demand for the Colmans, Rathbones, and Dame May Whittys ebbed fast.

But I was working through the 1950s in my fourth career as an internationally recognized TV writer and director. Many of my screenplays were broadcast live in the United States for *Fireside Theatre, Climax! Chrysler Theatre, Lux Video Theatre,* and *Schlitz Playhouse of Stars.* I also wrote for the *Ford Television Theatre, The Christophers,* and *Cavalcade of America.*

Among my many stories, one surely made television history. On September 2, 1954, the *Climax! Chrysler Theatre* asked me to adapt and script a comparatively unknown novel called *Casino Royale,* the year 1954 being long before James Bond became a world-famous character. It was to be an hour-long show—meaning around fifty-three minutes, allowing for commercials. The show was shot—live—on October 2, starring Peter Lorre as the heavy, Le Chiffre. As the producers had decided that James Bond was hardly a known literary character (and certainly not a cinematic one), the fact that the hero was originally written as an Englishman could be forgotten. So that Barry Nelson, an American actor, could play the lead, Bond became an American.

An amusing situation took place at Le Chiffre's death. The director forgot to press the necessary button, and instead of jumping the scene to the next, the cameras remained on "dead" Peter. Lorre rose to his feet, and—believing himself to be off-camera and out of sight of his perhaps twenty million viewers—sauntered off, smiling whimsically, toward his dressing room and, I have no doubt, a pleasant drink with which to solace himself upon his recent death.

Ah, Peter! I have observed the meaner the actor's role on-screen, the pleasanter the actor is in real life. Peter Lorre was the ultimate example of this, but with a twist. He was an adorable, very kind, very gentle, very sweet man with a big sense of humor. Peter carried his personal gentleness into his characterizations, and this was a great part of his magic. Peter Lorre the heavy could kill—calculatedly, malevolently—and still remain amusingly lovable. His was practically a new art form. I was very fond of him and happy that he starred in seven of my opuses.

Despite my distaste for writing for television, there were a few gratifying moments. I was pleased that my teleplay *Edge of the Law* (1952) came so early in the development of the medium. *Take Off Zero* (1955) was headlined in *Variety* as "Cavalcade's Finest!" And *The Gift of Dr. Minot* was awarded the Christopher Award for Best TV Direction of 1955. TV also provided the enjoyment of my writing and directing my way across Europe with *The Count Of Monte Cristo* series and as associate producer of *The New Adventures of Charlie Chan*.

It has been suggested that another story of mine is likely to break records with its four consecutive sets of options. This was *Miss Moffit and the Thunderbird* (also known as *Thunderbird*), which made quite a lot of money without ever achieving production. I wrote the gangster role in 1950 in remembrance of my recent tenant, Bugsy Siegel. The murderous mobster exemplified the suave villain character type I have so often favored. *Miss Moffit* is a suspense–love story, told against the wild country of northern Arizona and Nevada. The first option was to MGM for Robert Taylor—crazy about the lead role as the Bugsy Siegel–type gangster Johnnie Luther—and Greer Garson as Miss Moffit, an anthropologist researching among the Anasazi ruins. Everything was in order—all except for the signing of the contract. Stephan Ames was set to produce.

Suddenly, in 1951, Louis B. Mayer was maneuvered out of MGM and Dore Schary became studio head. He immediately canceled my deal because I was known as an avowed anticommunist. The general opinion was that he turned against me because I had held proxies in a 1950 vote opposing a communist takeover of the Directors Guild. Schary was wildly procommunist and flatly refused to have MGM do any business whatever with anticommunists. We have heard a lot about the Hollywood Ten— communists who went to jail. What nobody ever mentions is the fact that far too many good writers, producers, and directors were pilloried for their known anticommunist points of view. Schary was pushed out of MGM a few years later, paid off because of the money the studio was losing, but that didn't help me.

ANTONY: I should do Brutus wrong, and Cassius wrong,
    Who, you all know, are honorable men.
    I will not do them wrong: I rather choose
    To wrong the dead, to wrong myself and you,
    Than I will wrong such honorable men.
(*Julius Caesar*, act 3, scene 2)

Within three weeks I had sold an option to Loretta Young, who wanted to play Miss Moffit, and Tyrone Power was interested in the gangster role. But Loretta dropped the option when she realized the story entailed the gangster's suicide, which as a strict Catholic she couldn't go for. I wouldn't drop the suicide then—oddly enough, I have done so since—so that was that.

Then the fine director John Farrow wanted to make the thing, and he took it to Alan Ladd. Farrow died; but Alan eventually bought an option, and four weeks later, in January 1964, he died in Palm Springs. Alan's death is lost in Hollywood myth, but it was said he committed suicide. Not, I hope, because he optioned my script.

After Alan's death, I immediately sold a fourth option to a group of Mexican film financiers intent on shooting it in Mexico. But I said No! The background is Arizona, and I insisted that the picture be shot in its true Navaho setting. I shall never forget the multimillionaire owner of the company remarking in the Beverly Hills Hotel Polo Lounge, "Charles, what you don't seem to realize is that Mexico looks more like Arizona than Arizona does." Anyway, my insistence called the thing off.

Discouraged, I said the hell with it—until recently. Remembering what a good story it was, I revised the screenplay and novelized it as *Thunderbird.* But this has not sold because of continuing concern for filming in the Arizona backcountry. Oh, well, the story made me quite a bit of money in its options, and I've had the satisfaction of seeing five of Hollywood's top stars wanting to play it. I think it is the best story I have ever written.

ANTONY: If you have tears, prepare to shed them now.
(*Julius Caesar,* act 3, scene 2)

When Danny Peary was writing *Cult Movies 2* (1983), he sent me a copy of the draft. I was upset to find he had omitted my movie *Night of the*

*Demon* (1957). He discusses it in the published edition, but its early-on omission caused some reflection on a career turned sour. As Danny pointed out, despite its British setting, out-of-the-ordinary characters, and psychological suspense–mystery, *no* critic noticed any parallel to my Hitchcock films—which only goes to show how far my name recognition had plummeted in twenty years.

> ANTONY: But yesterday the word of Caesar might
> Have stood against the world: now lies he there,
> And none so poor to do him reverence.
> (*Julius Caesar*, act 3, scene 2)

But the story is infinitely sadder than that. *Night of the Demon* could have been a great film, the film that would turn my career back to its glory days. A screwup cost me the opportunity to direct the movie of my life! Danny graciously calls it "the best horror movie of the science fiction dominated fifties, [and] the most intriguing film ever made with a witch-craft theme," and, of course, "well constructed." But it could have been so much more!

I had purchased the rights to Montague James's story *Casting the Runes,* then wrote a screenplay that generated considerable excitement in Hollywood. Several well-known actors, including Robert Taylor and Dick Powell, wanted to play the lead, but no one had yet set up the deal, so I went off to England to direct *The Count of Monte Cristo* TV series for Eddie Small. I had an active writer-director membership in the Association of Cine-Technicians there, which gave me the right to work in England without union or labor ministry objections.

On the day I was leaving England to return to the States, a Mr. Hal E. Chester was waiting in the foyer of my residence at 39 Hill Street, off Berkeley Square. He said, "Look, I can set this picture up with Columbia Pictures. Will you just give me your signature now?" Very tired, I signed the option agreement, and then boarded the plane. Two days later I learned that RKO had given the okay for my screenplay to be shot, exactly as I wanted to make it, and I would be directing my own screenplay. But it was too late: I'd signed this paper on the way out to my plane. I'd signed it away. I had to sit back and watch Chester destroy my picture, rewriting it and taking a screenwriter credit. Then a further idiotic thing happened. Columbia said, "Oh, we can't use (the title) *Night of the Demon.*" So they called it *Curse of the Demon,* maybe to vie with Warner's *The Curse of Frankenstein* (1957). But I hated that title because it made it a B picture immediately, a title like that.

ANTONY: This was the most unkindest cut of all.
(*Julius Caesar,* act 3, scene 2)

Here, as elsewhere, it should have read, "Screenplay by Charles Bennett, destroyed by another writer!" Hal Chester cut many of the better things out of the picture for the sake of making it cheaply, and the eventual result was a pale shadow of what it should have been. The moviemakers added a visible monster, which made me very angry. I had intended a psychological thriller. The monster should have been any pursuing horror that an audience could conjure in its mind. And Karswell (the villain) would throw himself in front of a train in sheer panic and terror. But I think the job the director Jacques Tourneur did with what Hal Chester gave him was awfully good. So, Hal Chester, if he walked up my driveway right now, I'd shoot him dead. Still, my script must have had *something* to it, because in spite of Hal Chester's destruction, it is still considered a cult classic.

ANTONY: O, now you weep; and, I perceive, you feel
The dint of pity: these are gracious drops.
(*Julius Caesar,* act 3, scene 2)

In the late 1950s the actor Glenn Ford was crazy about setting up my screenplay titled *Train Ride* (also known as *The Doomsday Express*). It tells the story of the notorious outlaw and southern "Robin Hood," John Wesley Hardin, apprehended by Texas Ranger J. L. Armstrong. *Train Ride* is a story about personal honor, and how honorable men behave when overwhelmed by antagonistic forces. It is a metaphor for those frequent occasions when I have faced odds stacked against me—escaping the brokers' men, receiving the Military Medal, finding success in multiple careers, my Hollywood efforts at spying and breaking the propaganda taboo, writing propaganda in Britain, opposing the studio system and the communist takeover of the Directors Guild, and so on. Currently I am opposing ageism in the Writers Guild. Like Ranger Armstrong, I have often been up against it and succeeded.

BRUTUS: For let the gods so speed me as I love
The name of honour more than I fear death.
(*Julius Caesar,* act 1, scene 2)

Only this time, there was a burr under the saddle—*Train Ride* had the appearance of a western.

A western? Not really, but for unexplained reasons, the making of westerns became taboo. And since the characters wore western hats, the money shied away. Again in 1983 the actor Jon Voight wanted to star. When everything was apparently set, Voight decided he might become labeled as a western star and be shunned. Again I was disappointed, but by this time I was all too familiar with the lunacy of Hollywood. Advancing age has made me more philosophical than I was on my crusade.

In 1958 I presented an innovative TV series, *Terror,* for which I outlined numerous stories and wrote a frightening pilot, "The Typewriter." The series sold to Louis F. Edelman, executive producer of the ongoing series *Make Room for Daddy* and the soon-to-be *Barbara Stanwyck Show.* Like so many other good ideas, *Terror* went nowhere—but I had been onto something. *The Twilight Zone* series started its broadcast a year later; and after five seasons and 156 episodes, Rod Serling made a fortune in TV rerun residuals.

But *Terror* started me thinking about the supernatural, the result being that in 1961 I came up with a TV series called *The Ghost Breaker* (also known as *Ghost Hunter*), about the adventures of a brilliant university professor of extrasensory perception, like J. B. Rhine at Duke University, whose avocation was the investigation of the supernatural—a sort of psychic detective. Sometimes the cases he had to solve were phony—fake spiritualism, for example—but most of the cases were ghostly psychic phenomena. I sold the series to 20th Century Fox TV, which decided against the supernatural six months later and made a settlement with me.

I promptly resold the series to Four Star. They made an hour-long pilot titled *The Clocks* with Joan Fontaine and David Farrar. This pilot was presented twice on the *Dick Powell Show* because it was so popular. A second pilot, *Fasten Seat Belts* (not produced), featured a murderous supernatural phenomenon on a New York to Los Angeles–bound 707—but owing to the wild desire on the part of the American public to see domestic situation comedy, the series did not sell. Both *The Clocks* and the *Ghost Breaker* series reverted to me.

In 1966 I tried for a third time to resurrect elements of *Ghost Breaker,* preparing a James Mason series idea titled *What Do You Think?* It featured unexplained occurrences and unsolved supernatural mysteries; it predated this successful genre of TV paranormal investigations by a decade. Once again, my idea was too far ahead of its time. And the enormously profitable *Ghostbusters* (1984) featured three parapsychology professors running a ghost removal service.

Something similar to what had happened with *Night of the Demon* occurred on a second film involving the director Jacques Tourneur, *War-Gods of the Deep* (1965)—a dreadful picture that I should never have had anything to do with. I had written a good script based on a tiny Poe poem; and while it was in production I was asked to go to England to make alterations. The wretched American International Pictures (AIP) came up with a lousy offer that my agent turned down. Their idea of money was absolutely so trivial that it would have *cost* me money to go. So AIP put on some other writer who completely annihilated the thing. He put a chicken in the movie as one of the main characters—oh, God, that was *awful!* That was stolen directly from *Journey to the Center of the Earth* (1959), made by 20th Century Fox. In *Journey,* it was a goose. I should have taken my name off it. Jacques Tourneur was a great friend of mine—I knew him very well and was awfully fond of him. He is a very good director. But Jacques, the poor devil, got the blame for the film, where actually he was not to blame at all—then he blamed *me* for not coming over! Jacques Tourneur did a good job with an impossible script.

In this chapter I revisited the turn in my postwar career. It did not work out as I had hoped; but lest I appear ungrateful, I wish to acknowledge my share of successes in the interval between the war and my alleged retirement in 1965. Over and above the twenty produced feature films, I can locate more than forty produced teleplays—and I also directed all or part of five films and more than thirty TV programs in Europe and the United States.

But that achievement was a far cry from what might have been. The sad fact is that I scripted at least an additional twenty films, wrote three novels and three plays, offered twenty proposals for *new* TV series, and wrote countless teleplays and treatments for film and TV—and many of those scripts were far superior to what was produced!

It is no wonder that I lost faith in the Swanson Agency, though my sense of loyalty overrode my good sense. Had *Madeleine Smith, Miss Moffit and the Thunderbird,* or *Night of the Demon* played in my favor, I would again have been top of the heap. Instead, my later reputation came from scripts written for Irwin Allen. Irwin Allen, God help me! From our first film, I must admit, I wished to God I'd been dead.

The first time I became mixed up with Irwin Allen was back in 1948. Someone at Howard Hughes's RKO made him coproducer with Irving Cummings Jr. on my film noir *Where Danger Lives* (1950), starring Robert Mitchum as our hero, Faith Domergue as a calculating villainess, Claude Rains as the jealous husband, and Maureen O'Sullivan. Maureen's husband, John Farrow, directed.

As a passing point of interest, Howard Hughes had leased my Coldwater Canyon home to keep his mistress in while I was in England. My Swiss gardener recognized Hughes in the yard, said, "How do you do, Mr. Hughes?" and got no reply.

Irwin Allen was the living end! After *Danger,* I wrote his every picture until *The Poseidon Adventure* (1972). I was his favorite writer, but I couldn't stand him—an impossible man with the most horrible swollen head. He always stole other people's credits—never wrote a damn thing but always wanted first credit on everything. I am choosing my words delicately; there was no real personal relationship between us.

Irwin had a tremendous respect for me, and he never dared to cross me in any way. I remember a time at 20th Century Fox at work on *The Lost World* (1960), when I actually threw him out of my office—and he was the producer! I said, "Get out of here. Get *out;* you're stopping me from working." And he had to take it, because he knew that I could write and he couldn't.

My second involvement with Irwin was on *Dangerous Mission* (1954), which W. R. Burnett helped write before I came to it, and which was a complete mess. It was already in production when the director Louis King implored me to straighten it out. Eventually, I made sense of the script, but it meant writing some dialogue for Victor Mature, which Victor objected to because it wasn't in the original script. But it was needed, and Irwin— who was afraid of Victor—said, "Leave it to Victor." So I had to fight Mature just to rescue Irwin's bloody film. And this was not the first time I saved Irwin's neck—once I lent him three hundred bucks to pay his landlady. Nor was it the last time I fought Victor Mature on Irwin's behalf.

In 1957 I had just come back from England when Irwin implored me to work on *The Story of Mankind* (1957) in which the human race is put on trial, prosecuted by the devil and defended by an angel. I didn't realize when I started off that it was really going to be just a collection of snippets from old pictures. I had never read Hendrik van Loon's book *The Story of Mankind*—and I don't think Allen had either. But whatever I wrote, Irwin wanted cut out. The Marx brothers were just given a free hand—Groucho Marx's segment was the sale of Manhattan by the Indians. Nobody wrote his stuff—they were just told to do it themselves. It was dreadful. I hated everything to do with that picture. It was revolting and should never have been made. But I'm a writer—I was being paid quite handsomely, so that was that.

I know Ronald Colman hated *Mankind* and I don't think Vincent Price liked it either. Vincent Price was a dear friend of mine. I had him in seven different movies. I suggested a TV series for him, and I wrote a film with him in mind, *Satan Returns.* He has always been to me a fine, fine actor. But I don't know that he enjoyed playing the devil in *The Story of Mankind.* I don't think anybody enjoyed any part of it.

I remember the sneak preview at a theater in the San Fernando Valley, and Jack Warner was there. At the end we all went and talked about it around a table in a pub. I said, "It's *got* to be cut. This is no good in its present form."

Jack Warner said, "Oh, let's just release it."

And all his yes-men said, "Yes, Jack's right, let's release it." So they did.

Then came *The Big Circus* (1959). Columbia Pictures had sunk $90,000 into story development with Irwin and Irving Wallace; but their script was awful, and it came to the point where they told Irwin to get the hell out. I was reluctant to get involved, but Irwin prevailed on me to rescue the story and draft the screenplay—then Irwin went ahead and took first credit on my screenplay, which he didn't deserve. I should have received first screenplay credit on every movie I wrote for Allen.

But worse yet: the script made very little money for me but an immense amount of money for Victor Mature, an MCA client. Victor said, "I am not satisfied with the script. There are things I want altered."

Irwin, who was frightened to death of Victor Mature, said to me, "Charles, please, you go talk to George Jason [an MCA agent] and Victor Mature to straighten this matter out."

So I came up to a house in the hills above Hollywood with George Jason and an assistant—two top MCA agents—and Victor Mature. I said, "Well, what's the problem?"

George Jason said, "Charles, the problem is that you have Gilbert Roland walking the tightrope over Niagara Falls; and Victor thinks that, since it is he who is the star of the picture, it is he who should be walking across Niagara."

"Wait a minute," I said. "Roland is playing a wire walker. Victor isn't, he's playing the promoter of the circus."

Jason said, "Can't you alter the picture so that Victor Mature walks across Niagara?"

It went on like this with the utterly ridiculous, idiotic demands that only Victor Mature could come up with—and naturally he was backed up by MCA. Eventually I managed to say, "*No!* Get out of the picture if you don't like it." When I told Irwin, he was shaking with fright. I told him, "Victor Mature is not going to walk across Niagara." So Victor did not walk the tightrope, and the picture went ahead with him as the circus promoter. But I walked the tightrope to save Irwin's film and neck, and I didn't even get first screenplay credit!

*The Lost World* was a similar fiasco that Halliwell, in his *Film Guide,* panned as a "pitiful attempt to continue the success of *Journey to the Center of the Earth,* with the story idiotically modernized, unconvincing monsters, a script which inserts conventional romance and villainy, and fatal miscasting of the central part." I agree! The original silent film was better. As he had with *The Big Circus,* Irwin took multiple credits as producer, director, and first screenwriter—I should have taken my name off it.

Then I wrote the screenplay (practically the original tale) of the feature film *Voyage to the Bottom of the Sea* (1961). Irwin's girlfriend had said, "Why not a movie about a big submarine?" So he told me that this was a good idea for a movie. It was, let's face it, truly a spin-off of *20,000 Leagues under the Sea* (1954).

The Jules Verne epic was surely one of the major science fiction tales and movies of all time. The great submarine *Nautilus* had a mission. Commanded by Captain Nemo (superbly played by the English actor James Mason), it was bent on a monster hunt. According to Verne, in 1867 an unidentifiable monster was roaming the seven seas. *Nautilus* took off after it and, following many dramatic happenings, accomplished its mission. It was a first-class tale of adventure originally told so many years ago and offering everything that modern story craft can come up with—suspense, of course, but with one element missing.

What *Voyage* possessed was a plot element fundamental to, I suppose,

80 percent of my movies: the time limit. A fight against an inevitable, world-shaking disaster as time is running out. The suspense is heightened by crawling minutes or seconds. This was what Hitch and I had cashed in on so successfully with *The 39 Steps* screenplay. But Verne, like the novelist Buchan, who'd written *The Thirty-Nine Steps,* hadn't caught up with the time-running-out element.

I can't remember its MacGuffin. The fundamentally irrelevant story line had something to do with an explosion instigated by heavies somewhere in the far Pacific, a deep trench somewhere near the Philippines. But it created the suspense element—the sub had to get through with almost split-second timing to save the earth from annihilation—or else!

The same problem presented itself when Irwin asked me to write *Five Weeks in a Balloon* (1962). Dear old Jules again, a gentleman always good on suspenseful adventure, but who hadn't cottoned on to the time-limit element. So I had to invent one. Looking back—my memory is becoming pitiable—I believe it had mainly to do with a great slave-driving coup, which, to avert, our balloon had to cross the whole vastness of Africa from Zanzibar to the west coast, against a time limit. Naturally the balloon gets through, and the heavies are catastrophically defeated. Sir Cedric Hardwicke, Red Buttons—all of our heroes, including my favorite, Peter Lorre—survived. But I objected to the making of the *Five Weeks* with a woman who looked as if she had just walked out of a beauty parlor. I was a great fan of H. Rider Haggard's book in which the four main characters were men. Adding a woman was a damn silly idea—an error Irwin had made previously with the actress Jill St. John in *The Lost World.*

As I noted in the August 1992 edition of *Starlog,* I was in favor of writing the film *Voyage to the Bottom of the Sea,* but not the *Voyage* television series. I wrote the eight TV segments only when I had nothing better to do, and for the sake of the bloody money they paid. Once they paid me, I couldn't care less what happened to the scripts. The *Voyage* series was just something to fill up airtime.

Ironically, I *have* appreciated the few residuals they paid me over the years. In these last years my income has been pitiful—a negligible pension augmenting Social Security. I would be wealthy if I received a fraction of the ongoing profit to others from my life's creativity. But I am not wealthy, and except for these small residuals, there has been nothing. I was refused California state unemployment insurance as, it is said, I am self-employed. That's life! That's Hollywood!

Not long after *Five Weeks in a Balloon,* I came up with the idea of a space picture—people were starting to go up into space then. So I wrote a complete story with characters, called *Passage to the End of Space.* I suggested that it would be a good idea for a TV series or movie—but I went off somewhere and Irwin developed it without me. I was paid for the story, so I shouldn't complain; but he developed it as the *Lost in Space* television series. It was as simple as that.

In his *Backstory* interview of screenwriters, the author Pat McGilligan asked me why I stuck with Irwin for so long.

"Money!" I replied.

Astutely detecting regret in my voice, Pat pressed me, "Why weren't you writing stories that were particularly meaningful to you?"

I replied that I should have—for the money, fame, and personal enjoyment those would have delivered. But here I was, stuck in Hollywood. I concluded the interview by saying, "Hollywood is the greatest destroyer that a writer can ever meet with. I think the greatest thing that can ever happen to a writer—like my dear friends, Sidney Gilliat and Frank Launder [coauthors of *The Lady Vanishes*]—is the fact that they never came to Hollywood. The worst thing in the world for a writer is to come to Hollywood. It destroys you."

෧ ෧ ෧

## Excerpt: Bewitched

This is the original climax of *Night of the Demon.*

181. INT. A connecting link and corridor—long shot—Karswell, who comes tottering through. He looks terrifiedly back from the corner, then plunges on. But even as he *passes camera,* we get the weird impression that a HUGE AND WREATHING SHADOW FOLLOWS HIM. A long moment . . . then the POLICE APPEAR, hurrying forward . . .

182. INT. Another corridor—long shot—toward Karswell who reels on, *the music always with him.* His face is the face of a man who knows he is done for.

183. INT. At a connecting link—angle—Holden and Joanna hurrying down the train . . .

184. INT. A corridor—angle—toward Karswell who staggers towards a passenger in the corridor. The annoyed man gasps as Karswell pushes wildly by . . .

PASSENGER: Well, really! In all my life—

But right now he turns in shock . . . *as if something* ELSE *has pushed past him—something huge but unseen.* The man goggles . . . then he has heard the police coming . . .

185. INT. A corridor and connecting link way back—long shot—toward Karswell who is panting for breath, covered with sweat, emitting wildly desperate little *whimpers* of sheer terror. But even as he goes to reel *past camera* into the next coach, the connecting link is occupied by a fat man and wife, who are coming through, carrying bags. Karswell bumps into the Fat Man, staggers back as he sees that his way is barred by the even fatter Wife. He *gasps* in fright, turns aside as the Fat Man ejaculates:

FAT MAN: What's up, Mister?
KARSWELL (*squealing, looking back*): It's after me! It's *here!*
FAT MAN: What is?

But it is as if Karswell feels the claws of the pursuer on him, its breath on his neck. He snatches at his swelling throat, struggling as if to free himself, almost screaming. Then he is plunging to the door out to the track. His words are a hopeless *shriek* . . .

KARSWELL: I—No—*Anything—Nooo—*

*It is as if the huge shadow is present again, looming, blotting out the corridor light.* We get *one close glimpse* of Karswell's sweat-soaked, utterly terror-stricken face *as the shadow crosses envelopingly.* Then Karswell has thrown open the door to the track, *pitching precipitately through it into the night. The music rises to a wild and ultimate crescendo.*

186. EXT. Track beside boat train—angle—(process) along the side of the train. We see Karswell tumble headlong through the door. But even in this moment, an express train, *its whistle shrieking,* is coming the other way.

For a split second Karswell's body is falling . . . right into the path of the locomotive . . . then the express is racing past camera . . .

187. INT. A corridor—close shot—Holden and Joanna as Holden stops dead. *The shriek of the express train whistle can still be heard,* racing into the night . . . *but the music has stopped.* Holden looks like a man in a dream. Very slowly he looks at his watch . . .

188. Close shot—the watch face showing exactly *ten o'clock.*

189. Close shot—favoring Holden whose dazed eyes come to Joanna's face. His voice shakes but it is full of conviction . . .

HOLDEN: It's all over.

# 16

# Curtain Call

Retirement is to me a dirty word. If I'm not writing a picture, I'm writing something else, at least five hours every day well into my nineties. But I am interested in writing only what I really like, no matter what the payback. I get too many ideas, and like to work. I wish I could live to be 120 and get all the ideas down on paper. But I'm not likely to do that—not unless the devil is willing to strike another deal. I wish to live so long as I can hold a pencil—no longer.

During these years I have completed a considerable number of scripts, novels, and the like. But nothing has sold. I looked for excuses—in the early 1970s the studios were cutting back, or my agent wasn't performing (which he wasn't), or there was illness. But slowly the horrible truth began to dawn. One morning while I was shaving—I was ninety-one—my appearance in the bathroom mirror caught me by surprise. I realized I was getting old. My mind was young, sometimes razor sharp, but the face had aged. That's when I finally understood the problem—ageism!

No one should endure the frustrations I have endured—to have authored the seminal stories, and created the plot elements of the enduring thriller genre, then *not* to have sold a script for over twenty-five years—and to have to put up with the idiotic belief that young writers must be geniuses because they are young. In 1937 Hollywood writers were forty, fifty, sixty, and we didn't have this dilemma of younger writers taking over the industry.

I hate the talk of this being a young man's industry. I hate it! Not because I am an old man, but because I hate the notion you must be young to be *hot*. In many ways I feel my writing has improved. While many young writers have good ideas, they lack the technical experience of the older writer. Experience is terribly important, a tremendous help in writing. I have recently appealed to the Writers Guild to find ways to end this horrible ageism and to facilitate collaboration among its older and younger members.

There continues to be a willing audience for my ruminations. Friends pop over, bless their hearts; and since Betty died, a companionable practical nurse, Ruth Gross, looks after me. I go to parties—some very enjoyable, particularly the garden parties of our delightful British consul general, Merrick Baker-Bates and his wife, Chrystal. Merrick is a great addition to what's left of the famous British colony out here, and I'm glad to say he's a frequent guest at my home. At one of the consulate parties I met British Prime Minister Margaret Thatcher. She was simply charming. She talked to me for about eight minutes, and she knew all about me, what I'd done in the past and things like that. I knew damned well she'd been told—but what the hell! Shortly after, I met Britain's Princess Alexandra, first cousin to the queen, and her husband. Sweet, sweet people. Also I give nice dinner parties now and then—Ronald Neame and Roddy MacDowall and Anna Lee Nathan are comparative regulars. I try to pretend I'm fifty-four—not ninety-four.

But most rewarding, in 1990, as I was at work on the autobiography, there suddenly came an unexpected knock at my front door. It seems that 20th Century Fox had decided to remake my old play and Hitchcock's classic *Blackmail.* The coproducers came around looking for the film rights, believing I was dead. But I wasn't dead. Fortunately, the film rights had reverted to me from BIP, so 20th entered into a contract.

Nobody thought of inviting this experienced but ancient character with one and a half feet in the grave to write his own screenplay. Not a bit of it. As I've said, Hollywood is now a young man's industry, so a couple of young geniuses were called in, highly paid at that, to write a script. They immediately decided that my *Blackmail,* with its drama and twists—which many years ago had made better than a minor fortune for me—was old hat. So they threw away the story and wrote their own. It was *ghastly,* the worst script I have ever read, offering much filth and pornography in place of story and drama. The producers hit the ceiling. So I promptly did a forty-plus-page reconstruction of what they had to offer, taking the tale back to its successful beginnings. The honchos at 20th Century Fox were delighted, and I became the "genius."

The president of World Production asked, bewilderedly, "Why isn't Charles Bennett writing the script?"

I can imagine the horror. The answer, of course, was that I was ninety-one; and who had ever heard of a ninety-one-year-old being allowed to write a major movie in a young man's industry? But before long I was contracted to do so, with a cowriter and coproducer, Stuart Birnbaum. And that set a record—I was the oldest writer in the history of film under contract to a major studio to write a screenplay. We finished it, of course, but that's as far as it went. Their option expired, and the rights are back in my hands once again.

This publicity has done me a world of good. I am back on the "A-list" for Hollywood parties. The international press drinks at my bar, and my anecdotage is now recorded as film history. I have been interviewed by the press, TV networks, film historians, and the like for articles such as "Who's Who Right Now—Most Impressive Comeback," "True Brit Goes for a Remake," and "Bennett, 92, Back to Blackmail." I have also been honored with a lifetime membership to London's Green Room Club, an honorary membership in the British Academy of Film and Television Arts, Los Angeles (BAFTA-LA), and have been selected as a Telluride Film Festival honoree.

But when interviewers come to the subject of Hitchcock, they never seem to get it right. Hitch and I had the perfect relationship; he understood completely that the picture was completed once the story was written. I reiterate: Hitch knew that when the screenplay is finished, the picture is finished—"putting it before the cameras, putting it on the screen is nothing." Hitch, however, was completely vain, loath to credit *anybody*, above all a writer.

But film historians consider Hitch the sole responsible auteur—leaving me as a footnote to *his* career—though this is not the way we worked. Interviewers expect me to tell them how brilliant Hitchcock was. Of course he was brilliant, very brilliant—as a *director!* But he was the director, not the author.

Similar offense has occurred with the many Hitchcock retrospectives. I was recently invited to the showing of my film *Blackmail* at a local auditorium. As usual, the announcement was headed *Alfred Hitchcock's Classic Blackmail*. No mention of this author, the play basis, or that I own the film. I'm not going!

Of course, my conflict with directors is nothing new. As far back as my lecture "The Story in the Film" in January 1936, I recognized the error of giving a director the right to alter a story. After I finished the scenario of *King of the Damned* (1935), the director Walter Forde altered scenes, necessitating further alterations in consequence. I considered such alteration to the script to be very unfair: without a good script, no film could ever hope to be a success. But in those days I would give the director the benefit of the doubt, reasoning that *he* would take the blame if the picture was a flop.

But nearly sixty years later, I do not feel so generous. Studios routinely push for alterations to suit a usually brainless actor who happens to be a star, or a prospective director who considers himself a genius but usually isn't. There is nothing so important as the story!

So I have one conviction. Whatever happens to the entertainment industry—and I don't mean films only—I am very sure of one thing: there will always be *suspense*. Suspense has surely existed in 90 percent of entertainment since the birth of what we cynically describe as civilization. The gladiatorial contests of ancient Rome must have been full of it, undoubtedly accompanied by betting, the suspense of financial win or loss hanging on a bloody outcome. Will the Lion of Ephesus gore to death the Syrian Panther? Cut and thrust and stab, the audiences yelling and suspense mounting.

One finds suspense in practically every form of diversion—football, basketball, baseball, auto racing, possibly even Scrabble, but most certainly in movies. Ordinary suspense, as I know and love it, is frequently simple, even gentle. Take Noel Coward's *Brief Encounter*. Here was a very un-world-shaking tale, but suspense was there. A young man and a woman, both married, meet in a railroad station waiting room. Deep love develops, but will the two find happiness together? The ending was sad, the two had to part, but the question "Will it work out or won't it?" was always present. The huge moneymaker *Love Story* was also a gentle tale but never lacking in suspense. The wealthy parents were determined to break up the affair between their son and a girl whom they believed to be beneath his social level. Again the outcome was sad, but again suspense had carried the story.

It is interesting to me that theater, cinema, and TV haven't changed the form of presentation since way before the days of Punch and Judy. Except for very occasional excursions into the oval or into an almost enveloping three-sided screen, the square theater frame hasn't altered. The stage of the ancient Greek amphitheater remains the stage of films today. Theater has been known as the Fabulous Invalid, something that is always dying but never quite gives up the ghost. The same with movies. They were supposed to die when TV hit. But TV didn't win out, and movies are pulling in greater grosses than ever. And the old theater proscenium shape is still there.

Will it always be? What next? A swing back? Gladiatorial or jousting bouts? In the eighteenth century the hanging of highwaymen at London's Tyburn Tree was a vastly popular spectacle—and not framed by a proscenium arch. The burning of witches attracted much interest, or there could be bullbaiting, cockfighting, scores of other "pleasant" pursuits not recognized today as entertainment.

Surely it is only a matter of time before some form of instrument tuned into the brain will make thought a purchasable commodity. I am not thinking of some form of Orwellian mental dictatorship. I believe there will always be freedom of thought, but I am sure that forms of it will eventually be commercially procurable. Seek a notion, press a button in some probably pocket-size instrument, and an impulse will prompt a flow of previously stored ideas to the mind. Press a button and up comes entertainment, offering a mentally audible and visual performance—but only in the mind.

But one question remains; what form of entertainment will the mind behind the button come up with? Gentler than now? Kinder? Rougher? Who knows? The answer depends on what sort of minds accompany us into the twenty-first century.

Comedy? The great comforter, alleviator—laughter being the answer to unhappiness and worse. And why not? Comedy could be the fundamental balm of the future; and let nobody think that comedy or farce can lack suspense. I remember a glorious Laurel and Hardy episode in which the two struggled to get a heavy piano up a hundred feet or more of stone steps, completely unaware that they could have driven the piano up the hill by means of a street immediately alongside. The suspense was there, in reverse of the usual. Would the two comics get the piano to the top of the stairway without losing it and having it slide all the way down to the bottom again, something the audience was eager to see? Suspense must not disappoint, and the audience wasn't disappointed. Comedy or not, press button notwithstanding, I know that the art of storytelling will continue into the future. And with it will go the perpetual necessity—suspense.

# 17

# Where Danger Lives

## *John Charles Bennett*

The publisher has questioned why my father made such slight mention of my mother despite their marriage of thirty-seven years. I feel no satisfaction in writing this chapter—hers was a hard-luck story. But as Charles's memoir deserves its full telling, his omission requires my painting two unfortunate portraits.

People have asked, "What was it like growing up in Hollywood? Did you meet Hitchcock?" If I did, I don't remember it. I was bound to the old English expression "Children should be seen and not heard." Besides, few industry professionals would visit our house. Mom was the antithesis of my father's first wife, Maggie, who had been a popular hostess.

In fact, soon after my birth in 1947, Mom swore to destroy Dad's reputation. To his professional detriment, he drastically curtailed his social networking, partygoing, and hosting. This was evident as early as 1948 when, uncharacteristically, Dad failed to accept Lady Astor's invitation or renew a friendship with Gertrude Lawrence.

Betty Jo Riley (1922–84) was born of an *American Gothic* family. Walter Riley (1883–1968) was a Missouri farm boy who smoked a corncob pipe and worked the giant Ferris wheel at the 1904 St. Louis World's Fair. His father, Cornelius Riley (1858–1907), had been crushed by a locomotive in the Chicago train yard. Walter married Lena Bertha Smith, a farm girl, sometime before 1911, and sired Betty's sister in that year. In 1911 Walter was a clerk in the recently incorporated boomtown of Grandfield, Oklahoma. But after Lena's parents lost the family farm during the Depression, Lena became angry and emotionally abusive. At that time

Walter was "bringing home the bacon" as a hospital orderly in St. Joseph, Missouri; and on his meager wages his family ate ham, often day after day. Lena once told Betty Jo that she was an accident born ten years after her sister. And once, when Betty had her hair styled, Lena said, "Why did you waste your nickel? It didn't improve your appearance." Betty Jo resented both parents, as much Lena's caustic attitude as Walter's lack of ambition and failure to protect her from Lena.

In 1951 Betty Jo read aloud to me the Hans Christian Andersen story "The Little Match Girl." The tale is of a child beaten for not selling matches, who chooses to freeze to death while dreaming of her deceased grandmother. Betty Jo identified with this story to such an extent that she cried while reading it. Like the match girl, she chose a calamitous resignation that brought about a slow and chilling death.

Betty Jo specialized in resigned clichés such as "Better than a poke in the eye with a blunt stick" and "That's the way the cookie crumbles," "The world is going to hell in a handbasket" and "Damned if you do, damned if you don't." Yet she aspired to higher education and received an associate of arts degree at a junior college in St. Joseph, Missouri. In her early twenties Betty Jo was a reader immersed in the poetry of Wordsworth and T. S. Eliot and the philosophy of Ralph Waldo Emerson. She was also an award-winning bowler, and a brunette beauty named Tobacco Princess of Weston, Missouri. But after the death of her World War II pilot boyfriend, and some ugly, unrecounted abuse at the hands of her parents (for which she blamed her father), she boarded a Greyhound bus headed west and settled near Santa Monica, California. At twenty-one, she was working in payroll at Douglas Aircraft. She was married for a brief ten months in 1943, but was divorced on the grounds that she had acted in an extremely cruel and inhuman manner and caused her husband mental and physical suffering.

In the fall of 1945 Charles Bennett was writing *Ivy*, which would be cast with his colony friends Joan Fontaine, Herbert Marshall, and Sir Cedric Hardwicke, when he met Betty, working as a secretary in the office of his business manager, a former cavalry trooper. Charles was forty-six, recently divorced, rich, and an internationally recognized bon vivant. Betty was unpretentious, twenty-two, drop-dead gorgeous, and had a great figure. Charles was smitten. Their courtship was *Pygmalion* staged against the glamour and glitz of Hollywood. He fox-trotted Betty through a world of expatriates, film celebs, and studio bosses, drove her to Sequoia, and coaxed the acrophobic across Moro Rock. Hitchcock offered Betty a screen test—said he'd teach the beauty to act—but Mom refused. The studio mogul Jack Warner pressured Charles to bow out—but Dad refused.

Charles proposed to Betty in February 1947, within a week of returning from a five-month stint in London and Scotland, where he was planning *The Trial of Madeleine Smith,* about a girl who poisons her fiancé. The gossip columnist Louella Parsons reported their marriage in the February 21, 1947, issue of the *Los Angeles Examiner.* Their marriage was a civil ceremony in Beverly Hills, followed by a two-week honeymoon at a high-desert guest ranch. Betty was soon pregnant with me.

But around the time of my birth, Betty intercepted a letter that caused her to suspect that Charles, while overseas, had had an affair with the actress Annette Simmonds. Charles denied this, and he then wrote to Annette (in England), telling her never to write to him again. Unfortunately, his evasion dovetailed with Mom's learning about Peggy Field—the mistress during his marriage with Maggie. Now feeling degraded and vengeful, Betty threw away the wedding ring and swore off sex.

On the day of my birth, December 23, 1947, the nonchalant Charles noted in his diary, "Rode Mex." (Mex was his polo pony.) And secondarily, "Betty, a mother." There was no mention that Betty had nearly bled to death and required an emergency C-section. The next night, he was celebrating at the West Hollywood pub the Cock 'n Bull, where my name was burned into the wood of a red piano.

Betty said my birth kept them together. That may be so, but only because she was ill and needed his financial support. In August 1948 we flew to London. While we were there, a mysterious ailment caused her weight to plunge forty-five pounds. Mom was unable to travel to Monte Carlo, where Charles was contracted to direct the lovely Margaret Lockwood in *Madness of the Heart.* She was started on insulin treatment; and her diabetes, or whatever it was, did not persist. During those months caring for me, Betty was sick and friendless in the postwar ruin. Furious that Charles had abandoned her—"insult added to injury"—she nonetheless enjoyed my first word, "duck," spoken along the Serpentine in Hyde Park.

*Madness of the Heart* was notable as Charles's first film credit as a director. It also presents a dark and self-fulfilling prophecy of his future life with Betty. It tells of a nobleman who leaves his fiancée to travel to France. During his absence, she experiences brain degeneration, goes blind, and enters a convent. Sadly, this scenario would be approximated by events playing out in their lives a mere seven years in the future.

Returned from London in June 1949, Dad was soon at work on *Where Danger Lives,* about a suicidal woman who, having married for money, murders her husband, who is old enough to be her father. A young doctor, Jeff, is then seduced into assisting Margo's escape to Mexico through an Arizona border town. Though Jeff's judgment has been compromised by a brain concussion, he eventually tries to foil Margo's escape. In retaliation, Margo attempts to smother him and, when that fails, tries to gun him down. Border police save Jeff and end his drama by shooting the madwoman. Starring Robert Mitchum and Faith Domergue, this film noir classic is, like *Madness,* another prognostication of my mother's mental illness.

In my earliest memory, Mom was sweet and protective. She said she kept Dad away from my crib "to stop him dropping cigarette ash on the baby." Mom entertained me by singing "Three Little Fishies": "Down in the meadow in a little bitty pool, swam three little fishies, and a mama fishie too." We watched swans glide across stream-fed pools at the Bel Air Hotel. She read me Beatrix Potter stories and asked simple logic questions such as, "If all dogs are brown, and Henry is a dog—is Henry brown?" (Henry was an old cocker spaniel who passed gas under the dining table.) Also, Mom pretended to steal the nose off my face, her right thumb tucked between her forefingers.

"Mommy, give it back," I'd plead.

The fact that my father was fatherless weighed heavily against his ability to parent me or remain faithful to Betty. But to my four-year-old mind we seemed a happy family, just like our three cats: Poppa Cat, Momma Cat, and Baby Cat. There was in our sixteenth-century game cabinet a Victorian-era card game, Happy Families, which illustrated families engaged in occupations—cobbler, miller, baker, and so on. It was played like Go Fish, and if one asked for "Charles Bennett, film writer," the game reply was, "Not at home."

In 1951 Dad was on location in Mexico, codirecting *The Great Cardinal* (1952), also known as *The Prince of the Church* or *Un Principe de la Iglesia,* after which he traveled to the south of France and Cannes to film *The Green Glove* (1952), also known as *The White Road.* That original thriller presents a complete "Bennett scenario," with its hapless hero, disinterested heroine, suave villain, double-chase suspense, and MacGuffin. Its construction is intriguing, as it places the denouement at the start of the film.

But the actor Glenn Ford gave a lackluster performance, and the direction by Rudolph Maté was not on par with Hitchcock's direction of *The 39 Steps*. Dad's continuing travel did not endear him to my mother; and I am certain she soon wished he was out of her life for good.

Mom's mood lifted when Charles boarded the Super Constellation flight for Europe or Mexico. While I played in my bedroom with marbles and toy soldiers, she entertained her boyfriends Bob, Dick, or Wally during long afternoons behind her closed bedroom door.

On one of my early birthdays, Mom let me stay up past my bedtime, in anticipation of his long-distance phone call from Europe. I felt hurt when he didn't phone. But I also got to witness her frustration up close and personal. "That son of a bitch father of yours will have hell to pay," she fumed, sending me off to bed.

When in town, Dad entertained himself by tickling me, building apprehension as he marched his fingers up my arm, chanting, "Round and round the market like a teddy bear, one step, two step, tickle him right there." The tickling was merciless, and I would scream for Mom to make him stop. I also became painfully ticklish for the next twenty years. Sometimes his intoxicated sense of humor let fly with facetious remarks like "Children are revolting" or "All children should be destroyed."

By 1952 Dad decided it was time for a divorce. He had learned of Betty's lovers and blamed his own stupidity. Mom's retaliation was furious, and not without cause—I remember the name Peggy Field savagely whipped about during Betty's tirades. And later he told me that, while "Peitsy" was married to Louis Hayward (they divorced in 1950), she often phoned him late at night to drive over and collect her off the street.

At work on *No Escape* (1953), he traveled to San Francisco to direct the film while Mom remained in Los Angeles. But they did not divorce; for reasons of health and money, no escape was possible.

When I was four and Charles was in Europe, Betty had briefly employed a governess, Margaret Williamson—a nun novitiate from Nova Scotia who left the convent before taking her vows. A year or so later, Margaret was reemployed full time. Thankfully, she sheltered me from Mom's brooding belligerence and dad's neglect. I loved Margaret, though I was bruised by her authoritarian, no-nonsense manner.

Before Margaret, my closest brush with religion had probably been mom's insistent phrase "come hell or high water." But Margaret had me enrolled in kindergarten at the Beverly Hills Catholic School, where nuns swatted children with rulers—then prayed for forgiveness. In first grade I remember being refused a donut because I wasn't Catholic and didn't take confession. Also in first grade I wrote a poem that characterized my father as our Poppa Cat. I wrote, "The cats were thinking of getting a divorce with their wives. And the wives become mountain lions and try to seek revenge."

In second grade a nun explained, "Cats don't go to heaven"—so I decided I didn't want to go there, either. But I was fascinated by the martyred saints. Those images, and the emotions they evoked, fit my home life. I would kneel at my bedside and pray my parents' fighting would stop.

In 1953 Dad was admitted to a hospital with bleeding ulcers, which required stomach surgery and multiple blood transfusions. Mom took me to the hospital to say "Good-bye," in case he didn't survive. Later he told me his hospitalization was for gout in his right big toe, which was really perplexing when I noticed a foot-long suture up his abdomen. Earlier in their marriage, Mom had suggested that Dad take his savings and open a Beverly Hills hamburger stand; but now no savings remained—they mortgaged the house to pay his hospital bill. And Mom's mounting resignation explained, "The road to hell is paved with good intentions."

Usually, after dinner, Dad slugged Scotch and soda—writing while listening to 78-RPM records or the KFAC Gas Company Evening Concert. Mom did not like his choice of music, shouting, "Turn down the phonograph, and shut the study door." She was particularly distressed when he played Tchaikovsky's fatalistic Sixth Symphony, *The Pathétique*—saying its third movement brought on her episodes of sleepwalking.

My parents did not share activities. Mom resented his golf membership at the Riviera Country Club. She did not participate in his inebriated pastime of home-recording *Julius Caesar* on a reel-to-reel tape recorder. (I have interspersed some of this in chapter 15.) When Charles was visited by British drinking buddies, such as the actor Tom Conway or the fetish artist John Coutts (also known as John Willie), Betty stayed alone in the study, reading.

And she exploded with fury! During her frequent tirades, she snapped about his financial extravagance and club memberships. She crucified his friends, such as Prince Vladimir Rashevsky, castigating their pretensions. Recalling their fights, I am certain the underlying issues were abandonment, emotional unavailability, and sexual withholding. I grew up in a derisive and emasculating atmosphere.

My parents played poker on occasional Saturday nights with Dorita DeSa, the Nazi spy, her husband, Alfredo, and the Austrian actor Carl Esmond and his wife, Ruth. Mom despised Dorita, and Ruth Esmond told me at mom's funeral that "Betty's anger broke up the poker game—she drove us away."

My parents' arguments would escalate, much like the opening scene of *Young and Innocent* (1937), in which the wife is strangled by her estranged husband.

"This marriage was the worst thing that ever happened to me." Betty threw Dad's glass of Scotch against the wall. "You're a *has-been* and a lousy writer."

Dad went to the liquor cabinet behind the bar to pour a drink, and another. Mom was terrified by a butcher knife stored in the cabinet. Sometimes he left the house. One time he smashed his car into a tree down the street. Paramedics transported him to the hospital for facial stitches.

Dad was oblivious to my Catholic indoctrination—his scenarist imagination was actively scripting scenarios of terror. But sometimes he surprised me and consented to play Prince's Quest, an English board game from his childhood. A variation of Snakes and Ladders, it pulled me into a fantasy world populated by witches, dwarfs, castles, and flying dragons.

But more often than not, Dad ignored us, working at his desk. Mom warned, "Don't bother your father when he is writing." As he wrote daily from ten in the morning to ten at night, except for meals, there was little opportunity for interaction. I learned not to ask anything from either of them, since I was certain to be disappointed. I became extremely shy and introverted.

I played alone, climbing old avocado trees or building mud canals on an adjacent vacant lot owned by the costume designer Edith Head. Our two ranch-style houses were sister properties with terra-cotta-tiled roofs and flagstone patios, built in 1934 either by the actor Robert Armstrong or by the art director of *King Kong* (1934). We had a large walk-in monkey cage, where Dad, before World War II, kept a spider monkey. When "Kong" escaped and climbed a tall pine tree, the LA Fire Department captured the primate, and Dad donated it to the zoo. Years later I built a fort in its rooftop crawl space—miraculously, I didn't get lockjaw from protruding rusty nails. I also concocted poison in leftover alcohol bottles, mixing bleach, perfume, and drugs heisted from Mom's medicine cabinet.

On the afternoon that I dropped a stinky bottle of poison on the study floor, she abruptly terminated my apothecary experiments.

Betty was psychologically tested and found to be of superior IQ, but defensive and afraid of dependency, emotionally precarious, and suffering "free-floating anxiety." She was seen by an eminent Beverly Hills psychiatrist, Dr. Nathan Rickles, who specialized in female anger. Mom's takeaway was: "Psychiatry is a waste of time. I cannot be hypnotized." Also, "I should have divorced Charles and married the psychiatrist." She said this frequently enough that I have questioned whether there was an affair. For his part, Dr. Rickles wrote in a landmark study, "The Angry Woman Syndrome," "Treatment is at best palliative and is usually resisted."[26]

By 1956 Mom's health had crashed. Dr. Augustus Rose, professor of neurology at UCLA and later the first chairman of the Department of Neurology, diagnosed her with grand mal epilepsy and Huntington's chorea, a genetic neurodegenerative disorder that affects muscle coordination and leads to cognitive decline and psychiatric problems. She was prescribed anticonvulsants (Mysoline and Dilantin) and a bromide medicine. Panicked by the possibility of my carrying an inherited disease, Mom wrestled with the decision whether to have me sterilized.

Fortunately, by year's end her health had improved, which indicated a misdiagnosis. Dr. Rose quickly reversed his opinion, suggesting she was suffering neuritis, malnutrition, and bromide toxicity. Charles wrote in a memo, "Rose blames himself for . . . bringing about her panic. . . . I was very relieved to hear that Betty is suffering from a very bad vitamin deficiency." But the underlying cause of her illness went undiagnosed; Mom continued to use anticonvulsants, and Charles remained dutiful; as he had previously provided for his mother, or his mistress, he could now provide for Betty.

In 1956 Betty was hospitalized at Las Encinas Sanitarium in Pasadena. Charles was often in Europe, writing or directing *The Count of Monte Cristo* TV series and sending home the bucks for her private care. I was placed at the eighty-acre Mountain Oak Boys' Ranch, east of Redlands in the badlands of Riverside County. The ranch housed a handful of delinquent, autistic, and normal kids supervised by "Uncle Jack"—a child molester. Uncle Jack kept his hands off me, though bullies at Beaumont's Palm Elementary School flushed my head in a public toilet. Being very shy, I told no one of my humiliation. Through the next school year, I sat withdrawn and alone on a bench during lunch period.

One weekend, on a trip home from the ranch, I visited Mom in the hospital. A nurse told me she was dying and this good-bye would be my last. But she recovered. And after a year at the sanitarium, with multiple unnecessary electric-shock treatments, she was diagnosed with severe endocrine dysfunction—hyperadrenalism, hyperthyroidism, and psychoneurosis marked with features of hysterical conversion. The doctor speculated that there had been a traumatic head injury to her pituitary gland when, as a teen, Betty Jo was thrown from a car. After removal of her thyroid gland, and being given multiple prescriptions, she returned home under the care of an endocrinologist.

Charles continued to bounce between California and Europe as associate producer of *The New Adventures of Charlie Chan* (1957–58) for the producer Eddie Small. While at home, he completed a charming Christmas drama, *Sermon in the Snow,* about Franz Gruber's composing of the carol "Silent Night." This should have been filmed, and with Dad's direction it would have been an instant Christmas classic. But his partner in the project, Otto Klement, the producer of *The Amazing Adventure* (1936), did not sell the script.

Returned to Los Angeles, I was enrolled at St. John's Military Academy, a Catholic boarding school where each morning we saluted the cross and stood for bed inspection. When I complained, my parents moved me to the California Military Academy, where cadets were taught leadership and were spanked with heavy wood paddles. I played trombone in the CMA marching band and paraded in the honor guard.

At this point Betty suffered the toxic side effects of her medications and chronic anger; and since Dad was overseas, I suffered through her extreme back pain, delirium and tremors, narcolepsy and unconsciousness, sleepwalking, incoherent speech, and smoking in bed. I was twelve and had no one to ask for help. One day she said, "Johnny, go to the bathroom for me," so I went in and closed the door, and cried. Withdrawn and depressed, I have no memory of how I managed those months. But I do remember wishing to be invisible. After Dad returned, the endocrinologist adjusted her meds, and the situation improved. At my ninth-grade graduation from CMA in 1962, I was named both "Honor Cadet" and "Most Likely to Succeed." No one noticed that I was now picking into my right hand with sharp tweezers, trying to dig out a freckle.

During her rehabilitated period, Mom invited friends to the house and Charles invited his non-industry acquaintances. These included the

Beverly Hills architect Gerry Colcord and his wife, Ginny, and Georgene Wyatt—who married a mayor of Beverly Hills. I also remember Bob Rost, who, I think, was the illegitimate son of the mafioso Joe Adonis.

Betty had a mouthful of teeth repaired, twice—without novocaine. Denial of physical sensation came easily to her. "I put my mind on something else," she remarked. My introduction to orthodonture was her remark, "You're getting braces. You could eat corn on the cob down a shotgun barrel."

It is only a slight exaggeration to say Charles ignored Betty, as though she lived on a separate planet. They never saw films together, or did anything else together, for that matter. Mom quit dining with us, which caused me to complain that dinner conversation with Dad was little more than a nightly cross-examination. He offered slight recognition of her on Mother's Day or her birthday.

Our annual family excursion was to Christmas dinner at the West Hollywood pub the Cock 'n Bull. There were cocktails before dinner, Welsh rarebit, medium-rare roast beef with mashed potatoes and gravy, or leg of lamb with new potatoes, Yorkshire pudding, and English trifle. I loved the trifle! But the evening would drag on, with more drinks after dinner . . .

Some nights Dad and I played chess or backgammon, or searched the night sky for Echo 1, a communication satellite. To this day I cherish his written challenge: "I, Charles Bennett, father of my wretched son, will not allow him to win the next ten games. Signed, 'The Great Spotter of Satellites' [with a drawn image of 'The Black Hand and the Cross Bones']."

But the improvement in mom's health did not last, and, before long, depression spiraled her down into an angry, walking nightmare. She mixed phenobarbital (an antiseizure medication), Seconal (a sleep barbiturate that can cause hallucinations), and booze. Mom lived on the couch in front of the TV, moving only for beer or cigarettes, or to mix herself a vodka and V8. Her hair was often tangled and filthy. She seldom put on day clothes, wearing stained negligées and a frayed, burned bathrobe. Eating once a day, around two o'clock in the morning, she'd sometimes wake me to butter her baked potato. Or she'd pass out and sleep around the clock, and in the morning I would find a charred meal in a 450-degree oven.

Charles ignored her silent screams for attention. When not writing for television, he returned to his first love, writing for the theater. In 1960 he optioned a play titled *Once upon a Midnight* (not produced) to the Broadway producer Julian Olney. But the supernatural was not a timely topic, so the option reverted. In 1964 he wrote another play titled *A Little Night Music,* whose antagonist was a sexually frustrated, manipulative drunk, not unlike Blanche DuBois in *A Streetcar Named Desire. Night Music* was optioned in 1967 to the Broadway producer Elliot Martin. But Mom said the play was about her, so when the option reverted to Charles, Betty incinerated all copies of the manuscript. Years later I returned a copy he had lent me—but Dad had moved on to other scripts. "Too bad," he lamented. "The title was stolen for a Broadway musical."

By the mid-1960s Dad's income was plummeting—his stories were not selling—so Mom berated him, "You write lousy dialogue. You always have. No one will employ you!" So he turned to writing novels. *The Hinges of Hell* (ca. 1963, unpublished) is an interpersonal drama among a handful of nuclear war survivors racing to save humanity from a malevolent, extra-terrestrial slime. *Hinges* was followed by two other novels, *Fox on the Run* and *Thunderbird. Fox* is a race to prevent the assassination of the Prince of Wales, and *Thunderbird* is a romance between a female archaeologist and a mobster hunted by the mafia and the police. Dad scripted both *Fox* and *Thunderbird* as feature-length films. But by that point, his name recognition having faded, he could sell only an occasional Irwin Allen TV script. And Betty, unimpressed by his efforts, remarked, "There's no hope in hell of your selling anything."

Presented with financial problems, Mom got to repeat her Depression-era experiences. She eliminated my piano lessons, though kept me enrolled in an Episcopal military academy. Dad terminated his club membership, bought a Honda Civic for its gas mileage, and switched from Scotch whiskey to a Paul Masson chardonnay. We ate ham four nights out of seven. When Dad and I dined out, he substituted fried calf's liver at the Armstrong-Schroder diner for roast leg of lamb at Frascati's. We'd bring home a burger for Mom, who, more often than not, would go ballistic over something unpredictable like insufficient mayonnaise or its lukewarm temperature.

I enjoyed the ham but was troubled by mom's manipulations. "I can read your mind," she'd say, "and I know everything you're thinking." Then she'd slap me for thinking what *she* thought I was thinking. Alternatively, she'd demand, "Do what I tell you or you'll be disinherited."

"Go ahead," I'd reply. "I don't want your money."

A child of the Depression, she had money foremost in her mind. Though Dad blamed Mom's ill health for costing him dearly, her financial acumen allowed them to pay off the mortgage. In 1965, when Occidental College offered me a scholarship for music composition, Mom insisted that I attend the California Institute of Technology, saying, "We don't need another broken-down artist in the family; you need to support me in my old age."

In 1968 Charles was diagnosed with and treated for colon cancer. The surgeon removed his cancerous intestine, and he wore a colostomy bag for twenty-seven years. Fortunately, the Directors Guild paid his medical expenses. Home from the hospital, he wrote *Sierra Nevada* (1970, not produced) about a kidnapped heiress (Patty Hearst) in love with a gang member. The heiress marries him; but the story ends tragically when he falls to his death during the police manhunt.

By the late 1960s Betty was also falling. Any trip out of the house ended at Ye Little Club in Beverly Hills with her tiresome refrain, "Just one more beer." Typically, Charles drove her home—but sometimes she fell on the way to the car and dragged him down to the alley pavement. And occasionally Charles would lose patience, saying, "Find your own way home." Then Betty would be brought back by taxi, or by some man from the bar.

She justified her atrocious behavior by remarking, "Most people live lives of quiet desperation." But I didn't buy it, and told her, "You are wasting your life," or "You ought to go back to work." Clearly I did not understand the dimension of her problem, but my patience had worn thin.

With Mom in such bad shape, no one came to the house. Dad visited his friends, including the actresses Queenie Leonard, Anna Lee, and Joan Gardner (who married Zoltán Korda), the poet Robert Nathan, the actor Reginald Gardiner, the Honorable Cecil Howard (the second son of the 19th Earl of Suffolk), and Cecil's wife, the actress Frances Drake. After Mom's death, Dad considered marrying Frances Drake, but he chose not to—a pity, as her millions would soon be commandeered by a Hollywoodite, David Brown, offering a 1992 marriage for the uncontestable control of her property and eighty-year-old body.

I protected myself from Mom's dominations by a simple visualization, what I termed my "silver wedge." That psychic defense cut apart all insults hurled at me. In the mid-1970s, when I was toying with the idea of becoming a teacher, she asked, "Why teach? You don't like children." My wedge split that projection to pieces, and I have become a successful high school science teacher. Not surprisingly, I have specialized with my "Most Likely to Succeed" fourteen-year-old age group.

Over time Mom came to hate me as she hated Charles. During weekend visits from Caltech, I'd lock my bedroom door, afraid she'd suffer a psychotic break and stab me with that butcher knife. My emotional pain was devastating. I tried to remember the maternal comfort of my childhood. I tried to recognize her inner spirit, a black swan, and I forgave her mental illness. I tried to ignore the tantrums and treat her as though she were pleasant—that disconnect infuriated her. So one afternoon I phoned to ask how she was doing.

She replied, "If you don't drop out of law school, I'll kill myself."

To which, emotionless and detached, I said, "Your suicide is none of my business. Do what you want." She didn't kill herself. But with my trauma and college debt stacking up, and my body experiencing spasms and twitches, I dropped out of the USC Gould School of Law. As an adult, it took twenty-five years to reconnect to my emotions and effect a spiritual recovery. I did not marry until my late forties.

Meanwhile, dad's imagination continued to tick along, now brilliantly alive in a script titled *Satan Returns* (1972, not produced). It was a romantic sequel to *Curse of the Demon,* about the accidental conjuring of an ancient curse that threatens the protagonist. It did not sell; studios possibly balked at the expense of filming at a remote monastery in Spain's Cordillera Penibética.

By the mid-1970s Mom had gained considerable weight and fell ever more frequently, now too heavy for seventy-five-year-old Charles to lift. Her face was often black and blue from head injuries, her brow and eyes horribly swollen. She was angry, unreasonable, and uncommunicative for weeks at a time. "Go back to sleep" became Charles's consistent remark. What we weren't recognizing was that by 1982, at age sixty, Mom had early-onset Alzheimer's. By 1984 she was asking me, deep distress showing in her eyes and tone of voice, "Have you seen Charles? He's left me." Actually, he was standing beside her, still looking after her as dutifully as he had Lilian; but Betty, in her three-year-old's mentality, thought Charles to be her mother.

Mom died in 1984 of a mercifully aggressive lung cancer. I felt sad she'd lived such a tormented life. And a few days before her death, I told her I was sorry she was dying, and that I loved her. With remarkable lucidity, she replied, "I know . . . Every cloud has a silver lining." This cliché meant either she had now admitted my love, or she looked forward to dying—probably the latter. Either way, death found her at home in front of the TV, soon after the conclusion of the 1984 Olympics.

Eighty-five-year-old Charles was exhausted and devastated. He employed Betty's caregiver to look after him, rationalizing that he was keeping Ruth out of a Hollywood homeless shelter. His psyche had circled back to Lilian and his empathy for the derelict women of London. My recurrent nightmare was that Mom was alive and homeless in Hollywood, selling matches.

Charles outlived Betty by eleven years. After the Hitchcock films were rereleased on videotape, Dad was rediscovered and employed by 20th Century Fox studio. He was visited by the international press and the Hitchcock biographers, and he made new friends, including the actress Carrie Fisher, the actor Michael Caine, and the writer Stuart Birnbaum. His social standing recovered—he was back on the Hollywood A-list. It's a pity no one in Hollywood thought to ask if he had original plays, screenplays, or novels for sale.

One morning in 1985, while standing in the kitchen beside the stove, Dad asked me about Betty, "Do you think I was responsible?" He looked bewildered.

I shook my head no. I could not find it in my heart to remind him of what he had surely known since earliest childhood, "Hell hath no fury like a woman scorned."

# 18

# The Avenger

*John Charles Bennett*

Avenger: one who inflicts punishment in return for an injury or offense.

*—merriam-webster.com*

My father was the second of three sons born to Lilian Bennett, the eldest child of a wealthy shipping magnate. Lilian was the caretaker of eight siblings; and when inevitably she rebelled, she was cruelly cast off. Described by Charles as "wildly stagestruck" and by her cousins as "a bit frisky," Lilian hooked up with itinerant actors and a theatrical con man.

Her sons were bastards. Charles was told that his father—unbelievably surnamed Bennett—had died in a London boiler explosion when Charles was four. But that story doesn't stand up to scrutiny—Charles's earliest memory of the brokers' men, presumably by age four, placed Lilian's extreme poverty before her husband's death. Anyway, she was producing melodramas as the Miss Lilian Bennett Repertory Company in 1900 and 1901, which eliminates any husband from the picture. Penniless, Lilian "shot the moon" to escape her lodger-spies and dragged her starving children from one flat or city to the next—etching Charles's identification as the original man on the run.

Lilian's father, following attitudes of Victorian-era gentry, identified the family name with a seventeenth-century landowning family, Bennett of Pythouse, Wiltshire. In 1929 Lilian asked Charles to motor to Dorset to research that fabled Bennett lineage. Charles believed he found the missing ancestral link, a seventeenth-century south-of-Shaftesbury landowner, William Bennett, Gentleman. Research at the London Society of Genealogists indicated William was the uncle of a Thomas Bennett, Gentleman, the personal secretary to Prince Rupert, nephew of King Charles I, and commander of the Royalist cavalry. That discovery elevated Charles in his saddle and was the basis for one of his celebrated stories.

Unfortunately, my research told a different tale. Charles's ancestors descended from Pythouse through a cadet line of Quaker millworkers and tanners. The family endured a shameful 1767 bankruptcy, disclosing its illiteracy by an "X" signed on a relocation document. I believe that Lilian sensed her family's denial of its blue-collar roots. Abandoned by her own father and her sons' father(s), Lilian placed an emotional burden on her boys. Her shame imprinted Charles's psyche and conditioned his plays and films. Eventually it festered out of proportion, making its most graphic appearance as an extraterrestrial slime imperiling humanity in *The Hinges of Hell* (ca. 1963, unpublished novel).

Lilian sparked Charles's interest in Victorian melodrama. She taught him to read and encouraged him to write stories such as "The Mill Mystery" (1907). She directed him to find work as a child and teen actor with multiple touring companies. And throughout his career, Charles provided Lilian her financial support. After his younger brother committed suicide, Charles became her devoted caregiver. He dutifully accepted responsibility for this "great woman" and put off marriage to assist her. After Lilian's death, he often wired flowers to her graveside; and, in his nineties, the only photo at his bedside was an eight-by-ten, silver-framed portrait of his mother.

The reader will by now recognize Charles as a master of mimesis, routinely projecting his personal drama onto stage and film. In 1915 he was the orphaned tanner's apprentice, the silent-screen John Halifax, intent on rising above his lowly status. In 1916 he contemplated illegitimacy while acting as Edgar in *King Lear*. In his early twenties he was a repertory Romeo seducing country lasses. In 1927, at the apotheosis of his acting career, he strutted as King Theseus in *A Midsummer Night's Dream*. His older brother, Eric, was the World War I soldier remembered in Charles's first play, *The Return*. The molestation of a woman friend inspired his second play, *Blackmail*. Experiences of self-fulfilling prophecy prompted *The Clairvoyant*. His "shooting the moon" with Lilian instigated the "man on the run" Richard Hannay handcuffed to Pamela in *The 39 Steps*—neither Pamela nor the handcuffs appeared in the John Buchan novel. He populated his scripts with suave psychopaths, who were as emotionally absent as his father. And this pattern continued throughout his writing.

Charles's first play, *The Return*, teems with issues of maternal codependence, patricide, abandonment, illegitimacy, and shame. He divided Lilian's personal issues between two female characters—the widowed Mrs. Norcott, who takes a load of village gossip, and Miss Mary Dunn, who assumes the shame of giving birth out of wedlock.

The play's prologue stages the battlefield death of a soldier, Eric Norcott. Eric is reluctant to pass into the light because his mother will be left grieving and alone. *Enter Ishtar*—the earthbound spirit of a stillborn fetus, charged to live an honorable life. Ishtar offers to switch identities with Eric.

> ISHTAR: I want you to give me the chance that you have had, that I may the sooner gain my place in heaven. I want to prove . . . I *too* am worthy.
> ERIC (*thoughtfully*): You want to take my place. (*He looks up.*) But I don't see how you can. You are dead, too, for the matter of that. A spirit isn't a man.
> ISHTAR (*with conviction*): I can *look* like a man.
> ERIC: Perhaps you can . . . but that's not all. . . .
> ISHTAR: I can make your mother happy. Let me do *that*. It may be enough.

Eric cautions that he promised to marry a village girl, Mary Dunn. Ishtar explains that though a spirit cannot marry, Eric is not to worry.

> ISHTAR (*as if stilling his doubts*): She is young and will forget. Your mother is old.
> ERIC: My mother! Yes . . . that's the main thing.

Back in the village, after Eric's death, Mary tells Ishtar that she is pregnant. When Ishtar refuses to wed, Mary lapses into a deep depression. Hearing gossip of the pregnancy and Ishtar's refusal, Mary's father, Mr. Dunn, bursts into the Norcott sitting room.

DUNN: My daughter is here . . . out of my way . . .

*The door from the hall bursts open and Dunn stands in the doorway—
swaying slightly. He is crimson with fury and has evidently been
drinking heavily. His eyes light on Mary.*

So you are here. I knew you would be. I suppose you've come to your
fine friends to ask them to help you. (*Bitterly.*) Well . . . are they
laughing at the joke too?

MARY (*staring at him*): Joke?

DUNN: I've just heard it. I've just heard it. (*He suddenly lurches
forwards towards Ishtar.*) My God . . . let me get at you.

MARY (*seizing his arm*): Father . . . !

DUNN (*shaking her off*): Don't touch me . . . (*To* Ishtar.) By God, I'll
make you pay for this . . .

MARY (*quickly*): It wasn't his fault.

DUNN (*turning on her*): No . . . perhaps it wasn't. Perhaps you asked
him to . . . to . . . (*He buries his face in his hands.*) Oh God! (*He
pauses a moment—then goes on jerkily.*) I heard it just now at the
"Lion." That drunken sot Gunning shouted it in my teeth. I
thought I'd 'a killed him.

MARY: Father . . .

DUNN: You're no daughter o' mine. I've done with you. Done with
you . . . d'you hear?

MARY (*desperately*): But I loved him, Father . . .

DUNN: Did you think he'd marry you then? I could 'a told you
different. (*At* Ishtar.) The bloody swine!

Feelings of betrayal and shame compel Mary to suicide. Mrs. Norcott is
shamed both by her son's abandonment of Mary and by his seeming deser-
tion from a World War I battlefield. At the play's climax, Mary's avenging
father shoots Ishtar.

But the spirit Ishtar cannot die. Instead, he reunites Mary with her
murderous father, explaining that he interceded in Mary's suicide. The
bewildered families then learn that Eric had been killed in the war, but all
will be redeemed by the birth of Eric's son.

ISHTAR: Eric died gloriously that you might live, even as years
before, One died that the *world* might live. Your son's child
will soon be born. . . . Comfort each other, for the sake of the

one you both have lost. [Mrs. Norcott *holds out her hand and* Mary *comes to her slowly. For a moment they look into each other's eyes . . . then* Mary *kneels and her head falls gently forward on to* Mrs. Norcott*'s lap.* Mrs. Norcott *strokes her hair. Her eyes are alight with a newfound happiness.* Ishtar *is gazing at them fixedly, strange longing in his eyes . . . then [he] goes out through the French windows and away into the darkness of the night.*]

Church bells peal miraculously across the fields. Ishtar, the spirit of a still-born, has succeeded in his transcendental mission. Mrs. Norcott and Mary, mother and mother-to-be, are joyfully united in their love of the illegitimate and fatherless fetus. The curtain falls.

Charles selected the archetypical Ishtar, the part he played on opening night, to redeem Lilian's shame by an interplay of mythological and messianic archetypes. Though the mythological Ishtar was a wrathful Babylonian goddess of love and war, her characterization in *The Return* was beneficent, devoted, androgynous, and unable to wed (like Charles). But in Charles's later films, Ishtar reemerges in her wrathful aspect—as a murderous and vengeful she-demon.

Charles's second play, *Blackmail,* explored Lilian's issues more proactively. Working-class Alice knifes a rapist in self-defense. An itinerant collects evidence that places Alice at the murder. But his effort to blackmail the family backfires when Alice's boyfriend, a detective, is appointed lead investigator.

One encounters a problem attempting to study *Blackmail*'s third act. The version that the producer Al Woods insisted on, and which the press panned, is presently unknown. Because Tallulah Bankhead's fans behaved riotously, one suspects that Alice's integrity was compromised by the Al Woods version. But Charles said the play reverted to its original ending on tour and was then successful. In the 1934 published edition—presumably the repertory version—Alice is released from jail into the detective's arms after the blackmailer dies in a prison hospital.

My favorite is an unpublished version titled *24 Hours.* A sensational trial, occurring during the curtained interval between the second and third acts, acquits Alice of murder because she acted in self-defense. Returning home from jail, she is introduced by her mother, Mrs. Jarvis, to Miss Potter, a nasty Victorian spinster. Miss Potter has been tasked to force the terrified girl into a workhouse, where, locked away, she will atone her family's disgrace by ironing.

> MISS POTTER: You must remember that this is going to take a lot of living down. Your parents have their livelihood to consider. If you were *here* . . . Well . . . It isn't a very pleasant reflection, is it? I mean . . . the disgrace . . .
>
> ALICE (*breaking out*): But I don't see. *What* disgrace? I've been acquitted . . .
>
> MISS POTTER: Acquittal isn't everything . . .
>
> ALICE (*losing control of herself*): But they said. . . . Oh . . . you ought to have been there to hear them. It was proved I wasn't to blame . . .
>
> MISS POTTER (*soothing her . . . irritatingly*): Now try to keep calm. It's all right. It won't be for long. You can come back here in a year or so's time.
>
> ALICE: A year or so! And where do you expect me to go in the meanwhile?
>
> MISS POTTER: That has been arranged. You will live for the next few months at the Southwark branch of the Fallen Women's Aid Society . . . (*Alice gives a gasp but Miss Potter continues*) You will find your surroundings friendly and congenial and you will have time to reflect and to think about making a new start in life. You will . . .
>
> ALICE (*suddenly . . . unable to bear it any longer*): Be quiet! You . . . dreadful . . . woman!
>
> MISS POTTER (*staggered . . . and shocked to the depths of her soul*): What . . . !!
>
> ALICE (*tensely*): So you want to put me in a prison after all. Yes . . . that's what it means . . . Aid Society! Why . . . (*desperately*) I'd rather go on the streets!
>
> MRS. JARVIS: Alice!
>
> ALICE (*to her mother*): You. Do *you* consent to this?
>
> MRS. JARVIS: It's best, Alice.
>
> ALICE: Best! (*She turns away on the verge of hysterical laughter—but faces them again.*) And *this* is my home. You don't want me here. I killed a man to save myself from . . . from . . . (*Her voice breaks but she carries on.*) And yet you'd send me to a home, among women of that sort . . . as if . . . as if . . . (*She is crying again.*)

Alice won't have any of it—instead, she brazenly decides to sell her story to the press for an astronomical three hundred pounds, and then announces her engagement to the detective. Alice (that is, Lilian) emerges blameless, vindicated by strength of character.

But Alfred Hitchcock's dark film adaptation offered no such atonement. Hitch's ending planned for Alice to be pursued and jailed for the artist's murder; an ending that was changed for commercial reasons. Instead, Alice's detective boyfriend chases the blackmailer to his death, and then Alice feels conscience-ridden and decides to confess. At police headquarters, the detective silences her to protect his reputation. He *privately* justifies the murder as self-defense, and he appears relieved that his concealment of evidence will not be exposed. The viewer is made aware that Alice's conscience is subordinated, and she will remain emotionally scarred.

Hitchcock's *Blackmail* is similar to his silent melodrama *The Lodger* (1927), which followed police efforts to apprehend a serial killer identified as "the Avenger." The film audience is alarmed for the safety of its working-class heroine infatuated with a mysterious lodger. A frenzied crowd chases the lodger to within an inch of death, but he is saved by her detective boyfriend. The twist is offered that the observant lodger was doing his own police work. And its denouement finds the heroine and lodger in each other's arms, planning to wed—it is the detective who is forgotten.

It is commonly held that *The Lodger* was the first story of a falsely accused man on the run. But this is not accurate. Hitchcock did not intend the lodger to be falsely accused—he was the serial killer. The producers insisted that the plot be reconstructed so that Ivor Novello would *not* be cast as a murderer.[27] On close inspection, one finds Hitchcock cunningly maintaining his original intention. By *not* filming Ivor in a flashback to a ballroom murder scene, Hitch implies that Ivor murdered his sister, with whom he had been dancing. There can be no other explanation for his absence from the scene. There is no reason to believe that the camera angle is shot in his point of view, and as in the law, *fatetur facinus qui judicium fugit:* he who flees judgment confesses his guilt. Thus, Hitchcock created a film ending that was truly horrific—glad parents delivering their daughter to a serial killer. In consequence of this, Hitch's *Blackmail* was the first intentional and unambiguous thriller of a falsely accused man on the run.

In both *Blackmail* and *The Lodger,* Bennett and Hitchcock play female innocence against domination. But their intentions are different. Charles's *24 Hours* version is reminiscent of Charles's admiration for Keith

Chesterton, who championed the downtrodden women of London: it vindicates Alice, and she profits from the murder. On the other hand, the film version leaves Alice wallowing in guilt and Hitchcock's career profiting at her expense.

So where did Charles learn his melodramatic elements? Simply put, since 1916 he had acted repeatedly in sixteen or more of Shakespeare's plays. This had taught the dramatic construction of Shakespearean suspense. It taught him Shakespeare's varied themes of blackmail, emotional and otherwise, weaving through *Measure for Measure, The Merry Wives of Windsor, Macbeth, Julius Caesar, Hamlet, The Merchant of Venice,* and so on. He studied chivalric vengeance when, for example, his Romeo murdered the interfering rival Paris. He learned to characterize independent women, such as Beatrice in *Much Ado about Nothing,* Katherine in *The Taming of the Shrew,* Rosalind in *As You Like It,* Viola in *Twelfth Night,* Cordelia in *King Lear,* Portia in *The Merchant of Venice,* and Lady Macbeth.[28] And he learned how comedy can build or prolong suspense by the interplay of hero and villain.

Thus, Charles's next play, *The Last Hour,* featured a smart heroine, Mary, abandoned by her true love. To correct matters, Mary saves her father from emotional extortion, outwits an unscrupulous spy and blackmailer, and then rescues a British secret agent from impending death. Of course, that agent is her lover in disguise.

Mary's victory was Charles's stage triumph. The *Sunday Times* of London critic's comparison of Charles with the Jacobean dramatist John Webster was a long-winded acknowledgment that both had learned their craft from Shakespeare. Even the title of *The Last Hour* is evidence of Shakespearean influence, lifted from a question put by the Duke to the villain Shylock:

> Shylock, the world thinks, and I think so too,
> That thou but lead'st this fashion of thy malice
> To the last hour of act, and then 'tis thought
> Thou'lt show thy mercy and remorse more strange
> Than is thy strange apparent cruelty.
> (*The Merchant of Venice,* act 4, scene 1)

Which provokes the question "What type of suspense is represented in *The Merchant of Venice*?" Anxiety or apprehension? Clearly these terms are in need of better definition; and I do not know how Charles defined either. I am, however, aware of subtle differences of usage in family conversations. *Anxiety* is discomfort arising from a continuing oppressive or unconscionable circumstance, where *unconscionable* means nonconformance to dictates of conscience. *Apprehension* is a state of foreboding, a dread and fearful anticipation of a future happening. Thus, Shylock's claim on Antonio's pound of flesh presents a neat instance of apprehension.

Charles's plays *The Return* and *Blackmail* created melodramatic *anxiety* in the context of their heroines' familial and social circumstances, without apprehension of any particular future event. Both built audience discomfort by prolonging their heroines' emotional trauma, and both achieved atonement by her surmounting the obstacles. *The Last Hour* was Charles's first suspense play staged against the apprehension of a time limit—the midnight export of a death ray. And to audiences' satisfaction, Charles atoned his heroine's anxiety by her saving her lover's life.

But Charles's partnership with Hitchcock disrupted this theme of atonement. Hitch's ending of *Blackmail* had compromised female integrity—of course, Charles was not part of that rewrite. Charles's story *The Man Who Knew Too Much* preserved atonement by Jill's skillful sharpshooting. But *The 39 Steps* was a radical departure, even from Bennett's other crime dramas. Buchan's story about a man on the run resonated with Bennett's core issues of being on the run with Lilian from the brokers' men. To this Bennett added apprehension for Hannay's safety during an escape with a time limit. His film *Sabotage* returned to female anxiety, but it twisted the female lead—no longer a heroine—into a knife murderer. Conrad's story resonated with Charles's Shakespearean sense of vengeance, but it was darker than any earlier stories. *Sabotage* also intensified apprehension by the ticking of an entirely extrinsic device, a time bomb.

The redirection of the maturing Bennett scenario came at a cost. When he turned the heroine into a murderess and built external apprehension, there could no longer be cause for atonement. And this led to the very disturbing, male-dominant denouement presented in *Sabotage*.

That incongruity of an avenging Romeo successfully partnered with a misogynist led me to ask numerous dark questions about my father's emotional health: Why was he obsessed with a wrongly accused and hotly pursued male protagonist (*The 39 Steps, Young and Innocent*)? Why did he have a compulsion to seduce an uncooperative woman (*The 39 Steps, Sabotage, Young and Innocent, Foreign Correspondent*)? What primal instinct scripted women killing men—a naive girl knifing a rapist (*Blackmail*), a depressed wife knifing her heartless husband (*Sabotage*), or a mother shooting her daughter's kidnapper (*The Man Who Knew Too Much*)? What psyche thought to knife or strangle women to propel a story line (*The 39 Steps, Young and Innocent*) or dominate women by concealed evidence (*Sabotage*)? Why kidnap or kill children (*The Man Who Knew Too Much, Sabotage*), and privately quip that all children should be destroyed? Why did he have such a ubiquitous reliance on terror and mayhem (*Sabotage, The 39 Steps, Secret Agent, Foreign Correspondent*)? In other words, what monstrous obsession underlay his fascinations?

The answer is simple enough, initially. Charles was not maniacal; he was a slum child motivated by desire for money, recognition, and the recovery of his birthright. His stage experience made him skilled at pulling elements from a Shakespearean armory. But his work was permeated with Lilian's issues, which, although misinterpreted, had not gone unnoticed.

It has been twenty-five years since I encountered a feminist critic's analysis of rape in Hitchcock's film *Blackmail*. The plot was discussed as an "elaborate joke on the heroine, who in a Freudian paradigm is ultimately transformed into an object between two male subjects."[29] This is certainly an interesting analysis, and one that identified Hitch's misogyny; but it did not correctly identify the Freudian undercurrent of the play *Blackmail*—which was narcissistic revenge. "As defined by Sigmund Freud, narcissistic injury occurs when you take as a personal attack, an injury to a member of the group to which you belong."[30] Also, "A patient experiencing a narcissistic rage may become homicidal, particularly if he has a need to seek revenge."[31]

Lilian's hatred of male pretension, rape, and abandonment had been projected onto Charles. So in *Blackmail*, Alice kills the rapist, escapes parental domination, and finds love with her detective. It was Hitchcock who turned the film story to the emotional blackmail of Alice. And I doubt that Charles was pleased by that revision of his scenario.

After *Psycho*, Charles accused Hitch of sadism. He privately chastised studio heads (and producers) for their demeaning treatment of women. And by his mid-career film noir scripts, Charles had torqued his chivalric code tighter—his revenge now turned to women murdering men. In other words, Charles became an avenger, scripting female characters to deliver his offscreen intentions. The actress killing her husband or lover had sniper Charles pulling the trigger.

"Well, fair enough," someone might object; "if Charles's story was ultimately about Lilian, the brokers' men, shame, and narcissistic revenge, then why did he *not* write about a woman on the run?" Actually, he did so in his original noir film, *No Escape.* He was the writer, director, and lyricist for this United Artist release. Its plot was a further inversion of *Blackmail:* the actress Marjorie Steele is framed for murder and chased in a San Francisco dragnet. Regrettably, Charles avoided any mention of *No Escape* in his memoir—saying elsewhere that it was the "worst movie I ever made, something I want to forget." Small wonder that he felt this way, given his half-century emotional investment. His lyrics written for the composer Bert Shefter suggest that the film ran close to Charles's emotional core.

> No escape from the dreams that have haunted me.
> Schemes that have taunted me through the years.
> No escape from the nights that have brought despair,
> Nights that were everywhere, full of tears . . .
> No escape from you.

Like *No Escape,* much of Charles's contribution to film noir has been forgotten. This is a pity, as we find therein the maturing obsession that reflexively illumines his thriller psychology. Its emergence began with Laurence Olivier's *The Trial of Madeleine Smith,* which reveals a fascination for the femme fatale, the beautiful and intelligent siren who lures men to their death. That development continued toward a broader characterization—what I call the vengeful woman.

In her darkest composite, the vengeful woman is a demonic or tortured soul whose hatred twists her into an insane murderess bent on destroying the men dearest to her. Depending on context, she is the femme fatale or seductress, the fiancée, alcoholic wife, demon—whatever the story construction requires.

She was

- The fiancée poisoner Madeleine Smith in *The Trial of Madeleine Smith*
- The murderous wife and seductress Ivy Lexton (Joan Fontaine) in *Ivy*
- The crippled wife and mother Leah St. Aubyn (Susan Peters) in *The Sign of the Ram* (1948)

- The suicidal and crazed wife-murderess Margot Lannington (Faith Domergue) in *Where Danger Lives*
- The drunken wife in the play *A Little Night Music*
- And the stalking terror in *Night of the Demon*—without the objectionable appearance of the demon.

The mislabeled "typical Hitchcock scenario" presents naive stories populated with police, blackmailers, and spies. But as Charles exhausted those scenarios, his mind probed deeper toward its roots, into terror. In the "mature Bennett scenario" the tag-along heroine has morphed into a vengeful woman who gives the ultimate chase. Her contempt is proof of the protagonist's moral failure; and her rage is directed toward his annihilation. As an avenging shadow, she is the agent of his need for self-punishment. The vengeful woman is an unconscious force to be reckoned with; and ultimately she must die.

Charles's obsession brings us back to Betty's psychologist, who wrote the article on the "angry woman." Dr. Rickles observed that the husband of an angry woman reacts with an "intensification of weak masculine drive." In film the *weak* masculine drive is scripted as the suspenseful chase—in the passive sense of being chased as an innocently accused man on the run. The Freudian doctor continues: "Most of these men had mothers with . . . strong attachments to their sons and were largely instrumental in inspiring their drives for education and becoming more successful than their fathers. [The husbands] . . . feel a strong debt to womanhood and so accept the abuse that their wives heap upon them. They are attracted to beautiful women and seem to need the vilification as a purification by fire to exorcise the *Demon* of incest and to accept their role of masculinity."[32] Thus, both the thriller and vengeful-woman plots are, in Dr. Rickles's Freudian terms, Charles's reach for his masculine expression, overcoming a narcissistic codependence with his mother. Dr. Rickles uses the term *incest*; but as this is too narrowly associated with sexual relations between family members, I prefer the term *narcissistic revenge*. In the deepest sense both emanate from the same motivations and archetypes, and Charles's stories are his sublimation of its unconscious impulse.

Charles was ever the Janus of two minds—profligate and protective. By the time he married Betty, his sexscapades had cost him dearly, both financially and emotionally. Of course, none of that should have been brought into his marriage—he broke his vows. But by his rehearsed

Shakespearean chivalric code, wrathful evocations, and self-fulfilling prophecies, his emotional abandonment of Betty necessitated an avenger, some dark spirit—Ishtar or demon—to punish him. And ironically, there could be no better avenger than Betty herself. She fit the role, able to reenact her mother's emotional cruelty while revenging herself on her weak father. Mom's character played straight into Dad's lifetime construction.

And she succeeded admirably in her role. Betty disassembled his essential, professional social network. She incinerated his play *A Little Night Music* and blocked his return to England and the stage. And she cost him a fortune in medical care.

Their melodrama felt Shakespearean—not much different from *The Tragedy of Macbeth*, in which Charles had acted. It was similar even to the point of Lady Macbeth's blood-obsessed narcolepsy, where her doctor—reminiscent of Betty's misdiagnosing neurologist—laments:

> This disease is beyond my practice. . . .
> Foul whisp'rings are abroad; unnatural deeds
> Do breed unnatural troubles; infected minds
> To their deaf pillows will discharge their secrets.
> More needs she the divine than the physician.
> God, God, forgive us all!
> (act 5, scene 1)

So how could Charles end a personal melodrama whose narcissistic revenge sprang from ancestral denial, abandonment, illegitimacy, and shame? He had built a successful career on this foundation—and it had destroyed his marriage and my childhood. As in *Night (Curse) of the Demon*, Charles could not put the curse back in the book, nor the avenging Ishtar back in her temple.

Betty's curse necessitates the inevitable, final question, "How does a man on the run survive an avenger?" In *Night (Curse) of the Demon*, Professor Karswell is killed by the demonic archetype he has conjured. But Charles could not be murdered by rageaholic Betty. Neither was suicide an option—that scenario had been explored in early drafts of *Miss Moffit and the Thunderbird*, and had been rejected. His sole honorable alternative was to outlive Mom. The apprehension mounted through Charles's near-death illness of 1953, Betty's near-death and misdiagnosed chorea of 1959, his near-death intestinal cancer of 1968, her Alzheimer's diagnosis of 1982 and cancerous death in 1984.

Charles taught that a suspense thriller must present its resolution in its final scenes. So was theirs a "happy ending," or a nightmarish denouement to hell? At her end, Alzheimer's-afflicted Betty asked, "Where is Charles?" And Charles, intimating feelings of guilt, questioned whether he bore any responsibility for her condition. This was an unexpected admission from a man who seldom disclosed any personal emotion.

His answer was a new, remarkable screenplay, *Blow, Bugle, Blow* (1984, not produced), completed in the year of Betty's death. In it Charles moves suspense back toward his roots: he strives to diminish, but not eliminate, apprehension while reestablishing anxiety—anguish, conflicted conscience, and emotional endurance. Very notably, the story is not about the atonement of a woman; instead, it atones the anxiety of an old man, Mickey (that is, Charles), who sacrifices all for honor and conscience. And this is implicit in its story title, a line by the World War I poet Rupert Brooke: "Blow, bugles, blow! . . . Honour has come back, as a king, to earth; . . . And we have come into our heritage."[33]

I do not attend thriller movies. My family experience has left me resenting the genre. From shame to fury, the films glorify unresolved anger. Their justifications (MacGuffins) are arbitrary. The heroine walks a tightrope between emotional extortion and vengeance. Audiences are worked up by apprehension without atonement. The creator of the genre is cursed and destroyed by his vengeful creation. His obsession drives his wife to madness, and his genius is minimized by partner and critics alike. Well, that is my experience.

But having delved so deeply into Charles's psyche, I can now understand his avenging chivalric code, reconcile my mother's anger, and bear the ancestral family cross. My effort at this memoir has enriched my understanding of human nature, for which I am grateful. And I am reminded that a life worth living is a life of personal honor. All the rest is forgiven. Blow, bugles, blow!

~ ~ ~

## Excerpt: *Blow, Bugle, Blow*

My father wrote the following lines coincident with my mother's death. The story pits an everyman's personal honor against a suave villain's emotional extortion. It describes *Mickey O'Grady,* a fan of the LA Stealers baseball team, whose bugle call rallies a hometown batter to hit a home run and tie a pennant race. *Howard Simpson*—a suave villain—twists Mickey's sense of honor around a deceitfully attained contract, prohibiting his bugle call during the tie-breaker. *Joey* is an admiring bartender. *Mr. Fairlie* is the wealthy nonagenarian owner of the defeated out-of-town team who admires Mickey's sense of honor. The concluding lines (after the break) are spoken by Mickey to his wife, *Martha,* who after many years of marriage is fed up with his shenanigans. The following lines occur before the Climax and Close.

Camera moves close on Mickey and Simpson.—At the bar—
    *A beat, then Simpson is saying—*
SIMPSON: Well, guess that lays the matter on the line. Not that I foresee
    any hurdles. (*Indicating the papers*) Oh, you can still tear up the
    agreement . . . but you won't.
MICKEY: Why you so sure?
SIMPSON: Simply because a man of honor doesn't go back on his word.
MICKEY (*defensive*): I never gave no word not to blow my bugle at
    tomorrow's game.
SIMPSON (*winningly quiet*): But you *did* sign, and know something? Short
    as has been our acquaintance, I know you're not one to shame
    yourself by balking at a minor stipulation. . . .

Angle—Including the bartender, Joey
JOEY: Going, gentlemen? Not one for the road?
SIMPSON: Thanks, no. I'm sorry to have occupied your bar without a cent
    crossing it, except here—(*passing some bucks*)—Have one on me.
    Keep the change and—(*lifting his water glass to Mickey*)—please
    drink to a man of honor.
JOEY (*happy with his tip*): Well, thanks, sir, but half a mo' . . .
*He has grabbed for an ad leaflet on the shelf behind him and is already*
    *tearing it apart as—*

Close shot—The rending leaflet
*which reads*—HONOR BRITE BEANERY—OPEN ALL NITE.
    Come try our dusk to dawn snacks at West Hollywood's answer
    to—*Joey's hands have tossed away most of the leaflet, leaving only the*
    *opening word*—HONOR.

Med. shot—Joey, Simpson, and Mickey
    *as Joey, using a pin from his lapel, sticks the word* HONOR *on Mickey's*
    *chest, saying to the recipient—*

JOEY (*pouring liquor, lifting his glass*): To a man of honor and—Mickey—
    Los Angeles'll always love you for what you did today, and will do
    again tomorrow if need be. . . .
[*Next day, after a bugle-blowing come-from-behind pennant victory,*
    Mickey *is on the phone with* Fairley . . .]

Int. Mickey's living room—Close shot—Mickey
*Responding bewilderedly with—*
MICKEY: Jesus! Sorry but . . . guess I'm not hearing right.
FAIRLIE'S VOICE (*over the line*): You are . . . because . . . Mickey, today you
    did what you truly believed you should do. And I want you to know
    that the greatest attribute I admire in this world is integrity . . . which
    you have.
MICKEY (*actually moved*): Sir . . .
[ . . . ]
FAIRLIE'S VOICE: Thank yourself for being who you are.
(*changing tone with an apparent yawn*)
But now . . . mind if I hang up? I'm a very old man and I'm tired. It's nice
    to know you, Mickey. Goodnight . . .

Int. Fairlie's great living room—Close shot—Fairlie
    *as he hangs up, sits back amid his cushions, closes his eyes—*

Int. Mickey's living room—Angle—Mickey
    *emotionally drained as he too hangs up, sits back, mutters*—Je-sus!
*There are tears on his cheeks . . . but right now Martha is coming in, almost*
    *preceded by her usual [furious] approach . . .*
MARTHA: What's going on in here?

MICKEY (*wiping his cheek*): Quite a bit. But best of all . . . Soon as th'
baseball season's over you can be packing . . . for Europe, Hawaii,
Hong Kong . . . wherever.

MARTHA (*gazing at him*): Oh, Lordy me, drunk again! And crying drunk
at that!

MICKEY (*understandingly*): Yes . . . crying . . . but only out of happiness.
*(softly, sympathetically)*

Martha, we'll be together, like always. Mind if I hold your hand?

*Martha hesitates . . . then a sudden change comes over her . . . warmth,
affection. She takes the extended hand—*

FADE OUT

# A Tribute

PROSPERO: You do look, my son, in a moved sort,
    As if you were dismay'd: be cheerful, sir.
    Our revels now are ended. These our actors,
    As I foretold you, were all spirits, and
    Are melted into air, into thin air:
    And, like the baseless fabric of this vision,
    The cloud-capp'd towers, the gorgeous palaces,
    The solemn temples, the great globe itself,
    Yea, all which it inherit, shall dissolve,
    And, like this insubstantial pageant faded,
    Leave not a rack behind. We are such stuff
    As dreams are made on, and our little life
    Is rounded with a sleep.
(*The Tempest,* act 4, scene 1)

# The Works of Charles Bennett

Not inclusive of scripts sold and not produced

## Theater

### Actor onstage (work, [role], venue)—Incomplete list

| | |
|---|---|
| 12/1911 | *The Miracle* (chorister), Olympia |
| 8/1914 | *Drake*, His Majesty's |
| 1914? | *The Marriage Market,* Daly's Theatre and on tour |
| 191? | *Alice in Wonderland,* Savoy |
| 12/1915 | *Goody Two Shoes,* a theatre in Woolwich |
| 191? | Play about *Mr. Wu* (the erring son), Empire? |
| 4/1916 | *King Lear* (Edgar), with Herbert Tree |
| 1916? | *The Speckled Band,* Horsefield & Woodward touring company |
| 1916? | *Diplomacy* |
| 1917? | *Raffles,* Gerald Alexander touring |
| 1919+ | *Brewster's Millions,* Brewster's Millions touring company |
| ???? | *Polly with a Past* |
| 1920 | Repertory roles, Compton Comedy Co. |
| 1922 | Repertory roles, Lena Ashwell Players |
| 1922+ | Repertory roles, Gertrude Elliott Touring Co. |
| 1/1923+ | ?, Inez Bensusan |
| 3/1923 | *You Never Can Tell* (Philip), Jersey? |
| 5/1923 | *Two Orphans* (Pierre), Alexander Marsh Shakespearean Touring |
| 7/1923 | *Tancred* (Lord Fitzheron), Kingsway |
| 9/1923+ | *Romeo and Juliet* (Romeo), Alexander Marsh Shakespearean Touring |

| | |
|---|---|
| 1/1924+ | *Twelfth Night* (Orsino), Alexander Marsh Shakespearean Touring |
| 1924? | Repertory roles, Alexander Marsh Shakespearean Touring |
| 1924? | *Antony and Cleopatra*, Henry Baynton Co. |
| 1924? | *Midsummer Night's Dream*, Henry Baynton Co. |
| 9/1924 | *Mrs. Gorringe's Necklace*, Bristol Little Theatre |
| 9/1924 | *The Return of the Prodigal*, Bristol Little Theatre |
| 9/1924 | *The Two Virtues*, Bristol Little Theatre |
| 9/1924 | *The Enchanted Cottage*, Bristol Little Theatre |
| 9/1924 | *The Mollusc*, Bristol Little Theatre |
| 9/1924 | *Magic*, Bristol Little Theatre |
| 9/1924 | *The Romantic Young Lady*, Bristol Little Theatre |
| 10/1924 | *Hobson's Choice*, Bristol Little Theatre |
| 10/1924 | *The Young Idea*, Bristol Little Theatre |
| 10/1924 | *Doormats*, Bristol Little Theatre |
| 10/1924 | *Her Husband's Wife*, Bristol Little Theatre |
| 11/1924 | *Me and My Girl*, Bristol Little Theatre |
| 11/1924 | *Mixed Marriage*, Bristol Little Theatre |
| 11/1924 | *Smith*, Bristol Little Theatre |
| 11/1924 | *Young Imeson*, Bristol Little Theatre |
| 1924? | *Hamlet* |
| 1/1925+ | *Julius Caesar* (Mark Antony), Ben Greet Players |
| 1/1925+ | *Romeo and Juliet* (Romeo), Ben Greet Players |
| 1/1925+ | *The Tempest* (Antonio), Ben Greet Players |
| 1/1925+ | *As You Like It* (Amiens), Ben Greet Players |
| 1/1925+ | *Merchant of Venice*, Ben Greet Players |
| 1/1925+ | *Twelfth Night*, Ben Greet Players |
| 3/1925+ | *Macbeth*, Ben Greet Players |
| 3/1925+ | *Julius Caesar* (Julius Caesar), Ben Greet Players |
| 3/1925+ | *Taming of the Shrew* (Vincentio), Ben Greet Players |
| 3/1925+ | *Merchant of Venice*, Ben Greet Players |
| 3/1925+ | *Othello*, Ben Greet Players |
| 3/1925+ | *The Winter's Tale* (Camillo), Ben Greet Players |
| 4/1925+ | *A Midsummer Night's Dream*, Ben Greet Players |
| 8/1925 | *You Never Can Tell* (Bohun), Edward Stirling, English Players |
| 9/1925+ | *The Importance of Being Earnest* (Moncrieff, Chasuble), English Players |

| | |
|---|---|
| 9/1925 | *The Speckled Band* (Watson), English Players |
| 10/1925+ | Repertory roles, Ben Greet Players |
| 12/1925+ | *A Message from Mars* (Dicey), Playhouse |
| 1/1926 | *The Man Who Was Thursday,* Everyman |
| 2/1926 | *The Jealous Wife,* East London University College |
| 2/1926+ | Repertory roles, Ben Greet Players |
| 4/1926 | *The Needle's Eye,* Brighton West Pier |
| 9/1926 | *Pygmalion,* Edward Stirling, English Players |
| 9/1926 | *The School for Scandal,* Edward Stirling, English Players |
| 10/1926+ | Repertory roles, Ben Greet Players |
| 12/1926+ | *A Midsummer Night's Dream* (Theseus), Winter Garden |
| 3/1927 | *The Donovan Affair* (Duke of York) |
| 4/1927 | *Othello,* Shakespeare Memorial Theatre Fund, Apollo |
| 4/1927 | ?, Playroom Six |
| 5/1927 | *The Return* (Ishtar), Everyman |
| 7/1927+ | ?, Playroom Six |
| 9/1927 | *Mrs. Dot,* Lena Ashwell Players |
| 11/1927+ | *Cyrano de Bergerac* (Aramis), Apollo |
| 11/1927+ | *The Donovan Affair,* Apollo |
| 6/4/1928+ | *Blackmail* (Peter Hewitt), Regent, King's Cross |
| 9/1928+ | *Julius Caesar* (Julius Caesar), Ben Greet Players |
| 9/1928+ | *The Merchant of Venice,* Ben Greet Players |
| 9/1928+ | *Twelfth Night,* Ben Greet Players |
| ca. 11/1928 | *Blackmail,* Regent Theatre, King's Cross |
| 5/1929+ | *Blackmail* (Tracey), Langley Howard Touring |
| 11/1930 | *One Day More,* New Faculty, Piccadilly |
| 2/1932 | *Big Business,* Edward Stirling, Monte Carlo |
| 1/1936 | *Page from a Diary* (opening night), Garrick |

## Playwright (title, lead, venue)

| | |
|---|---|
| 5/1927 | *The Return*\* (Peggy Ashcroft), Everyman |
| 2/1928 | *Blackmail* (Tallulah Bankhead), Globe |
| 6/1928 | *After Midnight*\* (one act), Rudolph Steiner Hall |
| 12/1928 | *The Last Hour*\*\* (and Anna Lee, in rep.), Comedy Theatre |

---

\*Directed opening production
\*\*Directed after opening

| 9/1929 | *The Danger Line* (collaboration), Greenwich Theatre, Greenwich, Conn. |
| 10/1931 | *Sensation,** Lyceum |
| 1932 | *Big Business,** Comedy Theatre |
| 1/1936 | *Page from a Diary,* Garrick |

## Film

### Actor

| 1915 | *John Halifax, Gentleman* (dir. G. Pearson/prod. Samuelson) |
| 1915? | A small part in a film starring Milton Rosmer |
| 1935 | Walk-on cameo with Hitchcock in *The 39 Steps* |

### Screenwriter: seventy-nine listed—fifty-five credited, nineteen uncredited, five uncertain (possibly BIP)

#### England

| 1929 | *Blackmail* (Alfred Hitchcock/BIP), play basis, co-adaptation |
| 1930 | *The Last Hour* (Walter Forde/Nettlefold), play basis, screenplay |
| 1930? | *Death on the Footplate,* aka *Phantom of the (Footplate?)* . . . (?/BIP), story |
| 1930? | *The Parrot Whistles* (?/BIP), story |
| 1931 | *Midnight* (George King), play basis, co-screenplay |
| 1931? | *High Speed* (?/BIP), story |
| 1931? | *Love My Dog* (?/BIP), story |
| 1931 | *Number, Please* (George King), co-screenplay |
| 1931 | *Deadlock* (George King), co-screenplay |
| 1931 | *Two Way Street* (George King/Nettlefold), co-screenplay |
| 1932 | *Men of Steel* (George King), uncredited contribution |
| 1932? | *Fireman Save My Child* (?/BIP), story |
| 1932 | *Partners Please* (Lloyd Richards), screenplay |
| 1933 | *Matinee Idol* (George King), screenplay |
| 1933 | *Hawley's of High Street* (Thomas Bentley/BIP), co-screenplay |

| 1933 | *Paris Plane* (Paddy Carstairs), screenplay |
| 1933 | *The House of Trent* (Norman Walker), co-screenplay |
| 1933 | *Mannequin* (George Cooper/Twickenham), screenplay |
| 1934 | *Warn London* (T. Hays Hunter), co-screenplay |
| 1934 | *The Secret of the Loch* (Milton Rosmer), co-screenplay |
| 1934 | *Gay Love* (Leslie Hiscott), co-screenplay |
| 1934 | *Big Business* (Cyril Gardner), play basis, adaptation |
| 1934 | *The Man Who Knew Too Much* (Alfred Hitchcock), story, co-screenplay |
| 1935 | *Night Mail* (Herbert Smith), co-screenplay |
| 1935 | *The 39 Steps* (Alfred Hitchcock), co-adaptation |
| 1935 | *The Clairvoyant* (Maurice Elvey), story, co-screenplay |
| 1935 | *All at Sea* (Anthony Kimmins), screenplay |
| 1935 | *Blue Smoke* (Ralph Ince), story |
| 1935 | *King of the Damned* (Walter Forde), co-screenplay |
| 1936 | *The Secret Agent*, aka *Ashenden* (Alfred Hitchcock), co-screenplay |
| 1936 | *Sabotage* (Alfred Hitchcock), co-screenplay |
| 1937 | *King Solomon's Mines* (Robert Stevenson), co-screenplay |
| 1937 | *Shadow of the Wing*[34] |
| 1937 | *Young and Innocent* (Alfred Hitchcock), co-screenplay |

**United States**

| 1938 | *The Adventures of Marco Polo* (Archie Mayo), uncredited contribution |
| 1938 | *The Young in Heart* (Richard Wallace), co-adaptation |
| 1939 | *The Real Glory* (Henry Hathaway), uncredited contribution |
| 1939 | *Balalaika* (Reinhold Schünzel), co-screenplay |
| 1939 | *Hidden Power* (Lewis Collins), uncredited contribution |
| 1939 | *Good Girls Go to Paris* (Alexander Hall), uncredited contribution |
| 1940 | *Foreign Correspondent* (Alfred Hitchcock), co-screenplay |
| 1941 | *They Dare Not Love* (James Whale), co-screenplay |
| 1942 | *Lucky Legs* (Charles Barton), uncredited original story |
| 1942 | *Joan of Paris* (Robert Stevenson), screenplay |
| 1942 | *Reap the Wild Wind* (Cecil B. DeMille), co-screenplay |
| 1942 | *Saboteur* (Alfred Hitchcock), uncredited contribution |

| 1943 | *Forever and a Day* (René Clair and six others), co-screenplay |
| 1944 | *The Story of Dr. Wassell* (Cecil B. DeMille), co-screenplay |

**England and Scotland (uncredited)**

| 6/1944+ | Ten propaganda newsreels for the British Ministry of Information, including *We the People, a Scottish Local Government Film*, 12/1944 |

**United States**

| 1947 | *Ivy* (Sam Wood), screenplay |
| 1947 | *Unconquered* (Cecil B. DeMille), co-screenplay |
| 1948 | *The Sign of the Ram* (John Sturges), screenplay |
| 1949 | *Black Magic* (Gregory Ratoff), original screenplay |
| 1949 | *Madness of the Heart* (Charles Bennett), screenplay |
| 1950 | *Where Danger Lives* (John Farrow), screenplay |
| 1951 | *Lorna Doone* (Phil Karlson), uncredited contribution |
| 1951 | *Kind Lady* (John Sturges), co-screenplay |
| 1952 | *Un Principe de la Iglesia* (Miguel Delgado), screenplay |
| 1952 | *The Green Glove* (*The White Road*) (Rudolph Mate), original screenplay |
| 1953 | *No Escape* (Charles Bennett), screenplay |
| 1954 | *Dangerous Mission* (Louis King), co-screenplay |
| 1955 | *The Phenix City Story* (Phil Karlson), uncredited contribution |
| 1956 | *The Man Who Knew Too Much* (Alfred Hitchcock), story |
| 1957 | *The Story of Mankind* (Irwin Allen), co-screenplay |
| 1957 | *Night of the Demon* (Jacques Tourneur), adaptation, screenplay |
| 1959 | *The Big Circus* (Joseph Newman), co-screenplay |
| 1960 | *The Lost World* (Irwin Allen), co-screenplay |
| 1961 | *Voyage to the Bottom of the Sea* (Irwin Allen), co-screenplay |
| 1962 | *Five Weeks in a Balloon* (Irwin Allen), co-screenplay |
| 1965 | *War-Gods of the Deep* (Jacques Tourneur), co-screenplay |

## Film Director

| 1916? | *The Cost of a Kiss* (silent film), exterior shooting |

| | |
|---|---|
| 1949 | *Madness of the Heart* |
| 1951 | *Un Principe de la Iglesia,* codirector |
| 1953 | *No Escape* |
| 1962 | *Five Weeks in a Balloon,* exterior scenes |

## Television

### Associate producer

| | |
|---|---|
| 1957–58 | *New Adventures of Charlie Chan,* prod. Edward Small |

## Writer: fifty-eight teleplays identified (* indicates CB's direction)

| | |
|---|---|
| 1952 | "Edge of the Law," *Ford Television Theatre* |
| 1954 | "One Man Missing," *Ford Television Theatre* |
| 1954 | "Actor's Wife," *Fireside Theatre* |
| 1954 | "Afraid to Live," *Fireside Theatre* |
| 1954 | "Which of Our Sons," *Fireside Theatre* |
| 1954 | "Argument with Death," *Fireside Theatre* |
| 1954 | "The Failure," *Fireside Theatre* |
| 1954 | "The Mural," *Fireside Theatre* |
| 1954 | "I Came to Kill," *Fireside Theatre* |
| 1954 | "Marked for Death," *Fireside Theatre* |
| 1954 | "Casino Royale," *Climax!* |
| 1954 | "Nightmare in Copenhagen," *Climax!* |
| 1954? | "The Gingerbread Man," *Climax!* |
| 1955 | "Take Off Zero,"* *Cavalcade of America* |
| 1955 | "One Rugged Night,"* *Cavalcade of America* |
| 1955 | "The Palmetto Conspiracy,"* *Cavalcade of America* |
| 1955 | "The World Starts with Jimmy,"* *The Christophers* |
| 1955 | "Sensation Club,"* *Schlitz Playhouse of Stars* |
| 1955 | "Best of Everything,"* *Schlitz Playhouse of Stars* |
| 1955 | "Volturio Investigates,"* *Schlitz Playhouse of Stars* |
| 1955 | "Underground,"* *Schlitz Playhouse of Stars* |
| 1955 | "The Creaking Gate," *Lux Theatre* |
| 1955 | "Nor All Your Tears," *Lux Theatre* |
| 1955 | "The Softest Music," *Lux Theatre* |

| 1955 | "The Browning Version," *Lux Theatre* |
| 1955 | "The Suspect," *Lux Theatre* |
| 1955 | "Ivy," *Lux Theatre* |
| 1955 | "Marseilles,"* *Count of Monte Cristo* |
| 1956 | "The Pen and the Sword,"* *Count of Monte Cristo* |
| 1956 | "The Texas Affair,"* *Count of Monte Cristo* |
| 1956 | "London,"* *Count of Monte Cristo* |
| 1956 | "The Black Death," *Count of Monte Cristo* |
| 1956 | "The Art of Terror," *Count of Monte Cristo* |
| 1956 | "Bordeaux,"* *Count of Monte Cristo* |
| 1956 | "The Barefoot Empress,"* *Count of Monte Cristo* |
| 1956 | "Monaco," *Count of Monte Cristo* |
| 1956 | "Condemned to Glory," *Conflict* |
| 1956 | "Captain without a Country," *Conflict* |
| 1956 | "Who Is Byington?"* *DuPont Cavalcade* |
| 1956 | "Disaster Patrol,"* *DuPont Cavalcade* |
| 1956 | "The Stobo Story,"* *DuPont Cavalcade* |
| 1956 | "Light One Candle,"* *The Christophers* |
| 1957 | "Gentle Warrior,"* *The Christophers* |
| 1958 | "The Brioni Story," *Behind Closed Doors* |
| 1962 | "The Clocks," *Dick Powell Show* |
| 1965 | "Secret of the Loch," *Voyage to the Bottom of the Sea* |
| 1965 | "Dead Man's Doubloons," *Voyage to the Bottom of the Sea* |
| 1965 | "Escape from Venice," *Voyage to the Bottom of the Sea* |
| 1966 | "The Sky's on Fire," *Voyage to the Bottom of the Sea* |
| 1966 | "Night of the Eccentrics," *Wild, Wild, West* |
| 1966 | "Here Is Tomorrow," Jack Denove Productions |
| 1967 | "Murder-Go-Round," *Time Tunnel* |
| 1967 | "Death from the Past," *Voyage to the Bottom of the Sea* |
| 1967 | "The Heat Monster," *Voyage to the Bottom of the Sea* |
| 1967 | "The Deadly Dolls," *Voyage to the Bottom of the Sea* |
| 1968 | "The Terrible Leprechaun," *Voyage to the Bottom of the Sea* |
| 1968 | "Terror-Go-Round," *Land of the Giants* |

## Director: thirty-two identified (The following are not listed as written by CB)

| 1955 | *The Hostage, Cavalcade of America* |

| 1955 | *The Gift of Dr. Minot, Cavalcade of America* |
| 1956 | "A Toy for the Infanta," *Count of Monte Cristo* |
| 1956 | "The Island," *Count of Monte Cristo* |
| 1956 | "Flight to Calais," *Count of Monte Cristo* |
| 1956 | "The Lichtenburg Affair," *Count of Monte Cristo* |
| 1956 | "Mecklenburg," *Count of Monte Cristo* |
| 1956 | "The Carbonari," *Count of Monte Cristo* |
| 1956 | *The Story of Two Men, The Christophers* |
| 1957 | "The Sweater," *New Adventures of Charlie Chan* |
| 1958 | "The Noble Art of Murder," *New Adventures of Charlie Chan* |
| 1958 | "No Holiday for Murder," *New Adventures of Charlie Chan* |
| 1958 | "Man with a Hundred Faces," *New Adventures of Charlie Chan* |

## Print Media

| 1927? | "Signs by the Way," travelogue, sold for publication, publisher unknown |
| 1928 | *The Return,* London: E. Benn |
| 1934 | *Blackmail,* London: Rich and Cowan |
| 1934 | *The Last Hour,* London: Rich and Cowan |
| 11/1939 | "War in His Pocket" (aka "Havoc"), *Blue Book Magazine* |
| 6/1944+ | Propaganda and war news for British Ministry of Information |
| 11/1945 | "Rank Enthusiasm," *Screen Writer* |
| 6/1972 | "Gripe, Gripe, Gripe," *Writers Guild of America, West, Newsletter* |
| 5/1977 | "Those White Cliffs," for Royal Oak Foundation of California |
| 1978 | "Laurence Olivier: The Power and the Glory" and "Peter Lorre: Gentlest Murderer," in Danny Peary, *Close-Ups: Intimate Profiles of Movie Stars by Their Co-Stars, Directors, Screenwriters, and Friends,* New York: Workman |
| 1984 | "The Jules Verne Influence on *Voyage to the Bottom of the Sea* and *Five Weeks in a Balloon*," in *Omni's Screen Flights/Screen Fantasies,* ed. Danny Peary, 120–23, Garden City, N.Y.: Doubleday |

1987        *Fox on the Run* (novel), New York: Warner Books

1994        "L.A. Nostalgia," in Arnold Schwartzman, *Anglafile: A Guide to the Best of British in Los Angeles,* Los Angeles: AngLAfile

# Charles Bennett's Awards and Distinctions

| | |
|---|---|
| 12/1918 | Awarded the Military Medal for Bravery |
| 4/1927 | Member of all-star cast *Othello,* Shakespeare Memorial Theatre Fund, accorded royal patronage |
| 1929 | Writes play basis and is co-scenarist of *Blackmail,* distinguished as first European full-length talkie; first full-length talkie, England; first Hitchcock talkie; first British International Pictures talkie; Banned by Australian censor |
| 1930 | *The Last Hour* becomes the first Nettlefold Studio talkie |
| 1931 | *Deadlock* is the first British talkie using a "Talkie Studio" as a set |
| 9/1932 | *Deadlock* achieves more than 1,400 theater bookings |
| 12/1933 | Nominated Corresponding Honorary Member of the Institut Littéraire et Artistique de France |
| 1934 | *The Secret of the Loch* is the first talkie filmed in Scotland |
| 1/1936 | Cited as Britain's "Most Successful Screen-Story Writer" in the *Era* newspaper on a crucial film forum question: "Should British film producers put international appeal before national character?" |
| 1937 | Is the first major British screenwriter to be signed by Hollywood |
| 1940 | Selected among twenty-three best scenarists of the year by the editor of *Starr-Dust* |
| 1941 | *Foreign Correspondent* is nominated for six Academy Awards, including Best Original Screenplay and Best Picture |
| 12/1941–43 | Becomes commander of Company D, 4th Regiment, California State Militia, First Mounted Patrol |

| | |
|---|---|
| 10/1942 | Annual New England Writers' Award is given to *Reap the Wild Wind,* as reported in *LA Daily News* |
| 1942, 1943 | *The 39 Steps* and *Foreign Correspondent* are selected for New York University writing study |
| 2/1943 | Honored on four "top 10" lists for *Reap The Wild Wind,* as reported in *LA Daily News* |
| 1943 | Awarded fifth-time "box-office champion writer" for *Reap The Wild Wind,* in an unspecified "national trade publication exhibitors poll," according to *LA Daily News,* June 22 |
| 4/1946 | Receives state certificate for voluntary military service to the state of California |
| 1949 | Selected a Lord Calvert (whiskey) "Man of Distinction" |
| 8/1954 | Receives certificate of charter membership, Writers Guild of America |
| 1955 | Headlined in *Variety* as "*Cavalcade*'s Finest" for *Take Off Zero* |
| 1957 | Receives Christopher Award for Best TV Direction of *The Gift of Dr. Minot* |
| 1944–1962 | Receives box-office Blue Ribbon Awards for *The Story of Dr. Wassell, The Man Who Knew Too Much, The Lost World, The Big Circus,* and *Five Weeks in a Balloon* |
| 12/1972 | *The Secret Agent* and *Foreign Correspondent* are screened at "Written for the Screen," a salute to screenwriters at the Los Angeles County Museum of Art |
| 7/1975 | *The 39 Steps* is screened in "50 Years of British Cinema" at the Bing Theater, Los Angeles County Museum of Art |
| 1979 | *Blackmail* is screened in the "Fifty Years of Film" series by the British Film Institute at the National Film Theatre, London. |
| 8/2/1979 | Receives poem titled "To Charles at Eighty" from the poet Robert Nathan |
| 4/1987 | Profiled in *Writers Guild of America, West, Newsletter:* "Charles Bennett, Born to Write" |
| 1991 | Becomes the oldest writer in the history of film under contract to a major studio to write a screenplay |
| 3/18/1992 | Becomes an honorary member, British Academy of Film and Television Arts, Los Angeles (BAFTA-LA) |

| | |
|---|---|
| 1993 | Recognized for his "lack of specialization within the American film industry" (Anthony Slide, *International Directory of Films and Filmmaking*, 1993) |
| 3/1993 | *Blackmail* is screened at the Louvre Auditorium: Cinéma muet en concert |
| 9/1994 | Is a Telluride Film Festival honoree |
| 10/1994 | Is selected as one of the "100 coolest people in Los Angeles," *Buzz Magazine* |
| 3/1995 | Receives Writers Guild of America, West, Laurel Award for Lifetime Achievement |
| 3/17/1995 | Receives congratulatory letter for WGA Laurel Award from Merrick S. Baker-Bates, British consul general, Los Angeles |
| 3/17/1995 | Receives congratulatory letter for WGA Laurel Award from Rt. Hon. Stephen Dorrell, MP, Secretary for National Heritage, DNH Ministry, U.K. |

# Notes

1. The referenced actresses are Joan Fontaine, Edna Best, Paulette Goddard, and Anna Lee Nathan "Boniface"; the Charles Bennett film titles are italicized.

2. For more about the film *The Last Hour,* see *Bioscope,* July 2, 1930.

3. Mace is quoted in Randall Clark, ed., *Dictionary of Literary Biography, Screenwriters,* vol. 44, 2nd ed., pp. 24–31.

4. Charles Bennett to John Belton, 1980, in possession of John Bennett.

5. Danny Peary, *Cult Movies 2: Fifty More of the Classics, the Sleepers, the Weird, and the Wonderful* (New York: Dell, 1983), p. 108.

6. The application of the label *auteur* to Hitchcock was initially presented in Robert E. Kapsis, *Hitchcock: The Making of a Reputation* (Chicago: University of Chicago Press, 1990). A synopsis is available at http://press.uchicago.edu/ucp/books/book/chicago/H/bo3684265.html.

7. See www. http://dictionary.reference.com/browse/auteur.

8. John Belton, "Charles Bennett and the Typical Hitchcock Scenario," *Film History* 9.3 (1997): S. 320–32.

9. Rupert Brooke, "III. The Dead" (1914), in *Collected Poems* (New York: John Lane, 1915).

10. The evidence includes multiple cabinet photos, a very early glass photo, an autograph, Kyrle Bellew's birthdate entered in Lilian's personal family collection, and a press announcement of Bellew's 1911 death. Someone has written across the obit, "Did you know this?" underscoring her interest in him. The Kyrle Bellew paternity was later confirmed by a psychic medium who spoke to John Bennett as Charles's grandfather, John Chippendall Montesquieu Bellew.

11. Oliver Lodge's blurb was printed on the dust jacket of Charles Bennett, *The Return* (London: Ernes Benn, 1928).

12. "Drama and Psychology at the Grand," *Oldham Chronicle,* August 20, 1929, following a repertory production on August 17, 1929.

13. *Encyclopedia Britannica* (1944 ed.), 23:473.

14. See press announcement in *Bioscope* announcing BIP purchase of *High Speed,* May 20, 1931.

15. BBC *Omnibus* interview of Samuel Taylor, 1986.

16. This line, written in spring 1987, places her birth circa 1907–8.

17. Alfred Hitchcock, "My Own Methods," *Sight and Sound* 6.22 (1937), www.hitchcockwiki.com/wiki/Sight_and_Sound_(1937)_-_My_Own_ Methods.

18. Ivor Montagu, "Working with Hitchcock," *Sight and Sound* 49.3 (1980): 189–93, http://explore.bfi.org.uk/4e85e2047df93.

19. *Era* (film magazine), January 1936.

20. The Film Society, February 1936.

21. Anthony Slide, *International Directory of Films and Filmmaking*, vol. 4, *Writers and Production Artists* (Detroit: St. James Press, 1993).

22. As of January 2013 it is TCL Chinese Theatre.

23. The landing strip was at Giant Rock, near Landers, California, just east of aptly named Spy Mountain, and about thirty-three miles north-northeast of Palm Springs. The desert rat was Frank Critzer, an immigrant German miner and ham radio operator. From the early 1920s Critzer excavated chambers beneath the seven-story Giant Rock. He graded the runway and about forty miles of dirt roads. This was, at least, his cover. He was a lone eccentric, but whether Critzer was a spy is conjecturable—and would make an interesting search under the Freedom of Information Act. He died during a police siege in 1942 when an explosion occurred in his living quarters beneath the rock. The land was then leased from Bureau of Land Management by George Van Tassel, an aviation mechanic and flight instructor who retired from Hughes Aircraft in 1947. Under Tassel, Giant Rock became a focal point for UFO celebrations during the 1950s and 1960s.

24. Patrick Humphries, *The Films of Alfred Hitchcock* (New York: Portland House, 1986), p. 66.

25. Pat McGilligan, ed., *Backstory: Interviews with Screenwriters of Hollywood's Golden Age* (Berkeley: University of California Press, 1986), p. 19.

26. N. K. Rickles, "The Angry Woman Syndrome," *Archives of General Psychiatry* 24.1 (1971): 91–94.

27. Richard Combs, "Hitchcock Olympiad," *Film Comment* 48.6 (November–December 2012): 34.

28. Arlene Schulman, "Plays: Role of Women in Shakespeare," December 17, 2008, http://en.allexperts.com/q/Plays-1556/2008/12/Role-Women-Shakespeare .htm.

29. Tania Modleski, "Rape versus Mans/laughter: Hitchcock's *Blackmail* and Feminist Interpretation," *PMLA* 102.3 (May 1987): 304–15.

30. "Sigmund Freud—Psychologist and Confirmed Pacifist," www.bsu .edu/libraries/virtualpress/wolfe/word/sigmundfreud.pdf.

31. Butterfly Faerie, "Definition, Causes, Symptoms & Treatment" (August 26, 2006), www.psychforums.com/narcissistic-personality/topic14021.html.

32. Rickles, "Angry Woman Syndrome," p. 94, emphasis added.

33. Brooke, "III. The Dead."

34. See Terry Ramsaye, ed., *International Motion Picture Almanac, 1937–1938* (New York: Quigley, 1938), p. 96.

# Suggestions for Further Research

Unless otherwise stated, the following are located either in the Charles Bennett Estate Collection (CBEC) in the possession of John Bennett, San Clemente, or in the Special Collections of the Margaret Herrick Library.

Properties for sale (film and television scripts, plays, unpublished novels) including *Blackmail, The Last Hour, Heart's Desire, Night Music, Once upon a Midnight, Sermon in the Snow, Train Ride, Thunderbird, Satan Returns, Fox on the Run, Blow, Bugle, Blow,* and *The Hinges of Hell,* CBEC.

*Blackmail* draft screenplay for 20th Century Fox, CBEC.

Autographed and vintage scripts, plays, playbills, lobby cards, and movie posters, CBEC.

Awards, contracts, interviews, correspondence, letters, photographs, CBEC.

Lilian Langrishe Bennett Family Collection, CBEC.

Personal diaries, 1919–95 (excluding 1921, 1922, 1931–33, 1935, 1940–45, which are missing), MHL.

Exercise books containing draft screenplays, ca. 1930, MHL.

Press clippings, 1925–95. MHL.

Unpublished stories, screenplays, treatments, and teleplays, MHL.

## Personal Narratives and Short Stories

"Finis?" a 1925 unpublished short story, CBEC.

"The Magician's Dragon," a ca. 1925 unpublished fairy tale, CBEC.

"Magic in Montmartre," a 1925 personal narrative, published in this memoir, CBEC.

"Back to Mrs. Methuselah," a ca. 1927 unpublished personal narrative, CBEC.

"Early Risers," a ca. 1927 draft article, MHL.

"First Nights," a ca. 1927 unpublished personal narrative, CBEC.

"Grand Scale Humor," a ca. 1927 unpublished personal narrative, CBEC.

"Provocation," a ca. 1927 unpublished fable, CBEC.

"The Magic Street," a ca. 1927 unpublished personal narrative, CBEC.

"The Morning After," a ca. 1927 unpublished short story, CBEC.

"The Motorist Walks," a ca. 1927 unpublished personal narrative, CBEC.

"The 9.50 from Paddington," a ca. 1927 unpublished short story, CBEC.

"Pastorals," a ca. 1927 draft article, MHL.

"Signs by the Way," a ca. 1927 travelogue possibly published in the *London Sunday Express*, CBEC.

"The Greatest Practical Joke in the World," a 1928 unpublished personal narrative, CBEC.

Publicity page written in the third person, ca. 1929, MHL.

"Mr. Shakespeare Comes to Hollywood," a 1937 spoof published in this memoir, CBEC.

"My Most Unforgettable Character," a ca. 1965 personal narrative excerpted in this memoir, CBEC.

"The Story in the Film," address to the Film Society, February 14, 1936, MHL.

Text of opening address, International PEN, London, January 31, 1945, MHL.

"The Scenario Writer," address presented at a meeting, MHL.

"Laurence Olivier: The Power and the Glory." In Danny Peary, *Close-Ups: Intimate Profiles of Movie Stars by Their Co-Stars, Directors, Screenwriters, and Friends*. New York: Workman, 1978.

"Peter Lorre: Gentlest Murderer." In Danny Peary, *Close-Ups: Intimate Profiles of Movie Stars by Their Co-Stars, Directors, Screenwriters, and Friends*. New York: Workman, 1978.

DeMille tarantula story, in Jack Smith column, *LA Times*, July 25, 1979.

Oral History Collection on the Performing Arts, Southern Methodist University, ca. 1981.

"Night of the Demon." In Danny Peary, *Cult Movies 2*. New York: Dell, 1982.

"The Jules Verne Influence on *Voyage to the Bottom of the Sea* and *Five Weeks in a Balloon*." In *Omni's Screen Flights/Screen Fantasies*, ed. Danny Peary, 120–23. Garden City, N.Y.: Doubleday, 1984.

"LA Nostalgia." In *Anglafile: A Guide to the Best of British in Los Angeles*. Los Angeles: AngLAFILE, 1994.

## Print Interviews: The following list comprises an incomplete list of interviews archived at the MHL.
## (Sources are unavailable in some cases.)

Accinelli, Laura. "The Oldest Screenwriter." *Santa Monica Evening Outlook*, November 5, 1991.

"Actor Playwrights." *Daily Chronicle*, August 2, 1929.

Adolphe, Edward. Interview with CB on the state of British film. *New York Sun*, n.d.

"A.R.T. Dark Deeds Planned on Hampstead Heath." *Star*, December 29, 1928.

Avallone, Susan. Interview for *Film Writers Guide*, 4th ed. Los Angeles: Lone Eagle, 1993.

Brock, J. "Playwright/Screenwriter Bennett Brings Tales to 72 Market Street." *Argonaut,* November 1, 1991.

Broeske, Pat. "Now Here's a Real Comeback." *LA Times,* September 30, 1990.

"Can Love Blot Out the Past [*Blackmail*]?" *Woman's Life,* August 31, 1929?

"Charles Bennett, Born to Write." *Writers Guild of America, West, Newsletter,* April 1987.

"Contemporary Authors and Their Works." *LA Examiner,* April 11, 1942.

Cooper, Candy. "The Man Who Could Scare Alfred Hitchcock." Unidentified source, 1981.

Crocker, Harry. "Balalaika." Unidentified source, December 1939.

———. "Tells of San Francisco Séance & Hatpin." Unidentified source, 1939/40?

Davis, Ronald L. "Charles Bennett: Import from England." In Davis, *Words into Images: Screenwriters on the Studio System.* Jackson: University of Mississippi Press, 2007, pp. 3–18.

"Greer Garson Story." *Daily Mirror,* August 10, 1938.

Hiscock, John. "True Brit Goes for a Remake." *Sunday Telegraph,* October 14, 1990.

Kaukas, Bernard. "Heard in the Bar." *Drumbeat: The Savage Club Quarterly,* September 1992.

"Knife Accident at the Regent Theatre [*Blackmail*]." Unidentified source, June 5?, 1928.

Lewin, David. "*The Visitor.*" *London Daily Express,* March 24, 1949.

McCarthy, Todd. "Hitchcock Dish . . . at Telluride," *Daily Variety,* September 9, 1994.

McManus, John T. "Melodramatist Abroad," *New York Times,* March 1937.

Mines, Harry. "Meet Charles Bennett." *LA Daily News,* October 14, 1941.

"New Film with a Psychic Theme." *Psychic News,* August 10, 1935.

Phillips, Mark. "Giant Jellyfish & Time-Lost Dinosaurs (Part One)." *Starlog: A Quarterly Magazine* 182 (August 1992).

"Play That Is Based on Fact [*Blackmail*]." *The People,* February 26, 1928.

Robb, David. "Bennett, 91, Urges Older Writers to Keep Going." *Variety,* April 11, 1991.

"Romance of an Actor-Author [*Blackmail*]" *Daily Express* (London), January 21?, 1928.

Scanlon, Tom. "Gaining Fame from 'a Little Fat Man.'" *San Jose Mercury News,* n.d.

Shepherd, S. R. "A Stage Flop That Made Money [*Blackmail*]." *The People,* April 20, 1930.

Swaffer, Hannen. "My Greatest Story." *Psychic News,* June 24, 1961.

Weaver, Tom. "Charles Bennett." In *Attack of the Monster Movie Makers.* Jefferson, N.C.: McFarland, 1994.

———. "The Oldest Working Screenwriter Explains It All." *Starlog: A Quarterly Magazine* 193 (August 1993).

"When Peace Came." *Swindon Evening Advertiser,* February 22, 1935?

"Without a Hitch." *Southern California Senior Life,* March 1991.

Wright, Virginia. "Writing for DeMille: The Story of Dr. Wassel." *LA Daily News,* August 12, 1942.

———. "MOI Activities & Trial of Madeleine Smith." *LA Daily News,* August 30, 1945.

## Audiovisual Interviews

Reel-to-reel Shakespeare voice recordings, 1950s, CBEC.

Birthday party interview, August 3, 1985, CBEC.

Powell, Tristram. *Hitchcock: It's Only Another Movie.* BBC, September 26, 1986.

———. *Hitchcock: Sex, Murder and Mayhem.* BBC, October 3, 1986.

Birthday party interview, July 30, 1989, CBEC.

E! Entertainment Television interview, April 11, 1991, CBEC.

Fox News interview, April 12, 1991, CBEC.

Cable News Network interview, June 7, 1991, CBEC.

Miles, Tim. *Eye on America,* CBS News, June 16, 1991, CBEC.

Greener, David. Oral history interview, August 1991, CBEC.

*Real Life with Jane Pauley,* NBC News, September 19, 1991, CBEC.

Taped interview, 72 Market Street salon series, Venice, Calif., November 9, 1991, CBEC.

*Today Show,* CBS News, November 29, 1991.

*Blackmail* Criterion Laserdisc Collection, audio commentary, spine 154, 1992, CBEC.

Macleod, Tracey. "Britain's Missing Movie Heritage." British Film Institute, BBC, 1992, CBEC.

"Charles Bennett Interview." Broadcasting, Entertainment and Cinematograph Technicians, 1992, CBEC.

Charles Bennett reminisces with Ronald Neame at BAFTA-LA screening of silent *Blackmail,* June 11, 1992, BAFTA Los Angeles, CBEC.

Charles Bennett addresses guests at St. James Club, Hollywood, Classic Movie Night, 1992, CBEC.

BBC interview of Charles Bennett and Sidney Gilliat regarding early talkies, August 1993, CBEC.

Brownlow, Kevin, and David Gill. *Cinema Europe: The Other Hollywood,* pt. 5, "Opportunity Lost." BBC documentary, United Germany/Great Britain, 1995 (available on DVD), CBEC.

Writers Guild of America, West, Laurel Award presentation, videotape, March 18,1995, CBEC.

"The Writer Speaks." Writers Guild Foundation. 1999 broadcast date (available on DVD), Writers Guild Foundation & Shavelson-Webb Library, Los Angeles, CBEC.

"Unscripted Hollywood." American Movie Classics, April 28, 1995, CBEC.

# Books and Articles

Barr, Charles. "*Blackmail:* Charles Bennett and the Decisive Turn." In *Hitchcock at the Source: The Auteur as Adapter.* Edited by R. Barton Palmer and David Boyd. Albany: SUNY Press, 2011, pp. 67–76.

———. *English Hitchcock.* Moffat, Scotland: Cameron and Hollis, 1999.

Belton, John. "Charles Bennett and the Typical Hitchcock Scenario," *Film History* 9, no. 3 (1997).

Boller, Paul F., Jr., and Ronald L. Davis. *Hollywood Anecdotes.* New York: William Morrow, 1987.

Bouzereau, Laurent. *The Alfred Hitchcock Quote Book.* New York: Citadel Press, 1993.

Chandler, Charlotte. *It's Only a Movie: Alfred Hitchcock, A Personal Biography.* New York: Simon and Schuster, 2005.

Costello, Peter. *In Search of Lake Monsters.* New York: Berkley Medallion, 1974.

Curtis, James. *Between Flops: A Biography of Preston Sturges.* New York: Harcourt, Brace, Jovanovich, 1982.

Douglas, Sholto. *Combat and Command: The Story of an Airman in Two World Wars.* New York: Simon and Schuster, 1966.

Ebert, Roger, ed. *Roger Ebert's Book of Film.* New York: W. W. Norton, 1997.

*Film Comment* (New York), Winter 1970–71.

*Films in Review* (New York), June–July 1971.

Fontaine, Joan. *No Bed of Roses.* New York: William Morrow, 1978.

Gielgud, Val. *Years of the Locust.* London: Nicholson & Watson, 1947.

Gill, Brendan. *Tallulah.* New York: Holt, Rinehart & Winston, 1972.

Harris, Robert A., and Michael S. Lasky. *The Films of Alfred Hitchcock.* Secaucus, N.J.: Citadel Press, 1976.

Hisock, John. "The Scripted Life." *California* 16, no. 6 (1991).

Kabatchnik, Amnon. *Blood on the Stage, 1925–1950: Milestone Plays of Crime, Mystery and Detection.* Lanham, Md.: Scarecrow Press, 2010.

Kapsis, Robert E. *Hitchcock: The Making of a Reputation.* Chicago: University of Chicago Press, 1992.

Lasky, Jesse, Jr. *Whatever Happened to Hollywood?* New York: W. H. Allen, 1973.

Mace, Kevin. "Charles Bennett." In *Dictionary of Literary Biography,* vol. 44, *American Screenwriters,* 2nd ser. Detroit: Gale, 1986, p. 23.

McGilligan, Patrick. *Alfred Hitchcock: A Life in Darkness and Light.* New York: HarperCollins, 2003.

———, ed. *Backstory: Interviews with Screenwriters of Hollywood's Golden Age.* Berkeley: University of California Press, 1986.

Parker, John, ed. *Who's Who in the Theatre: A Biographical Record of the Contemporary Stage.* London: Sir Isaac Pitman and Sons, 1947.

Peary, Danny, ed. *Close-Ups: Intimate Profiles of Movie Stars by Their Co-Stars, Directors, Screenwriters, and Friends.* New York: Workman, 1978.

———. *Cult Movies 2: Fifty More of the Classics, the Sleepers, the Weird, and the Wonderful.* New York: Dell, 1983.

———, ed. *Omni's Screen Flights/Screen Fantasies: The Future according to the Cinema.* Garden City, N.Y.: Doubleday, 1984.

Perry, George C. *Movies from the Mansion: A History of Pinewood Studios.* London: Elm Tree Books, 1976.

Ramsaye, Terry, ed. *International Motion Picture Almanac, 1937–1938.* New York: Quigley, 1937.

Rebello, Stephen. *Alfred Hitchcock and the Making of* Psycho. New York: Dembner Books, 1990.

Rubin, Steven Jay. *The Complete James Bond Movie Encyclopedia,* rev. ed. Chicago: Contemporary Books, 1995.

Server, Lee. *Screenwriter: Words Become Pictures.* Pittstown, N.J.: Main Street Press, 1987.

Slide, Anthony. "Charles Bennett." In *International Directory of Film and Filmmakers,* vol. 4, *Writers and Production Artists.* Detroit: St. James Press, 1993.

Spoto, Donald. *The Art of Alfred Hitchcock: Fifty Years of His Motion Pictures.* New York: Hopkinson & Blake, 1976.

———. *The Dark Side of Genius: The Life of Alfred Hitchcock.* Boston: Little, Brown, 1983.

Stirling, W. Edward. *Something to Declare: The Story of My English Theatre Abroad.* London: Frederick Muller, 1942.

Swanson, H. N. *Sprinkled with Ruby Dust.* New York: Warner Books, 1989.

Taylor, John Russell. *Hitch: The Life and Times of Alfred Hitchcock.* 1978. Reprint, New York: Da Capo, 1996.

Thomson, David. *Showman: The Life of David O. Selznick.* New York: Alfred A. Knopf, 1992.

Vertrees, Alan David. *Selznick's Vision:* Gone with the Wind *and Hollywood Filmmaking.* Austin: University of Texas Press, 1997.

# Index

# Index

Bennett, Charles: acting commander in California State Guard, 138–39; admitted into Hollywood British film colony, 99–102; and Irwin Allen, 197–98 (*see also* Allen, Irwin); anger at press, xiv; anticommunism, 179, 190; apprehension during twilight war, 115–26; arrival in Hollywood, 85–86; as associate producer, 1, 190; awards and distinctions, x, 253–55; and Betty Bennett, 185, 210–22; and Lilian Bennett, 224; and Maggie Bennett, 25, 38, 83, 125–26, 157; Best Original Screenplay, nomination for, 134; birth, 4; *Blackmail* (film rewrite), 204–5; cause for alarm (apprehension), 87–88; and Keith Chesterton, 23–25, 29–30; as child actor, 7–9, 243; childhood, 1–9, 169, 224; convoy crossing, 144, 155, 167–68; crusade against ageism in WGA, xiv, 203–4; crusade against Hollywood studio formula system, x, 177, 179, 194; and Cecil B. DeMille, 135, 180–81; on directors' mistakes, 205–6; education, 6, 101, 234; empathy for homeless women, 27–28, 222; escaping brokers' men, 4, 193, 223, 231–33; father (Kyrle Bellew), 3, 257; Faustian deal, 21, 203; on film historians, xii, xiv, 205; and film noir, 196, 212, 232–33; Fleet Street party, 25–27; flight "almost into eternity," 181; and Errol Flynn, 108–10; friendship with Hitchcock (*see under* Hitchcock); genealogy, 5, 224; frustration with studio formula system, 177, 179; frustration with script rewrites, 33–34, 93, 181, 188, 192–93; giant squid in *Reap the Wild Wind*, 136; at Goldwyn Studio, 88–90; on Hitchcock's designation as auteur, xiii, 205; in Hitler's bunker, x, 183; Hollywood as greatest destroyer, 200; joining Writers Guild of America, 90; letter from Major General John Beith (Ian) Hay, 124–25; Lewis gunner, 14–16, 121, 124, 155, 168; making *The Man Who Knew Too Much,* 51–54; at MGM, 92–93; Military Medal, 14, 168, 193; most successful film writer in England, 57, 81, 258; mother's interest in melodrama, 2, 223–24; 1944 arrival in London, 153–59, 161–62, 164; opposition to communism as DGA proxy holder, 179, 190; in Paris during 1920s, 29–31; partnership with Hitchcock (*see* partnership, Bennett-Hitchcock); personal melodrama, 4, 235; as playwright, 33–41, 151, 219, 234–35; propagandist in England (MOI), 143, 156, 169, 173; propagandist in Hollywood, 123–25, 133, 136–38, 143, 193; retirement, 203; return aboard *Queen Mary*, 177; sailing to America, 84; secret agent in Hollywood, 140–42; Shakespearean actor, 19–21, 139, 243–45; spy at Split Rock, 110–14; as TV writer and director, 117, 188–95, 199–200; at Universal Pictures, 91; Vere's suicide, 36–37; visit to Dover, 172–73; wanderlust, 83–84; "white-listed" from MGM, 179, 190; work at British International Pictures, 47–48, 51–52; work at Gaumont British, 53–54; in World War I, 11–16; Writers Guild of America, West, Laurel Award, x

Bennett, Charles James Fox (uncle), 5

# Index

## Screen Classics

Screen Classics is a series of critical biographies, film histories, and analytical studies focusing on neglected filmmakers and important screen artists and subjects, from the era of silent cinema to the golden age of Hollywood to the international generation of today. Books in the Screen Classics series are intended for scholars and general readers alike. The contributing authors are established figures in their respective fields. This series also serves the purpose of advancing scholarship on film personalities and themes with ties to Kentucky.

### Series Editor
Patrick McGilligan

### Books in the Series

*Mae Murray: The Girl with the Bee-Stung Lips*
Michael G. Ankerich

*Hedy Lamarr: The Most Beautiful Woman in Film*
Ruth Barton

*Von Sternberg*
John Baxter

*Hitchcock's Partner in Suspense: The Life of Screenwriter Charles Bennett*
Charles Bennett, edited by John Charles Bennett

*The Marxist and the Movies: A Biography of Paul Jarrico*
Larry Ceplair

*Warren Oates: A Wild Life*
Susan Compo

*Jack Nicholson: The Early Years*
Robert Crane and Christopher Fryer

*Being Hal Ashby: Life of a Hollywood Rebel*
Nick Dawson

*Intrepid Laughter: Preston Sturges and the Movies*
Andrew Dickos

*John Gilbert: The Last of the Silent Film Stars*
Eve Golden

*Pola Negri: Hollywood's First Femme Fatale*
Mariusz Kotowski